News
and
Sexuality

In Memory of Roy Aarons

(1933–2004)

News
and
Sexuality

Media Portraits of Diversity

Edited by

Laura Castañeda
Shannon Campbell

The Annenberg School of Journalism
University of Southern California

SAGE Publications
Thousand Oaks ▪ London ▪ New Delhi

For information:

Sage Publications, Inc.
2455 Teller Road
Thousand Oaks, California 91320
E-mail: order@sagepub.com

Sage Publications Ltd.
1 Oliver's Yard
55 City Road
London EC1Y 1SP
United Kingdom

Sage Publications India Pvt. Ltd.
B-42, Panchsheel Enclave
Post Box 4109
New Delhi 110 017 India

Printed in the United States of America on acid-free paper.

Library of Congress Cataloging-in-Publication Data

News and sexuality : media portraits of diversity / edited
by Laura Castañeda and Shannon B. Campbell.
      p. cm.
Includes bibliographical references and index.
ISBN 1-4129-0998-8 (cloth) — ISBN 1-4129-0999-6 (pbk.)
1. Homosexuality—Press coverage—United States. I. Castañeda,
Laura, 1963— II. Campbell, Shannon B.
PN4888.H66N49 2006
070.4′49306766—dc22

                                          2005009851

06   07   08   09   10   9   8   7   6   5   4   3   2   1

Acquiring Editor:	Margaret H. Seawell
Editorial Assistant:	Sarah K. Quesenberry
Project Editor:	Claudia A. Hoffman/Astrid Virding
Copy Editor:	Catherine M. Chilton
Typesetter:	C&M Digitals (P) Ltd.
Indexer:	Julie Grayson
Cover Designer:	Janet Foulger

Contents

Preface and Acknowledgments

N ews portrayals of gay, lesbian, and other sexual orientation issues often reflect rhetoric, stereotypes, and plain ignorance. Part of the reason is that journalists with little background in sexual difference often fall into lazy habits that pollute coverage and alienate news consumers. This is unacceptable. In today's world, journalists must be equipped to bring a general knowledge of sexual diversity issues to the table as part of their professional education repertoire; those who consume media messages, whether or not they work in media, must be able to spot inaccurate or biased reporting.

Educators are well aware of the high-octane presence of sexual diversity issues in the news, but they often lack the knowledge and resources to teach about them. The purpose of *News and Sexuality* is to provide these instructors, especially those who teach journalism, with a tool with which to address these complex and often controversial issues.

Many outstanding academic works deal with gay men and lesbians and the media, such as *Up From Invisibility: Lesbians, Gay Men, and the Media in America*, by Larry P. Gross, and *Straight News: Gays, Lesbians, and the News Media*, by Edward Alwood. Others do an excellent job of covering news writing and reporting in general, including *Reporting and Writing Basics for the 21st Century*, by Christopher Scanlan, and *News Reporting and Writing*, by Melvin Mencher. However, no text exists that frames the intersection of press portrayal and broader issues of sexual difference in a practical way that can easily be translated to the classroom environment.

News and Sexuality aims to fulfill this need with original contributions written for the book. Educators can use this text to satisfy the new requirement by the Accrediting Council on Education in Journalism and

Mass Communication that makes the teaching of sexual diversity issues a requirement for all of its 104 accredited journalism programs in the United States. *News and Sexuality* also is intended for use in other journalism courses, such as history of journalism, journalistic ethics, minorities in the media, women in the media, and even basic news writing. Communications courses that will find the book useful include media and society, intercultural communication and gender, and media and communication. The book will also be useful in many courses in gender or gay and lesbian studies, such as social issues and gender or seminars in gay, lesbian, bisexual, and transgender history.

Each chapter in *News and Sexuality* includes a study guide section at the end in which books and Web sites are listed for further reading about the topic covered, discussion questions are posed that students can answer in class or as take-home written assignments, and other homework assignments are suggested for students. The National Lesbian and Gay Journalists Association (NLGJA) has graciously granted permission to reproduce its style guide, which is modeled after the Associated Press Stylebook and is included at the end of this book.

Anonymous reviewers read the manuscript and offered insights that helped shape this work. We wish to thank these reviewers: Rhonda Gibson, University of North Carolina, Chapel Hill; Loren Ghiglione, Medill School of Journalism at Northwestern University; Chuck Hoy, Bowling Green State University; Helene Shugart, University of Utah; Rodger Streitmatter, American University; and Federico Subervi, University of Texas, Austin.

We would like to thank the authors who contributed to *News and Sexuality* for their dedication and enthusiasm, as well as our colleagues, including Geoff Cowan, dean of the University of Southern California's Annenberg School for Communication; Michael Parks, director of the Annenberg School of Journalism; Patricia Dean, associate director of the Annenberg School of Journalism; and Annenberg journalism professors Bill Celis, Felix Gutierrez, and Ed Cray. In addition, Yolanda Retter Vargas of the University of California, Los Angeles, Chicano Studies Research Center Library and the NLGJA provided valuable research, photos, and materials. We are indebted to Margaret Seawell, Sarah Quesenberry, Astrid Virding, and Karen Wiley, the hardworking staff at Sage. We also wish to acknowledge the encouragement and inspiration we received from our families: Art Buckler, Olivia Buckler, and Ruben and Socorro Castañeda, and Frank and Susie Campbell.

News and Sexuality is dedicated to our friend Roy Aarons, a pioneer in the effort to improve coverage of gays in the media. Roy originally proposed the idea for such a book but bowed out of the project after he was diagnosed with cancer. He died from a heart attack in November 2004.

Roy's long career as a journalist began at the *New Haven* (Connecticut) *Journal-Courier*, took him to the *Washington Post*, and later to the the *Oakland Tribune*, where as editor he oversaw the newspaper's Pulitzer Prize photo coverage of the Loma Prieta earthquake in the San Francisco Bay Area.

He made headlines at the American Society of Newspaper Editors convention in 1989 when he came out as a gay man while presenting the results of a national survey of gay journalists. He eventually founded the NLGJA and served as its president until 1997. Today, the organization has 1200 members in 24 chapters across the United States, with affiliates in Canada and Germany.

Roy established and served as director of the USC Annenberg School's Sexual Orientation in the News program and developed a course titled "The American Press and Issues of Sexual Diversity," which became a model for other journalism schools across the country.

Roy was an elegant, kind, and brilliant man, and he is sorely missed. However, the work he began, to bring greater visibility to gay and lesbian journalists and improve the coverage of GLBT issues in the media, lives on. We hope *News and Sexuality* makes a positive contribution to these efforts.

—*Laura Castañeda*
—*Shannon B. Campbell*

LOUISA E. B. METSON, WHO WAS BETROTHED
TO MISS FAIRWEATHER AND IS NOW IN JAIL.

[*From a Sketch made recently in Los Gatos.*]

1

"A Tremendous Sensation"

Cross-Dressing in the
19th-Century San Francisco Press

Clare Sears

❖   ❖   ❖

In 1866, San Francisco's leading daily newspaper published a front-page story describing a "tremendous sensation" caused the previous night by a woman who appeared "in full masculine apparel" on the city's fashionable Montgomery Street ("Ad captandum vulgas," *Daily Alta California*, May 9). The *Alta* demanded the woman's arrest under a local law that banned cross-dressing, and Eliza DeWolf was apprehended the next day, launching a court case and newspaper scandal that lasted for 4 months.

Ten years later, in 1876, San Francisco newspapers reported that Jeanne Bonnet, a local woman who had "achieved a rather nonsensical notoriety . . . by persistently appearing in men's apparel" had been murdered in the bed of her "female companion," Blanche Buneau ("Murder at San Miguel," *Daily Alta California*, September 16, 1876). As an unsolved mystery, Bonnet's death generated a wealth of newspaper coverage, and her preference for men's clothing remained a central component of the stories told.

Cross-dressing grabbed the headlines once again almost 20 years later, when it was discovered that Milton Matson, a prisoner at the San Jose County Jail, was actually a woman who had lived as a man for more than 25 years. This "startling disclosure" launched a scandal that far outlasted Matson's legal troubles, as newspapers published numerous in-depth articles and interviews following his release from jail ("Posed as her brother," *San Francisco Chronicle*, January 27, 1895).

This chapter closely reviews newspaper coverage of DeWolf, Bonnet, and Matson to analyze the types of stories that reporters told about women's cross-dressing in 19th-century San Francisco. The facts of these cases did not speak for themselves through the pages of the press but were organized into meaningful, coherent narratives by reporters living in specific historical and social contexts.

As historical documents, these newspaper stories do not reveal the "truth" about cross-dressing and provide only a partial and distorted window onto the past. However, this partiality and distortion is what is interesting. When reporting on 19th-century cross-dressing, reporters crafted stories that would resonate with popular sentiments, and consequently, they provide a window onto the dominant ideologies and anxieties of the time. Moreover, in the process of turning facts into newsworthy stories, reporters organized events, characters, and emotions for their readers and hence created new ways of understanding sexual and gender difference.

This line of inquiry builds on the work of social constructionists who have shown that the ways that Western societies conceptualize gender and sexuality today are different than in the past. In particular, the concepts of lesbianism, homosexuality, and even heterosexuality did not exist for most of the 19th century, nor did the concepts of cross-dressing, transsexuality, or transgenderism (Foucault, 1980; Katz, 1995; Weeks, 1981).

This does not mean that people did not have sex with others of the same sex or dress, live, or identify as the "opposite" sex. Indeed, Jonathan Katz (1976, 1983) has compiled a wealth of evidence documenting male sodomy and cross-dressing in colonial America, and George Chauncey (1994) has documented an extensive social world among men who had sex with men in 1890s New York. It does mean, however, that the social and subjective meanings of these practices cannot be assumed. Instead, these meanings need to be investigated empirically so as to shed light on the past and provide insights into how and when contemporary conceptualizations of gender and sexual difference, as well as normativity, emerged. According to Lisa Duggan (2000), Judith Walkowitz (1992), and others, 19th-century newspaper stories were a key site where the social meanings of gender and sexuality were worked out.

This chapter also draws from the work of historians who have used newspaper stories about DeWolf, Bonnet, and Matson to document the existence of women's cross-dressing in 19th-century San Francisco. In particular, press coverage of Bonnet and Matson has appeared in several studies of lesbian, gay, and transgender history (Rupp, 1999; San Francisco Lesbian and Gay History Project, 1989; Sullivan, 1990), and newspaper articles on DeWolf have informed research on women's dress reform (Chandler, 1993). These studies have performed invaluable historical and political work and are used as sources here. The main aim in this chapter, however, is not to provide more newspaper evidence of past cross-dressing practices (although some articles that have not previously been published are presented) but to ask a different set of questions about the stories told by newspapers.

First, what was the social content of the stories that reporters narrated? In other words, what social issues or questions did the press associate cross-dressing with in the process of making it newsworthy and "sensational"? For example, did reporters associate cross-dressing with women's rights, homosexuality, changing fashions, or something else entirely? Second, what was the social message of these stories? Did reporters characterize cross-dressing as threatening, ludicrous, or progressive? Did they characterize it as a public or political issue or a private, individual one? Finally, what alternative stories of cross-dressing emerged in this press coverage? Were there events or characters that reporters could not easily fit into the stories they were telling? Did these characters ever speak back? To answer these questions, stories are analyzed from San Francisco's five major daily newspapers in the second half of the 19th century: *Daily Alta California* (hereafter referred to as the *Alta*), *San Francisco Morning Call*, *San Francisco Chronicle* (also published as the *Dramatic Chronicle*), *San Francisco Evening Bulletin*, and *San Francisco Examiner*.

❖ ELIZA DEWOLF: "MUCH ADO ABOUT NOTHING"

On May 9, 1866, the *Alta* ran a front-page story describing "a tremendous sensation" that occurred the previous evening on Montgomery

Street caused "by the appearance of a female dressed in black doeskin pants, men's boots, riding jacket, hat etc., full masculine apparel" ("Ad captandum vulgas"). Eliza DeWolf was "leaning on the arm of what appeared to be a man although it might have been a woman" and her appearance drew "a mob of small boys, some hundreds in number" who shouted insults and needed to be restrained by a police officer. However, despite a local cross-dressing law prohibiting public appearance "in a dress not belonging to his or her sex," DeWolf was not arrested, prompting the *Alta* to comment: "as the police arrest every man caught on the street in women's clothing, we see no reason as to why the rule should not be applied to the other sex as well." The following day, DeWolf was arrested and charged with violating the city's cross-dressing law. When found guilty, DeWolf appealed her conviction, and the subsequent case generated a wealth of publicity, as newspapers reported on her every public appearance, both in court and on the city streets.

At the time of her arrest, DeWolf and her husband had been in San Francisco for 4 months to deliver a series of lectures on Spiritualism and women's dress reform, advocating that women adopt bifurcated pantaloons or "bloomers" as a rational and hygienic alternative to heavy skirts and petticoats. In organizing the facts of the case into a coherent news story, the press registered DeWolf's political and spiritual beliefs only to drain them of all seriousness through a series of unflattering characterizations, jokes, and dismissals. The *Alta*, for example, wrote of "the perambulating Doctress DeWolf," who "waddled awkwardly" and was "ridiculed by every body" ("The female in pantaloons case," May 13, 1866; "Who shall wear the breeches," May 16, 1866; "The DeWolf in men's clothing" August 8, 1866). Similarly, reporters claimed that DeWolf's case was not driven by her commitment to justice but by her "shameless hunting" and "panting for notoriety"; far from being an advocate of equality, she was an ungrateful upper-class snob who received special treatment from law enforcement ("Getting what she went after," *Alta*, August 17, 1866; "The Lees rising," *Dramatic Chronicle*, May 18, 1866). DeWolf's allies were also attacked by reporters, with her supporters dismissed as "long-haired men" who resembled inmates of "Insane Asylums" and her fellow dress reformers characterized as "a few ill-favored women, who had through natural defect failed to otherwise attract the attention of the opposite sex" ("Bloomerism," *Evening Bulletin*, August 23, 1866; "Female in pantaloons," *Alta*, May 13, 1866). Finally, reporters attempted to deride the cause of dress reform itself through comparing DeWolf's appearance to that of Chinese prostitutes and of cross-dressing men.

Alongside and in conjunction with these characterizations, journalists reframed the political issue of dress reform as a humorous but insignificant event. Journalists reductively mocked DeWolf's political beliefs through numerous puns on the association of "wearing the breeches" with marital dominance and henpecked husbands. For example, in an article titled "Who Shall Wear the Breeches?" the *Alta* framed the legal question at stake in DeWolf's case as "whether a married woman has or has not the right to wear the breeches if she sees fit, and her husband don't [sic] object" ("Who shall wear," *Alta*, May 16, 1866). Even the *Dramatic Chronicle*, which was generally more supportive of DeWolf than other newspapers, jokingly suggested that the "difficult" question of women wearing breeches could be resolved by altering wedding vows to reflect women's dominant position in marriage ("Theory and practice reconciled," *Dramatic Chronicle*, May 14, 1866). The real political question of dress reform, claimed the *Evening Bulletin*, had been obsolete for more than 20 years, and the current case was "Much Ado About Nothing" (*Evening Bulletin*, August 16, 1866). Indeed, the *Alta* even claimed that the court was only hearing the case to "humor" DeWolf and sarcastically commented: "We wait with breathless anxiety for the next chapter in the history of the case" ("What will they do with it?" *Alta*, July 30, 1866). Finally, the *Evening Bulletin* suggested that DeWolf's case was not worthy of legal attention at all, comparing women's increasing presence in the public sphere to cases of bad table manners that could be effectively policed by "those two great social detectives, Good Taste and Precedent" ("Bloomerism," *Evening Bulletin*, August 23, 1866).

There is, of course, a great irony in the press framing DeWolf's case as trivial yet continuing to draw public attention to it through countless articles on her every move. These articles, however, were not simply reflecting a pre-existing belief in the story's irrelevance but were actively creating this sense among their readers. Moreover, reporters were acutely aware of this. Early on in DeWolf's case, for example, the *Dramatic Chronicle* urged the press not to provide a platform for her husband, who supported women's dress reform:

The open antagonist of marriage should not be flattered by any serious discussion of his plans for regulating the fashion of a petticoat, much less for changing the family relations on which society is based. America is the home of purity and liberty, and not a theater for license and indecorum to exhibit their immoral pranks. ("Lees rising," *Dramatic Chronicle*, May 18, 1866, p. 3)

As DeWolf's case progressed through the courts, the *Dramatic Chronicle* reversed its position and argued that the legal issue at stake was "a grave and important one" and that "the mind that . . . can find in the matter nothing more than the subject for a wretched joke, must be one of the most feeble and frivolous cast" ("Cruel and demoralizing," *Dramatic Chronicle*, August 7, 1866). However, the rest of the city's newspapers disagreed and continued to ridicule DeWolf. Indeed, the *Evening Bulletin* openly advocated a trivializing approach, noting that England's Punch magazine had previously used caricature to mock dress reform clothing and observing "how mercilessly the jester pursued it to oblivion . . . Satire, mischievous pleasure and caricature undoubtedly helped it to the grave."

❖ JEANNE BONNET: "A DISSOLUTE LIFE"

Ten years after ridiculing DeWolf for her dress reform clothing, the San Francisco press announced that Jeanne Bonnet, a young local woman who had worn a "suit of boy's clothing" for several years, had been shot and killed in the neighboring town of San Miguel ("The last tragedy," *Chronicle*, September 17, 1876). The murder took place in the guest room of a local saloon: Gunshot burst through the window and struck Bonnet eight times as she lay in bed waiting for her "female companion" to undress and join her ("Coroner's intelligence," *Alta*, September 17, 1876). According to newspaper accounts of the murder, Bonnet's companion, Blanche Buneau, was a prostitute who had recently left her lover and pimp, Arthur Deneve, at Bonnet's urging. In response, Deneve and his friends had violently assaulted Bonnet and, in Buneau's words, threatened to "FIX HER So that she would never again allure a woman from her lover" ("Last tragedy," *Chronicle*, September 17, 1876). As Buneau succinctly stated at Bonnet's inquest: "Arthur was angry at Jennie because I . . . always went out with her and he believed she was the cause of my leaving him" ("San Miguel murder," *Evening Bulletin*, September 16, 1876). Bonnet's murder was never solved, but newspapers relayed strong suspicions that Deneve had killed her for disrupting his sexual and economic relationship with Buneau.

At the time of her death, Bonnet was no stranger to the San Francisco press. According to the *Chronicle*, she had been arrested more than 20 times for wearing men's clothing in violation of the same cross-dressing law that had earlier ensnared DeWolf. Newspapers reported regularly on these arrests, and in the months leading up to her murder, they had printed numerous stories on "The Irrepressible Jennie" (*Chronicle*, July 12, 1876), "Jennie Bonnet's Weakness" (*Chronicle*, May 12, 1876), and "Jennie's Persistency" in "wearing male attire" (*Morning Call*, August 3, 1876). These stories represented Bonnet as defiant or recalcitrant, and the *Morning Call* quoted her telling a Police Court judge: "You may send me to jail as often as you please but you can never make me wear women's clothing again" ("Tired of women's clothing," *Morning Call*, July 11, 1876). Generally, however, these articles lacked the sensationalist or mocking tones of earlier stories about DeWolf and appeared in the "local items" and "Police Court" columns as short, descriptive pieces. Once Bonnet was dead, however, the press crafted a remarkably durable morality tale of cross-dressing, prostitution, and murder that narrated the dangers of challenging gender norms and circulated in the city press for at least 20 years.

Two versions of this morality tale were told. In the first, reporters characterized Bonnet as a domineering villain, who lived a life "checkered with evil" and ruled her companions "as if they were her slaves" ("Jeanne Bonnet," *Morning Call*, October 19, 1879; "Murder at San Miguel," *Alta*, September 16, 1876). This tale centered on Bonnet's desire for independence, which led, domino fashion, to crime, cross-dressing, and murder. The *Morning Call* connected the dots as follows:

When she reached the threshold of womanhood, she envinced a disposition to "go it alone" . . . spurned the advice of relatives and friends, and hastened down the broad road to moral destruction. She became imbued with a spirit of that heroism so graphically depicted in dime novels, and at one time cursed the day she was born a female instead of a male. Her ambition was to become the Captain of a gang of robbers, which would terrorize the community as did the brigands of Sicily. To carry her ideas into effect she discarded those garments which fashion decreed should be worn by the gentler sex and donned those worn by men. In this apparel, and with hair cut short, she had the appearance of a beardless boy of eighteen. ("Jeanne Bonnet," *Morning Call*, October 19, 1879, p. 8)

Other reporters made the connections between Bonnet's cross-dressing and criminality less directly, by discussing her masculine appearance alongside heavy drinking and violence. The *Evening Bulletin*, for example, described testimony at Bonnet's inquest by a local stable foreman who had sought payment from Buneau for a buggy she had hired:

> He asked Blanche to pay him $10. She refused. Jennie said, "If you lay a hand on her, I will put a ball through you." Then Jennie blew out the light. Went over to them to strike them when I was informed that Jennie was a woman . . . They were all pretty heavy in the head and it was a bad neighborhood . . . Don't believe any of the party were in their senses. ("San Miguel murder," *Evening Bulletin*, September 16, 1876, p. 4)

Through such articles, reporters repeatedly characterized Bonnet as a hard-drinking, violent "hoodlum," who paid the ultimate price for straying from society's expectations of the "gentler sex."

In a second set of stories, reporters similarly traced Bonnet's journey to "moral destruction" but characterized her as a romantic, tragic victim rather than a cold-hearted villain. This version of the morality tale appeared predominantly in the *Chronicle*, which claimed Bonnet "was 'a character,' such as Dickens or Balzac would have delighted to portray, such as Beranger would have immortalized in a song" ("An unknown assassin," *Chronicle*, September 16, 1876). Bonnet's class and nationality appeared frequently in this set of stories, as reporters persistently identified her as the "French frog-catcher" or "French frog-girl" ("Hired assassin," *Chronicle*, September 20, 1876). On the one hand, this identification referred to Bonnet's involvement in a traditionally male occupation, which the *Chronicle* presented as the reason for her cross-dressing:

> After calmly surveying all the various spheres of human activity that offered a promising opening to a young woman with no special qualifications for teaching music or other desirable accomplishments, and with a strong distaste for domestic drudgery or running a sewing machine, she concluded to engage in the exciting and lucrative business of frog-catching as the means of earning a living. Having come to this conclusion, she adopted male attire from motives of convenience in the prosecution of her calling. ("Unknown assassin," *Chronicle*, September 16, 1876, p. 2)

The frequent use of the term "French frog-catcher," however, also allowed reporters to keep Bonnet's status as a working-class French immigrant at the center of their stories. In this way, they characterized Bonnet as a romantic "social outlaw" on the margins of respectable society who was tragically, inevitably doomed ("Unknown assassin," *Chronicle*, September 16, 1876). Reporters could then admire Bonnet's "protests against the tyranny of public opinion and the laws prohibiting women from wearing masculine apparel" and then sadly, knowingly conclude: "the conventionalities cannot be abruptly violated with impunity even by persons of a much higher social status than that of poor Jennie Bonnet."

To characterize Bonnet as a tragic victim, reporters had to cast other characters in the role of villain. On one occasion, Bonnet's dead mother was blamed for leading her daughter to "ruin and death" by setting a bad example of drunkenness and neglect ("Last tragedy," *Chronicle*, September 17, 1876). The absence of maternal guidance in Bonnet's life, reporters suggested, explained why she "led a dissolute life," "was wont to get drunk frequently," and "when in such a condition . . . WAS VERY TROUBLESOME And made a great noise on the streets" ("Last tragedy," *Chronicle*, September 17, 1876). Far more frequently, however, reporters cast "degraded Frenchmen who live with Frenchwomen of bad reputation" ("Last tragedy" *Chronicle*, September 17, 1876) in the villain role. These "discarded lackeys of debased Frenchwomen," the *Chronicle* insisted, were responsible for Bonnet's death, either murdering her with their own hands or hiring "assassins" to do the job ("Hired assassin," *Chronicle*, September 20, 1876). The role of "debased Frenchwomen" in Bonnet's life and death, however, proved more difficult for reporters to explain.

On the one hand, reporters characterized Bonnet as a vehement opponent of San Francisco's prostitution industry. According to the *Morning Call*, Buneau was not the first woman Bonnet had "rescued" from the immoral clutches of an exploitative pimp:

> Jeanne had formed a resolve to step in between as many women of Blanche's character and men of Deneve's stripe as she possibly could, and cause a separation. At the time she met Blanche, she had already caused a number of these unfortunate women to dismiss their lovers and cut them off from an easy but disgraceful living. ("Jeanne Bonnet," *Morning Call*, October 19, 1879, p. 8)

On the other hand, Bonnet was subtly, but persistently, represented as an integral part of the city's sex worker subculture. When the *Chronicle*, for example, reported that Bonnet "always brought her friends from Dupont Street" to the San Miguel saloon where she was killed, they indirectly announced that her friends were prostitutes by naming a popular site of prostitution in San Francisco ("Last tragedy," *Chronicle*, September 17, 1876). Similarly, press descriptions of her funeral emphasized her involvement with prostitutes, by focusing on "the peculiar circles of her acquaintance" in attendance ("Coroner's intelligence," *Alta*, September 17, 1876), specifically the "numerous women of the bad class and of French nationality" whose "tears had washed little furrows through the paint of their cheeks" ("Last tragedy," *Chronicle*, September 17, 1876). The press also used the phrase "fair and frail" to refer to Bonnet's friends, particularly Buneau, employing a popular euphemism for prostitute that had existed in San Francisco since the Gold Rush (Barnhart, 1986). Through this euphemism, the *Chronicle* even suggested that Bonnet worked as a prostitute: "Jennie was young and fair. Possibly she was also frail; but there is nothing thus far disclosed which shows that she had been guilty of anything which could justly provoke assassination" ("Unknown assassin," *San Francisco Chronicle*, September 16, 1876).

Despite their different characterizations of Bonnet, both versions of this morality tale drew similar conclusions concerning the fate that awaited women who dared to violate traditional gender norms. For even as the *Chronicle* insisted that Bonnet's murder was not warranted, it warned its readers: "Her career and fate furnish an illustration of the difficulties under which women labor when they undertake to disregard the conventional rules which are popularly regarded as constituting the law for their sex in the matter of dress" ("Unknown assassin," *San Francisco Chronicle*, September 16, 1876).

Strikingly, neither version of this morality tale provided commentary on the potential sexual character of Bonnet's relationship with Buneau. This absence is jarring, not least because Bonnet was allegedly murdered by a jealous ex-lover in another woman's bed. Moreover, the press did not shy away from reporting this fact, or from acknowledging Bonnet's commitment to and preference for women. The *Morning Call*, for example, claimed that Bonnet "turned man-hater, vowing to treat man only as she would a cur; at the same time declared that she would make herself, as far as lay in her power, the friend of those women of her nationality" ("Jeanne Bonnet," *Morning Call*, October 19,

1879). The press also noted the intimate relationship between Bonnet and Buneau:

> There is no doubt that the woman Blanche became strangely and powerfully attached to the dead girl Jennie, and followed her around all the time on all her excursions after frogs. On one occasion Jennie went to the Seventeen-Mile house and remained away all day, Blanche spent the day in weeping, and on the following day secreted Jennie's coat so that she could not go again. ("Last tragedy," *Chronicle*, September 17, 1876, p. 8)

It is important to note, however, that Bonnet's relationship with Buneau, as framed in the press, lacked sexual content, and she was represented as a thoroughly nonsexual figure. Newspaper reports did not even acknowledge the possibility of sexual attraction and activity between Bonnet and Buneau, and scenes that today appear to be a perfect vehicle for journalistic innuendo, such as the two women undressing and sharing a bed, are represented in innocuous terms. Moreover, the nonsexual representation of Bonnet did not operate in spite of her masculine appearance, but in conjunction with it. Specifically, Bonnet's cross-dressing rendered her inaccessible as an object of male desire (her one alleged suitor committed suicide as a result of unrequited love) but failed to transform her into an active sexual subject, with desires of her own. These silences highlight the lack of associations between women's cross-dressing and same-sex sexuality in the 1870s San Francisco press. The morality tale that reporters crafted about Bonnet was one of independence, cross-dressing, prostitution, and murder; it was not one of same-sex desire.

❖ MILTON MATSON: "ALL-AROUND SWINDLER"

In late January, 1895, the San Francisco press announced a "startling disclosure" ("Posed as her," *Chronicle*, January 27, 1895) and a "highly sensational denouement" ("A secret for years," *Morning Call*, January 27, 1895) to the case of Milton Matson, a prisoner at the San Jose County Jail—the jailer had just discovered that Matson was female. The "strange story," the press reported, had begun 2 weeks earlier, when Matson was arrested in San Francisco for passing a bad check in the town of Los Gatos, 50 miles south. Matson was arrested at the home of his fiancée, Ellen Fairweather, and then taken to San Jose County Jail to be locked up in a cell with several other men. Matson remained in that cell for 2 weeks, until the jailer received a bank telegraph, addressed to Luisa Matson care of the County Jail, and realized that Matson was female. Although Matson's sex does not appear to have been related to the criminal charge against him, it was nonetheless dropped after he was discovered to be female. Rather than mark an end to the case, however, the discovery of Matson's "true sex" launched a newspaper scandal that outlasted his legal troubles, with journalistic interest following Matson as he left jail in men's clothing and returned to San Francisco the following month ("Louisa has her say," *Morning Call,* January 28, 1895; "Secret for years," *Morning Call,* January 27, 1895).

Through the ensuing news stories, journalists crafted the facts of Matson's case into an overarching narrative that characterized gender difference as intentional fraud and simultaneously expressed moral outrage and prurient fascination. Newspapers emphasized the success of Matson's "male disguise," reporting that he had fully passed as a man for more than 25 years, was currently engaged to be married, and had successfully lived as a man among men in the close quarters of the County Jail. Even after Matson's "true sex" was publicly known, journalists wrote that he "truly makes a fine-looking man" ("Secret for years," *Morning Call,* January 27, 1895) and "looks like nothing so much as a solid, old English squire" ("She has been a man of the world for over twenty-six years," *Examiner,* February 10, 1895). Journalists conveyed the confusing disjuncture between Matson's masculine appearance and female sex through their use of gendered language. Although most reporters referred to "Luisa" or "Miss Matson," some referred to "Mr. or Miss Matson" ("She has been," *Examiner,* February 10, 1895) or placed "Miss" in quotation marks, as in "Miss" Matson ("Louisa has her," *Morning Call,* January 28, 1895). Journalists also occasionally mixed pronouns. One journalist who interviewed Matson reported that "the confusing knowledge that "he" was "she" and "she" was "he" would creep in" and described how "he (she) hid his (her) face in his (her) hands with vexation" ("She has been," *Examiner,* February 10, 1895). Matson only heightened this gender confusion by continuing to identify as a man, telling the *Morning Call:* "It seems outrageous . . . that a man cannot have any peace, but must be badgered to death by reporters" ("Louisa has her," *Morning Call,* January 28, 1895). In this chapter, I follow Matson's lead and use masculine pronouns when referring to him.

Journalists primarily interpreted this gender confusion as intentional fraud, characterizing Matson as a "pretender" or "masquerader," who wore a "disguise" for the purpose of "deception" and "concealing her sex." The press suggested ulterior, probably criminal, motives for Matson's cross-dressing, asserting, for example, that "officers do not believe the story she has told of her reasons for masquerading as a man and they expect further developments" ("Secret for years," *Morning Call*, January 27, 1895). Although no additional criminal charges arose, newspapers pressed forward to associate Matson's cross-dressing with economic deception, framing him as an "all-around swindler and deceiver generally" whose "victims in a monetary way embrace a Chinese laundryman, boarding-house keeper, bartender, druggist, restaurant proprietor, and people in numerous walks of life" ("Her betrothed is a woman," *Examiner*, January 28, 1895). The press also accused Matson of illegally occupying a house without paying rent, swindling money from his fiancée, and running up gambling debts.

In addition to accusations of economic fraud, the press associated Matson's cross-dressing with romantic deception, prominently featuring his relationship with Fairweather—and other "ladies"—as a particularly potent manifestation of gender fraud. Indeed, the first article to report on Matson opened with a description of Fairweather's plight:

Miss Ellen Fairweather, a substitute teacher in the Denman Grammar School, is mourning the loss of her betrothed. Neither death nor a prettier woman has stepped in to rob her. She has learned that her betrothed is a woman. ("Her betrothed is," *Examiner*, January 28, 1895, p. 12)

In these articles, the press consistently represented Fairweather as one of Matson's many victims, insisting that this respectable schoolteacher had not only fallen prey to his gender fraud but to his economic deception. The *Examiner*, for example, alleged that Matson had wooed Fairweather and then tricked her out of money by claiming to have a fortune tied up in divorce proceedings and promising to marry her once the case was settled. Their engagement, the *Examiner* wrote, was "the crowning piece of infamy perpetrated by Miss Matson . . . Miss Fairweather has evidently been Miss Matson's dupe from the start" ("Will again don woman's garb," *Examiner*, January 30, 1895). Matson's apparent success at tricking Fairweather, however, was a source of prurient fascination as well as moral condemnation, with the *Examiner* finding "the love affairs of the two women" far more interesting than Matson's economic scams and speculating about "the interesting secrets connected with her numerous love episodes" ("Has no love for petticoats," February 7, 1895; "Her betrothed is," *Examiner,* January 28, 1895).

Although the press centered the threat of gender confusion in their stories about Matson, they also attempted to contain this threat by describing characteristics that allegedly signified femaleness and undermined his male "disguise." In a typical account, the *Examiner* wrote:

> Louisa Matson is a heavily built woman of short stature and her strongly marked features are distinctly masculine. Her head is decidedly feminine in shape, the hair worn pompadour is fine in texture, and her voice high keyed ... Jailer Gardner's suspicions were aroused a day after her commitment when he saw her pacing back and forth in shirt sleeves and bareheaded. It struck him that she looked more like a woman than a man, and her piping voice strengthened this belief. Several times after that he mailed letters for her ... and the addresses were written in a feminine hand. ("Her betrothed is," *Examiner,* January 28, 1895, p. 12)

In this manner, journalists insisted that gender appearance was essentially immutable and—despite the cross-dressers' best efforts to the contrary—was still discernible to the naked eye. Nonetheless, this insistence existed in uneasy tension with the competing claim of gender confusion, as journalists continued to describe Matson's success at passing as a man. One day after the *Examiner* had described Jailer Gardner's suspicions, for example, they wrote: "Her ways were effeminate at times, but no one suspected she was not other than she represented herself to be" ("The woman in man's clothes," *Examiner,* January 29, 1895).

Such narrative contradictions became outright contests when reporters incorporated Matson's voice into the stories they told. In contrast to earlier newspaper reports on DeWolf and Bonnet, reports on Matson quoted him extensively, and several newspapers published lengthy interviews and artists' sketches. Subject to editorial control and reporting conventions, these interviews did not necessarily provide more accurate representations of cross-dressing than earlier articles, but they did allow other narratives of gender difference to be crafted.

Beneath headlines such as "Louisa Has Her Say," Matson criticized reporters for misrepresenting his story and disputed their accusations of fraud. Instead, Matson explained his clothing in terms of comfort and opportunity, suggesting that others would dress similarly if they understood its benefits:

> Why, I have been wearing this style of costume for the last twenty-six years . . . and I wouldn't wear any other. You wouldn't either, if you knew how comfortable it was. This thing of being skewed up in tight waists and subject to the flapping of petticoats is to me unbearable. . . . You see, I was always more of a boy than a girl in my tastes. I didn't like the restraints or humdrumness of domestic life, and it was a relief to get out in the world. ("Has no love," *Examiner,* February 7, 1895, p. 16)

The press certainly countered Matson's claims by focusing on his ostensible loss of femininity, but he was permitted to respond to such characterizations. The *Examiner,* for example, observed that Matson appeared happy but "was the only woman in the world who could not indulge in the luxury of a good cry and who had not chance to faint" ("She has been," *Examiner,* February 10, 1895). Unable to fathom Matson's rejection of these luxuries for the privileges of manhood, the newspaper continued: "Didn't you ever want to 'cling' to somebody?" Grabbing the opportunity to reply, Matson "lifted her face like a shot" and retorted "No, never!" Through such exchanges, dominant representations of cross-dressing as fraud were challenged, and alternative characterizations were glimpsed.

In newspaper interviews, Matson also challenged dominant representations of his relationship with Fairweather, claiming that she knew he was female and was not deceived economically or romantically. Moreover, Matson described his relationships with women in ways that emphasized pleasure rather than deception:

> Yes, I like the ladies and in my earlier days was quite a beau. I was a good dancer and I guess I pretty thoroughly understand all about the female weaknesses. I have been made a confidante by the fair ones more than once and have had some interesting experiences. It was lots of fun carrying on flirtations with the ladies and a real joy to make love to them. ("Has no love," *Examiner,* February 7, 1895, p. 16)

In 1895, "making love" had a slightly different meaning than today, referring to amorous advances and courtship rather than sex. Nonetheless, in quoting Matson's accounts of his courtships with women, newspapers associated cross-dressing with a same-sex pleasure that was potentially independent of fraudulent intent. Interviews with Fairweather furthered this association, even as she insisted that she had not known that Matson was female. Expressing embarrassment at this "mistake" and retracting her initial claim that she and Matson were engaged, Fairweather nonetheless defended their romantic relationship: "To those inclined to be merry at my expense I can say that it is better to have been loved by a woman than not to have been loved at all . . . I was loved, and that it was not a man is no fault of mine" ("Denies the impeachment," *Morning Call,* January 29, 1895).

❖ CONCLUSIONS

Taken together, newspaper coverage of DeWolf, Bonnet, and Matson illustrate the argument of Duggan (2000), Walkowitz (1992), and others that 19th-century newspapers not only reflected pre-existing beliefs about gender and sexual difference but also actively created and circulated new social meanings. On the one hand, coverage of these cases shows that reporters did, to a limited degree, register debates about gender and sexuality that were occurring at the time of writing, particularly debates about women's involvement in the public sphere and the possibility of alternative domestic arrangements. Newspaper coverage of DeWolf's case, for example, mentioned campaigns for women's equality; stories about Bonnet noted her desire for independence and adventure, as well as her preference for "female companions"; and reports on Matson registered questions of women's comfort and freedom, as well as the possibilities of same-sex pleasures. However, rather than report these cases as serious news events, in relation to concurrent public contests over women's political rights and economic opportunities, newspapers presented them as "sensational" stories and transformed central social issues into private eccentricities and individual moral flaws. DeWolf's cross-dressing was thus characterized as "much ado about nothing"—the ridiculous act of an ungainly individual with laughable beliefs. The political implications of Bonnet's cross-dressing were also obscured through a morality tale of a "dissolute life" that warned of the dangers of violating gender norms and straying from the respectable, family home. Finally, Matson's challenge to the confines of womanhood was reframed as the criminal act of an "all-around swindler" who victimized naïve, respectable women. In these different ways, newspapers emptied women's cross-dressing of its potential political significance and represented it as a private flaw of deviant individuals.

Newspaper coverage of these cases also structured social meaning by creating and broadcasting new cultural "characters" that readers could use to interpret their social worlds. As Duggan (2000) has argued, journalists introduced the masculine, inverted "girl-lover" into newspaper stories in the 1890s in response to women's increasing gains in the public sphere. The introduction of this character helps to explain the striking differences between newspaper accounts of same-sex intimacy in stories about Bonnet and Matson. In the 1870s, reporters paid no attention to the possible sexual elements of Bonnet's relationship with Buneau, and although female sexual immorality featured prominently in their stories, it was exclusively associated with the figure of the prostitute, whom Duggan identifies as a standard character in pre-1890s sex-scandal reporting. In contrast, reporters in the 1890s were fascinated by Matson's relationships with women, even if their titillation primarily arose from the far-reaching success of his male "disguise" rather than from a full recognition of same-sex desire. Unlike coverage of Bonnet, the coverage of Matson's case connected his masculine appearance to an active, even predatory, sexual interest in women. This connection was not articulated as homosexuality or lesbianism, but it nonetheless indicated the sexualization of women's cross-dressing, in reporters' imagination, and the emergence of a new cultural character: the sexually aggressive masculine woman.

This new cultural character was not necessarily flattering, and Lillian Faderman (1981) has suggested that its popularity at the turn of the century undermined women's relationships with one another. However, the stories about cross-dressing that San Francisco newspapers told were never monolithic, and alternative meanings could arise. In particular, these newspaper stories advertised the possibilities of doing gender differently even as they framed these possibilities as dangerous, criminal, or just plain silly, and some readers may have been inspired rather than repelled. Newspaper coverage of Matson, in particular, was susceptible to multiple interpretations, as the prurient fascination of reporters combined with interviews and artists' sketches to provide readers with viewpoints and visuals that could not be fully confined within the dominant narrative of fraud. Additionally, newspaper stories occasionally provided glimpses of communities that were supportive of gender or sexual difference, and these could counter, albeit partially, characterizations of cross-dressing as the act of isolated individuals. Reporters noted in passing, for example, that DeWolf's courtroom appearances drew crowds of supporters and that Bonnet's funeral was packed with distraught friends. However, although such glimpses of community may have aided alternative interpretations of newspaper coverage, they were nonetheless marginal to the stories reporters told. In the 19th-century San Francisco press, reporters characterized women's cross-dressing as ludicrous, dangerous, and fraudulent, crafting "sensational" stories about deviant individuals rather than meaningful social debate.

❖ DISCUSSION QUESTIONS

1. How useful are 19th-century newspapers for the study of lesbian, gay, and transgender history? What can they tell us about cross-dressing practices during this time? What can't they tell us?

2. What does the author mean when she claims that gender and sexuality are socially constructed? How might newspapers participate in this process?

❖ HOMEWORK ASSIGNMENTS

1. Locate some contemporary articles on transgender issues in your local or national newspapers. How are these articles similar to the 19th-century newspaper reports on cross-dressing discussed in this chapter? How are they different?

2. Keep a media journal that tracks representations of cross-dressing and cross-gender identification and representations of lesbians and gay men. How do these representations overlap? How do they differ? In what ways do you think these representations are accurate and in what ways are they distortions?

❖ REFERENCES

Barnhart, J. B. (1986). *The fair but frail: Prostitution in San Francisco, 1849-1900.* Reno: University of Nevada Press.

Chandler, R. (1993). Eliza Ann Hurd DeWolf: An early case for cross-dressing. *The Californians, 11*(2), 28–30.

Chauncey, G. (1994). *Gay New York: Gender, urban culture, and the making of the gay male world, 1890–1940.* New York: Basic Books.

Duggan, L. (2000). *Sapphic slashers: Sex, violence, and American modernity.* Durham, NC: Duke University Press.

Faderman, L. (1981). *Surpassing the love of men: Romantic friendship and love between women from the Renaissance to the present.* New York: Quill, William Morrow.

Foucault, M. (1980). *The history of sexuality: Volume 1. An introduction.* New York: Vintage.

Katz, J. (1976). *Gay American history: Lesbians and gay men in the USA.* New York: Thomas Y. Crowell

Katz, J. (1983). *Gay/lesbian almanac.* New York: Harper & Row.

Katz, J. (1995). *The invention of heterosexuality.* New York: Plume

Rupp, L. J. (1999). *A desired past: A short history of same-sex love in America.* Chicago: University of Chicago Press.

San Francisco Lesbian and Gay History Project (1989). "She even chewed tobacco": A pictorial narrative of passing women in America. In M. B. Duberman, M. Vicinus, & G. Chauncey (Eds.), *Hidden from history: Reclaiming the gay and lesbian past* (pp. 183–194). New York: New American Library.

Sullivan, L. (1990). *From female to male: The life of Jack Bee Garland.* Boston: Alyson.

Walkowitz, J. R. (1992). *City of dreadful delight: Narratives of sexual danger in late-Victorian London.* Chicago: University of Chicago Press.

Weeks, J. (1981). *Sex, politics and society: The regulation of sexuality since 1800.* New York: Longman.

❖ ADDITIONAL RESOURCES

California Historical Society, 678 Mission Street, San Francisco, CA 94105. Telephone: (415) 357-1848. Web site: http://www.californiahistoricalsociety.org/. (Their archive includes the Edward Byram scrapbooks, from which some of the material in this chapter was drawn.)

Irwin, R. M. (2003). The centenary of the Famous 41. In R. M. Irwin, E. J. McCaughan, & M. R. Nasser (Eds.), *The Famous 41: Sexuality and social control in Mexico, 1901* (pp. 169–189). New York: Palgrave Macmillan.

Katz, J. N. (1997). Coming to terms: Conceptualizing men's erotic and affectional relations with men in the United States, 1820–1892. In M. B. Duberman (Ed.), *A queer world: The Center for Lesbian and Gay Studies reader* (pp. 216–235). New York: New York University Press.

The presence of gays and lesbians in major cities across America became headline material for early tabloids such as *Broadway Brevities*.

2

Life as a Drag Ball

*Gay Men and Lesbians
in Media, 1920–1942*

Kevin Menken

❖   ❖   ❖

As Americans came home from fighting the "war to end all wars" (World War I) in 1919, there was growing evidence that the industrial revolution that had started to reshape American society during the last half of the 19th century would aid in the creation of the United States as a world superpower in the 20th century. War production created manufacturing centers in medium and large cities throughout the United States, and consequently, urban populations grew as people flocked to manufacturing centers in search of a better life.

By the dawn of the 20th century, metropolitan areas had already been established as centers for culture and diversity. During this time, immigration from European countries had created enclaves of neighborhoods within the expanded boundaries of large cities. In spite of conflicts between groups of differing national and ethnic heritage, urban areas developed a patchwork of diverse entertainment amid distinguishable neighborhoods. In addition to ethnic immigrants, the growth of centralized manufacturing attracted more people from rural areas of the country.

It was amid this era of community development that gay and lesbian citizens began to slowly discover each other and develop their own, albeit more hidden, communities. In locations such as New York City, gay men and lesbians were attracted to the artistic enclaves of Greenwich Village and the Bowery. They found more acceptance in these minisocieties, where eccentricity was more the norm rather than the exception.

The turn of the century marked the beginning of a period in which sexuality and traditional gender roles were being examined in new and innovative ways by social scientists. The rise of scientific research also brought more open discussions of divorce reform, prostitution, and debates over regulation of both public and private behavior (Senelick, 1999).

Scientific discoveries and the rise of the industrial nations had a direct, though gradual, influence on long-established traditions about family structure and social interaction. Western thought, beginning in the middle of the 19th century, began a process of reexamination as new theories about the origin of life (Darwin) and more complex theories about the human condition arose. This trend accelerated into the early decades of the 20th century at the same time that it became increasingly possible for large numbers of individuals to leave the structured agrarian family unit to create a new life in the cities. One of the most influential and prolific social scientists of the early 20th century was Sigmund Freud. The work of Sigmund Freud increased interest in the development of psychoanalysis, and his research during the last century both challenged established notions of homosexuality and created new ways of examining the complexities of the human condition (Kaiser, 1997).

It was Freud, along with British physician Havelock Ellis, who questioned traditional beliefs that all human beings were created het-erosexuals. His research examined causes for homosexuality based on biological influences, thus contending that the condition could not be altered. At the same time, he theorized that it was influenced by sibling rivalries and interpersonal issues experienced at a person's early age of development. Despite Freud's inconsistencies, he wrote in 1937 that although "homosexuality is assuredly no advantage . . . it is nothing to be ashamed of, no vice, no degradation, it cannot be classified as an illness" (Kaiser, 1997, p. 25).

Despite Freud's findings, social and medical science began to consider homosexual behavior as both an illness and a deviant behavior that warranted criminal codes and harsh punishments for those who chose to engage in the abhorrent sexual activity. Although Freud's analysis had some limited effects on the evolving treatment of homosexuals in Western society, most criminal laws remained on the books, and many members of the "enlightened" scientific community supported the idea that it was a curable illness for many decades to follow.

During the time between the two world wars, homosexual behavior was most often referenced under "sexual perversion" in mainstream media, and discussions surrounding the topic were generally limited to the debate over whether the homosexual act was equivalent to criminal behavior or stemmed from a legitimate medical illness. Yet, at the same time, curiosity about the subject often led to oversimplistic appraisals and assignments of stereotypes, particularly of gender behaviors or characteristics. These were not limited to people who might have identified themselves as gay—they often extended to damaging perceptions that calculated how influences of effeminacy or "mannishness" could damn even the most heterosexual person to a life with the label of homosexual.

Perhaps the most poignant example is an article that appeared in the magazine *Forum and Century* in August 1938. The author, Marion Joyce, wrote in "Flight from Slander" about a life of social flight stemming from the fact that she had been branded as a lesbian because of her tall stature, her low voice, and her large hands. Joyce wove a tale of labeling that displayed the destruction of her character, labeling that followed her through her life:

> I was eighteen before I learned that thoughtless remarks could blast a normal companionship and make of it a shameful thing. Public opinion, formed by cheap medical reprints and tabloid gossip, dubbed such contacts perverted, called such women Lesbians, such affection and understanding destructive. I am 50 years old and single and never before have I had the courage to speak frankly, because a woman has no defense against the slander of perversion. (Joyce, 1938, p. 90)

The notion that homosexuals engaged in criminal sexual behavior and the contention that homosexuality might be a curable illness illustrate the cultural understanding of the gay community at that time.

Homosexual intercourse was linked to other kinds of sexual crimes, including pedophilia, and was part of the "crimes against nature" policy that was an integral part of the criminal code. During this time, however, the underpinnings of homosexuality were popularly identified as a rejection of traditional gender roles. Consequently, widespread cultural beliefs suggested that homosexuals could be identified by a demonstration of effeminate behavior in men and masculine behavior in women.

Marion Joyce's article also points out how erroneous identification with gender stereotypes underscored the ways in which heterosexuals were ostracized when their own natural characteristics did not fit into the performative norm:

> I have reached the end of my personal endurance under the persecution that I have been forced to accept because I happen to have been born a woman well above the average in height, with a voice that is two octaves lower than it should rightly be, with hands that are broad at the knuckles and capable of swinging an ax or steadying a plow. Because I must earn my living, I am asking the right to live my life without the menace of ignorance made cruelly aware of misapplied clinical facts for commercial gain. (Joyce, 1938, p. 90)

Despite the criminalization of homosexual activity, the categorization of gay men and lesbians as mentally ill, and labeling based on gender appearance stereotypes, community members were increasingly becoming part of a growing arts and entertainment culture in major American cities and on the European continent. Although their presence in this culture brought more awareness about the existence of gays in society, identification was largely still formed in the public mind on the basis of appearance and mannerisms.

The United States was not the only Western nation dealing with homosexuality and its subsequent ramifications. Even prior to the Great War, fledgling organizations were founded in European locations, supporting some degree of emancipation for gay citizens. Following World War I, the concept of gay civil rights took on a particularly political tone. During the democratic composition of Germany, Magnus Hirschfeld, a German physician who later established himself as a popular sexologist, claimed that homosexuality was a trait that occurred naturally. As such, homosexuality warranted scientific study, and homosexuals deserved political emancipation. He had founded the first Institute for Sexual Research and organized the World League for Sexual Reform, bringing to them much of the research done by his Scientific Humanitarian Committee, which had been formed before the turn of the century. After World War I, Hirschfeld campaigned heavily for the repeal of Paragraph 175, the German law banning sodomy. His campaign encouraged homosexuals to reveal themselves. This revelation opened the door for Hirschfeld to petition the government to rescind the sodomy legislation. The movement garnered support from such luminaries as Thomas Mann and Albert Einstein in its unsuccessful attempt to permanently repeal the law (Kaiser, 1997; Melville, 2004).

One editor who followed, and at times opposed, Hirschfeld's institute created what would become the longest running publication advocating some form of relationships among men. *Der Eigene (The Exceptional)* was edited by German writer Adolph Brand, who founded the organization Community of the Exceptional around the turn of the century. Brand's position was a curious mixture of the right-wing concept of feminism as a threat to manhood and the embracing of male relationships as mentoring and prelude to marriage. The periodical operated for more than 30 years (ceasing publication in 1931). Meanwhile, Hirschfeld was hailed in many Western nations as an expert in sexuality research. American newspapers raved about his presentations. In fact, while on tour in the United States, one American journalist called him the "Einstein of Sex." That moniker eventually became the title of a German film biography of the sexologist by Chris Klaus and Valentin Passoni, released in 1999 (Klemm, 2002).

Even though Hirschfeld was a gay man, his private life and relationships were kept secretive. In the eyes of the public he maintained a celibate life. Although both European and American papers seemed responsive to his speeches encouraging the emancipation of homosexuals, the American press in general maintained a decidedly static view of homosexuals as deviants and criminals, when they bothered to cover the community in their papers.

By the early 1920s, American newspapers had embraced the notion that observant, unattached reporting was both responsible and a way of presenting information in a more "balanced" style. Papers sought to provide stories devoid of personal bias on the part of the journalist.

Edward Alwood (1996), in his book *Straight News: Gays, Lesbians and the News Media*, explained one of the flaws of the balanced reporting process:

By "straight" news they mean stories that are based on verifiable statements from recognized experts, public documents, and official sources—police, elected officials, public office holders—almost anyone's opinion but their own. But the unacknowledged drawback in this quest for objectivity is that the media are far more accessible to the defenders of the status quo than to advocates of change. In the case of gays and lesbians the standard of objectivity encouraged reporters to rely on information from politicians, police, clergy, psychiatrists—historically society's most forceful anti-gay detractors. (Alwood, 1996, pp. 9–10)

Since reporters were (and still are) overwhelmingly heterosexual, white males, along with the public and private officials of the day who were considered "experts," most stories appearing in print media reflected the mainstream and overwhelmingly oppressive social and cultural attitudes about homosexuals. Most mainstream newspapers in the 1920s simply ignored the plight or the existence of gay and lesbian Americans. In fact, the word "homosexual" did not appear in the *New York Times* until 1924, when the newspaper published a review of *The Doctor Looks at Love and Life,* a book by Dr. Joseph Collins in which he contended that most homosexuals were not degenerates. In 1922, the magazine *Vanity Fair* printed Gertrude Stein's "Miss Furr and Miss Skeene," a fiction that made use of the word "gay."

Book publishers, unlike their newspaper counterparts, seemed to display more willingness to tackle gay and lesbian themes. Even so, there were movements in Western nations to ban many books with gay and lesbian story lines or characters. The publication of *The Well of Loneliness* (1928), Radclyffe Hall's book with a lesbian theme, received widespread recognition and notoriety, but D. H. Lawrence's *Lady Chatterley's Lover,* published in France in the same year, was banned by Great Britain for the next 32 years.

Meanwhile, newspaper references to the American homosexual community remained largely relegated to criminal reports of arrests for various violations of decency laws. In the 1920s, gay communities began sponsoring popular "drag balls" in locations where participants often cross-dressed and danced or imitated the styles of the time. Molly McGarry and Fred Wasserman described these events in *Becoming Visible: An Illustrated History of Lesbian and Gay Life in Twentieth Century America* (1998), writing that in 1920s Harlem, men often danced together "decked out in tuxes and drag at fabulous balls, and mixed at speakeasies and cabarets." Lesbians often gathered at places such as Webster Hall, a Greenwich Village social club, for costume balls.

These balls may have reinforced existing social stereotypes of the effeminate male and masculine female, but they also signified the increasingly undeniable presence of gay men and lesbians in major American cities. This presence became so obvious that, by the early 1930s, tabloids such as *Broadway Brevities* started plastering headlines across their front pages about the onslaught of "queers" in New York's Times Square. In a 1933 front-page report about the "takeover," *Brevities* reported that "emboldened by the tolerance of the public and police alike, New York's hordes of third sexers have descended upon Broadway and Times Square with a whoop and are making life intolerable for normal passers-by" (McGarry & Wasserman, 1998).

One successful performer during this era was Gladys Bentley, an African-American artist whose risqué lyrics and penchant for double entendre gained her wide and celebrated recognition in New York. A product of Harlem, Bentley subverted gender roles in costume by performing in a tuxedo, backed by a "full pansy chorus line." She even claimed at one point to have married her white girlfriend.

Other artists used blues lyrics and song titles, such as "Sissie Man's Blues" and Bessie Jackson's "Bulldagger Women's Blues," to discuss and describe the homosexual community (McGarry & Wasserman, 1998, p. 68).

❖ FILM PORTRAYALS

By the 1920s, silent films had grown from a curiosity at the turn of the century to a full-fledged entertainment industry with millions of audience members devoted to the medium. In this last decade of motion pictures without sound, there were silent images that alluded to the presence of gays in society. Although many of these images reflected the social assumptions that homosexuality was decadent (*The Sign of the Cross*, 1928), comic depictions of the effeminate man (*The Soilers*, 1923) drew upon those notions and stereotypes that were publicly understood by the general audience. Later, Marlene Dietrich's kiss with another woman in the 1930s sound movie *Morocco* was displayed more as a brief erotic moment (Fejes & Petrich, 1993). Homosexual depictions, when present, most often served as a form of (not so) subtle comedic gender role caricatures. Characters in films such as *Our*

Betters (1933) and *The Gay Divorcée* (1934) were portrayed as "sissies" without any references to their sexual orientation. These caricatures of gay men were acceptable to audiences because they reinforced stereotypical perceptions of the gay population (Russo, 1987).

Popular films like *The Broadway Melody* (1929) and *Myrt and Marge* (1934) may have featured gay characters, but they were never projected as people who fell in love. Even when movies were based on real stories, such as 1933's *Queen Christina*, Hollywood veered from the lesbian aspects of the story about this Swedish royal family member to please an increasingly vocal religious element in the general public (Russo, 1987).

In an effort to appease religious protests that were intolerant of erotic depictions of hetero- or homosexuality, Hollywood turned to Will Hays, postmaster-general during the Harding Administration, to put together the first production code, aimed at underscoring the industry's commitment to culturally responsible (or responsive) entertainment. When the code was introduced in 1930, its statement included a tribute to the influence of the Catholic Church, which was increasing its threats to boycott the motion picture industry. Although the code was initially treated lightly in motion picture studios, religious protests, led by the Catholic Church, continued their offense. By 1934, the Legion of Decency, an organization led by Catholic bishops opposed to immorality in movies, had started rating movies by content. Congregations pledged not to attend movies with immoral story lines and, in many cases, boycotted theaters that ran the films.

Hollywood responded by adopting a stricter interpretation of the production code. Studios agreed not to violate the public morals by showing anything that might be considered objectionable. Among these restrictions, which censored such things as open-mouthed kissing, lustful embraces, seduction, and profanity, was any reference to "sexual perversion." For the next 35 years, the motion picture industry was subject to censorship of words, personalities, and plots in scripts under development and production.

Images of homosexuals may not have been completely eradicated from the local screens, but their images were gradually projected more frequently, although framed carefully in the story. From spoofs of heterosexuals masquerading as women in comedies to darkened versions of questionable characters who were menacing and villainous, characters that either hinted at sexual orientation or reinforced popular images popped up in the occasional motion picture. Examples of these movies include scenes in *Dracula's Daughter* (1936) and *Rebecca* (1940) (Russo, 1987).

Perhaps most telling concerning the power of the Hays Code was its influence in the planned film adaptation of the 1934 Broadway production of *The Children's Hour*. When Lillian Hellman's play, about two women who operated a school for girls, centering around a student's accusation that the two women were having a lesbian affair, opened, the reaction was characteristic of social policy in the era. Although the production received accolades from critics, the play was banned in several major American cities and was characterized as a primary reason for enactment of even tougher laws against displays of any sort of same-sex affection.

When the stage play was being adapted for the motion picture *These Three*, the Hays Code not only forced a name change but prohibited any reference to Hellman and *The Children's Hour* in marketing the movie. The character relationships were also altered, from the accusation about two women sharing a kiss to a portrayal of an illicit heterosexual affair. An affair was socially scandalous enough, but it was more palatable than the story line of one woman falling in love with another. This underscored the pattern in which a closeted gay and lesbian American public learned how to read inside the altered images (Westbrook, 2000).

Censorship policies also did not stop gay and lesbian Americans from searching for representations in movies. Film images of Greta Garbo, Marlene Dietrich, and Katharine Hepburn featured characters that, although carefully constructed, possessed some masculine traits. These were often the most encouraging images for gay viewers. For gay men, identification with certain stars, such as Judy Garland, was pervasive within the community.

❖ RADIO MAKES WAVES

Although motion pictures captured the hearts of the audiences of America, the development of radio captivated their imaginations. For the first time, people could turn on a box and automatically hear a variety of programming in the comfort and privacy of their own homes. The roots of radio lay with communication of messages between points on land and, later, ships at sea, so the federal government took an early interest in regulating the expanding media as it became more accessible to the public. After the S.S. Titanic disaster in 1912—an off-duty radio operator on a nearby ship never heard the distress signals from the sinking vessel—the government took steps to maintain some control of the airwaves, ostensibly in the public interest.

As radio made its way into millions of American homes, the number of broadcasting stations multiplied, and competing use of the airwaves forced the government to issue broadcast licenses as a means of regulating the use of frequency bands. The issuance of licenses also increased both government interest and regulation of standards of broadcasting, however, and for the first time, Congress had to decide how to regulate concepts of free speech on the airwaves.

When the Radio Act was passed in 1927, the prevailing interest was in the orderly regulation of assignment of frequency use. Mark Goodman, in analyzing the act, examined the elements of progressive influence in the document and concluded that the intent of regulating speech was partially affected by political fears of radical viewpoints, obscenities, or social reform being monopolized by those who owned broadcasting outlets (Goodman, 1999). The act, which gave government commissions the right to protect audiences from those who would not broadcast with concern for the "public interest, convenience and necessity," also embedded the value systems of the influential middle class into the regulatory system (Goodman, 1999).

In many ways, the standards of broadcast decency not only mirrored the regulations established in the 1930s that censored Hollywood motion picture productions but were even more stringent, because radio reached directly into American homes. Steven Capsuto (2000), in an excerpt from *Alternate Channels: The Uncensored Story of Gay and Lesbian Images on Radio and Television: 1930s to the Present,* wrote that the ability to reach into millions of homes also meant that there was no restriction on the demographics of the audience member who could listen. To effectively protect the public from hearing immoral or undesirable speech, the government monitored the broadcast programming of stations. This meant virtual elimination of depictions in this medium of gay Americans.

Capsuto (2000) wrote:

> Besides being immoral, any mention of homosexuality could have meant financial ruin for broadcasters. Angry sponsors and the United States government had closed stations over less controversial subjects. Homosexuality was so taboo that even antigay comments were dangerous.

In 1930, the Federal Radio Commission (FRC) decided not to relicense station KVEP in Portland, Oregon. The FRC cited numerous antihomosexual remarks by a local politician, Robert G. Duncan. (p. 14)

Newscasters routinely ignored any story about sexual "perversion." At the same time, the motion picture industry censors regularly changed the personalities of characters that could be perceived as gay, and adaptations of both plays and books were subjected to drastic alterations to make them palatable to established images of audience consumption. Capsuto also writes that radio censorship even extended to the airing of popular music. Although gay lyricists like Lorenz Hart and Cole Porter were already established musical luminaries, radio censors often changed popular songs and sometimes banned them altogether. Capsuto cites a 1946 column by *New York Herald-Tribune* columnist John Crosby, who wrote:

Porter's sophisticated lyrics have been a headache for the song-clearance departments of radio networks for years . . . The broadcasters took a long, long look at "My Heart Belongs to Daddy" before it was allowed on the air. Then, for obscure reasons of their own, they decided young ladies could sing it but young men couldn't. (quoted in Capsuto, 2000, p. 14)

Capsuto also writes about the police raid on the gay drag revue *"Boys Will Be Girls,"* which cut short a broadcast of the revue in 1933 by a San Francisco radio station. Listeners heard the police disrupt the performance and shut down the cafe where it was being held.

Although strict guidelines obviously influenced the presence of gay voices and characters in entertainment productions, there were a few recurring roles in which stereotypes were often reinforced for comic relief that apparently escaped the censorship pens. Derogatory, degrading, and heterosexist comments, as long as they made people laugh, were acceptable in most entertainment genres. Men could pretend to be women as long as the "drag" performance was an obvious attempt at soliciting (heterosexist) humor.

One of the most enduring homosexual characters on a radio series was developed by Ray Hedge, who played the high-strung, effeminate young costume designer named Clarence Tiffingtuffer. Tiffingtuffer's character appeared on the soap opera *Myrt and Marge,* which chronicled the adventures of two young women in the theater. The series ran for more than a decade.

❖ AMERICA STARTS TO GROW UP: WORLD WAR II

The movement toward increased government and industry self-censorship accelerated in the United States during the 1930s. That trend toward stricter notions of decency began very slowly to change to accommodate the nation's increased need for manpower and production to meet the war effort. Although the military, for the first time, instituted a screening process to eliminate homosexuals from serving in the armed forces, many homosexuals were able to become part of both fighting and support units.

The military's screening process grew out of the recommendation of American psychiatrists, who recommended that the armed forces examine recruits for mental disorders. These disorders, which included homosexuality, became subjects of stories in the popular press. Allan Bérubé traced the role of gay and lesbian Americans in *Coming Out Under Fire: The History of Gay Men and Women in World War Two* (1990):

> Newspaper and magazine editors did not shy away from publishing articles that announced the military's new efforts to screen out homosexuals. "We question [the selectee] about his sexual habits," wrote a physician in the *Saturday Evening Post,* "and, in general, about his relationship with the opposite sex. If there is a reason to suspect it, we try to find out whether the selectee is homosexual, a common enough aberration, but one which the Army has found it necessary to exclude from its ranks." (p. 21)

When the Nazis took over the German government, gangs of brownshirts raided and burned the contents of Magnus Hirschfeld's Institute for Sexual Research, and Hirschfeld himself was exiled. He died in France a couple of years after the institute was destroyed. Under the German government's new moral codes, the once bustling homosexual communities in Berlin were raided and closed down—by 1935, gay citizens were being either imprisoned or put to death. Even gay members of the Nazi hierarchy were eventually arrested and shot, and no one knows how many homosexuals ended up in concentration camps.

As Allied troops began liberating the occupants of Nazi camps during the closing months of World War II, the media began broadcasting information about the abhorrent conditions of the death camps, including the piles of Jewish (and other minority) bodies from the organized extermination efforts, to a stunned world. There was, however, no mention of the thousands of homosexual victims of Nazi atrocities.

❖ DISCUSSION QUESTIONS

1. What similarities, if any, do you see in the development and visibility of gay and lesbian Americans during the 1920s with their visibility today? What are some of the differences?

2. In the 1930s, a moral backlash resulted in increased regulation of the broadcast industry and self-censorship of the motion picture industry and drove many gay Americans underground. Were there any positive results from these policies?

3. In Alwood's *Straight News,* he criticizes the notion of objective reporting and balance as a myth, especially in regard to ideas and people who are not in power. Is it possible to establish meaningful professional standards of objectivity and balance in news reporting?

4. Discuss Alwood's contention that gay Americans were historically ignored and mistreated by the media.

❖ HOMEWORK ASSIGNMENTS

1. Write a paper or a news or feature story concerning the concepts of objectivity and balance on a subject relating to the experiences of gay, lesbian, and transgendered people. Make a list of sources for the topic you have selected and consider which may offer the best information for your paper or story. Keep notes on how you have made each decision about how you are going to represent each "side" in your story to satisfy the nature of your topic.

2. Create an analysis from representations of different media over a week's period and record the way stories are constructed about a particular subject. For example, compare coverage of a news

item on *Fox News* and *CBS*, looking for differences of construction and description that might indicate bias. Or look at the *Washington Post* and the *Washington Times*. What standards of ethical and moral integrity govern the manufacturing of news? Do these standards seem different today than they would have been in the 1930s, with the production code or the Radio Act? Compare the presentations today with how you believe information was constructed during the time between World War I and World War II.

3. Library assignment: Select some random dates from each decade of the 1920s, 1930s, and 1940s and record the ways and locations in which each of the following American groups are represented in newspapers: *women, Asian Americans, African Americans, gay men and lesbians, Hispanics, religious minorities*. Make a list of the areas where representations of these groups exist in newspaper coverage, including photographs or cartoons, and compare differences (if any) between the decades in which dates were selected for that newspaper. In what kinds of stories do these people appear? How are they described in the news?

❖ REFERENCES

Alwood, E. (1996). *Straight news: Gays, lesbians and the news media.* New York: Columbia University Press.

Bérubé, A. (1990). *Coming out under fire: The history of gay men and women in World War Two.* New York: Free Press/Macmillan.

Capsuto, S. (2000). *Alternate channels: The uncensored story of gay and lesbian images on radio and television, 1930s to the present.* New York: Ballantine.

Fejes, F., & Petrich, K. (1993). Invisibility, homophobia and heterosexism: Lesbians, gays and the media. *Critical Studies in Mass Communication, 10,* 396–423.

Goodman, M. (1999, August/September). The Radio Act of 1927 as a product of progressivism. *Mass Media Monographs, 2*(2).

Joyce, M. (1938, August). Flight from slander. *Forum and Century, 100,* 90–94.

Kaiser, C. (1997). *The gay metropolis 1940-1996.* Boston: Houghton Mifflin.

Klemm, Michael. (2002). Stonewall on the Rhine: The Einstein of sex. Retrieved April 19, 2005, from Outcome Buffalo Web site: http://www.outcomebuffalo.com/film_jan-04.htm

McGarry, M., & Wasserman, F. (1998). *Becoming visible: An illustrated history of lesbian and gay life in twentieth century America.* New York: Penguin Putnam.

Melville, R. (2004). Dr. Magnus Hirschfeld. Retrieved April 19, 2005, from Stone Wall Society Web site: http://www.stonewallsociety.com/famouspeople/magnus.htm

Russo, V. (1987). *The celluloid closet: Homosexuality in the movies*. New York: Harper and Row.

Senelick, L. (1999). *Lovesick: Modernist plays of same-sex love, 1894-1926*. New York: Routledge.

Westbrook, B. E. (2000, July). Second chances: The remake of Lillian Hellman's *The Children's Hour*. *Bright Lights Film Journal, 29*. http://www.brightlightsfilm.com/29/childrenshour1.html

❖ ADDITIONAL RESOURCES

Bostridge, M. (2003, November). All dressed up for the great drag ball. Private passions: Mark Bostridge uncovers evidence of an era that was [Review of book by Graham Robb]. *Sunday Independent*, p. 17.

Capsuto, S. (2002). "Queer" moments in old-time radio. Retrieved from Alternate Channels Web site: http://www.alternatechannels.org/radio.htm

Curtin, K. (1987). *"We can always call them Bulgarians": The emergence of lesbians and gay men on the American stage*. Boston: Alyson.

Freeman, J. (2004, February 24). Gay life: Out and about in the 19th century [Review]. *Seattle Times*, p. M8.

Johnson, P., & Keith, M. (2001). *Queer airwaves: The story of gay and lesbian broadcasting*. Armonk, NY: M. E. Sharpe.

Marcus, E. (1992). *Making history: The struggle for gay and lesbian equal rights 1945-1990*. New York: Harper Collins.

Sen. Joseph McCarthy chats with his attorney Roy Cohn during Senate Subcommittee hearings on the McCarthy-Army dispute.

SOURCE: Courtesy, Library of Congress.

3

From Invisibility to Subversion

*Lesbian and Gay Representation in the
U.S. News Media During the 1950s*

Marc J. W. de Jong

❖ ❖ ❖

Attempting to talk about "the news media" is a tall order, with the plethora of news media available: magazines, television, radio, newspapers, movies, and the Internet—talk about news media can quickly become overwhelming. Fortunately, there are several ways to tackle such a vast exercise in media analysis. For one, it sometimes makes sense to focus on a particular time period. Such a focus will often yield more in-depth insights. A particular time period often is chosen because it was host to some unusual event(s) that took place— events that continue to have social and cultural significance. For media representations of lesbians and gay men, the latter half of the 20th century is abundant with such events: some good, such as the gay and lesbian liberation movement of the 1970s, and some tragic; for example, the AIDS epidemic of the 1980s. Historically, the 1950s are particularly interesting. This time period is often remembered for its politically unstable climate and a raging moral panic—both reflected in McCarthyism. The term *McCarthyism* comes from Wisconsin Republican Senator Joe McCarthy. Accusing the Truman administration of not doing enough to identify and oust "subversives" from the federal government, McCarthy took it upon himself to purge alleged Communists and "sex perverts" from governmental positions. McCarthyism has come to symbolize the paranoia and political witch-hunt–like atmosphere surrounding communism and homosexuality in U.S. society during the 1950s and 1960s, fueled by a fear that foreign infiltrators were preparing attacks on America, with the help of American traitors. Lesbians and gay men were especially deemed suspicious because of their perceived inability to conform to mainstream middle-class moral standards. However, although the 1950s have become reflective of political and sexual intolerance, they also helped propel the homophile movement—the front-runner of the present-day lesbian and gay liberation movement—into existence (D'Emilio, 1983). This movement, particularly the foundation of the Mattachine Society, along with McCarthyism, will be used to examine the double-edged sword of media visibility.

❖ WHY THE MEDIA?

The mass media serve an important function in society—particularly for minority groups. In one way or another, all individuals in society interact with, and are shaped by, the mass media. However, particularly for those groups that historically have been and continue to be marginalized, mass media representation is of great significance. First, mass media images contribute to the construction of "social reality." Although most individuals do not rely solely on the mass media to make sense of the world around them—and their place in it—most people are affected by the images produced by the mass media. For example, media scholars Susan Douglas (1994) and Larry Gross (2001) argue that the mass media influence the way women and gay men perceive themselves; how they (re)evaluate their position in society; and how, accordingly, they interact with other men and women. Indeed, the entertainment media continue to produce an abundance of female stereotypes. Recently, however, there have been signs that, in general, media images of women are changing. Although popular television series such as *Buffy, The Vampire Slayer* and *Alias*, or blockbuster movies such as *Scream, Lara Croft: Tomb Raider*, and *Resident Evil* contribute to the perceived ideal type of female beauty (for example, all leads in these productions are thin, young, and fair-skinned and have long, straight hair), they also portray women as strong, aggressive, and independent. Women thus receive mixed messages about themselves. At the same time, these mixed messages allow many of them to free themselves from heteronormative and white stereotypical perceptions of femininity.

Similarly, as women's images in the entertainment media have changed, so have images of lesbians and gay men. One only has to be reminded of Vito Russo's 1981 study of homosexuality in the movies throughout the 20th century, *The Celluloid Closet*, or read Gross's 2001 study of lesbian and gay images in the U.S. media to realize how much lesbian and gay representations have changed during the 1990s alone. This change becomes particularly clear if one compares, for example, the cocky self-confidence displayed by Will and Jack, from the NBC sitcom *Will and Grace*, to the self-loathing and despair of lesbian and gay characters in Hollywood movies of the past.

Still, a closer look at *Will and Grace* or any other show featuring lesbian or gay characters, such as Bravo's style makeover show *Queer Eye for the Straight Guy*, uncovers that these shows still embrace stereotypical conceptions of what it means to be a gay man. Although most women depicted in entertainment media must be thin and young to be considered feminine and attractive, gay characters, on the other hand, such as Will, Jack, and four of the "Fab Five" (from *Queer Eye)* are camp, well groomed, white, and middle class.

Mass media's overrepresentation of gay men as well groomed, white, and middle class has relegated gay men who do not fit this mold (men of color, men who are very young or mature, men who are poor or working class, etc.) to invisible status. Because mass media often represent a window to the world for many viewers, readers, listeners, and so on, relegating certain disenfranchised groups to invisibility can have dramatic effects on their everyday life. When groups of people do not exist in the mainstream media, they are not discussed, critiqued, or examined by many people, including key decision makers. Lesbians fare even worse in terms of visibility. Other than Showtime's *The L Word*, sitcoms or programs featuring lesbian characters are hard to find on prime-time television. Lesbian invisibility in the media, however, is not uncommon. As far back as the 1950s, homosexuality was predominantly discussed as a domain reserved for white, middle-class males.

The mass media have the power to marginalize certain groups in society, because they are able to successfully perpetuate stereotypes. Their ability to perpetuate stereotypes is rooted in their ability to reach large audiences, as well as the function the mass media play in the way we perceive the world around us. For example, if the only images of gay men shown on television are those of white gay men, one may come to believe that homosexuality is a white men's trait. As social historian Allan Bérubé (1990) states, however,

> Despite the stereotype, the gay male population is not as white as it appears to be in images of gay men projected by the mainstream and gay media, or among the "out" men (including myself) who move into the public spotlight as representative gay activists, writers, commentators, and spokesmen. (p. 236)

Similarly, during the 1950s, the news media's systematic portrayal of homosexuals as "sex perverts" and "deviants" may have affected the way society treated and perceived homosexuality and, subsequently, how homosexuals perceived themselves. Visibility is often the first step toward negating stereotypes in the media, however. The role of visibility in negating stereotypes explains why media representation is often a double-edged sword for minority groups: Minorities are frequently stereotyped, yet they need the visibility to negotiate more accurate representations of themselves in the media.[1]

However, unlike most present-day media representations, during the 1950s, negotiated media visibility was a privilege not reserved for lesbians and gay men. In the news media in particular, homosexuality was something that was written about by "others"—closeted lesbians and gay men or heterosexuals—as a relational topic. Lesbians and gay men themselves rarely were given a voice in the news media. Instead, they were "represented" by medical experts and politicians, who often condemned homosexuality. Not until the foundation of the Mattachine Society did lesbians and gay men finally have a place to organize politically and, through this mobilization, allow for their voices to be heard. However, given the rampant homophobia and anticommunism during the 1950s, the Mattachine Society had limited avenues available for political activism and litigation. Given the social stigma of homosexuality, most journalists did not want to jeopardize their jobs by writing articles that could be perceived as pro-homosexual or, even worse, given the association between homosexuality and political ideology, procommunist. Furthermore, coming out in public had serious economic and social ramifications: Lesbians and gay men risked losing their jobs, friends, and families.

❖ THE FRAMING OF LESBIANS AND GAY MEN

This chapter focuses specifically on the news media for two reasons. First, the entertainment media during this time period were predominantly movie and radio oriented, and, as mentioned earlier, lesbians and gay men in the movies have already been discussed in Vito Russo's (1981) *Celluloid Closet*. Furthermore, with the television industry still in early stages of development, most Americans relied heavily on the written news media for their information. Newspapers and current affairs magazines significantly contributed to Americans' perception of society. Of course, the news media was not the only source of information, but, given the relative underdevelopment of information technology at the time, the written news media often helped to set the public agenda. The news media largely determined what society talked about, around the water cooler in the office or during parties with friends.

An examination of the news coverage of homosexuality during the 1950s should provide some insight into society's attitude toward homosexuality during that time period. That is not to say that the news media "produces" social reality—individuals do through interpretation and social interaction with others. The news media does, however, contribute to the construction of social reality. It is a stretch to suggest that the way the news media reports on certain events and topics is reflective of the way society feels about these events and topics. That would be an assumption impossible to measure. However, the news media's coverage of homosexuality—for example, related to Dr. Alfred Kinsey's reports on male (Kinsey, Pomeroy, Martin, & Gebhard, 1948) and female (Kinsey, Pomeroy, Martin, & Gebhard, 1953) sexuality, to McCarthyism, or to pedophile sex crimes—helped to shape the public perception of homosexuality itself, and "normal" sexuality in general during the 1950s.

Homosexual Invisibility:
Sex Perverts, Criminals, and Subversives

The Los Angeles Central Library's History Department's volumes of large, bound indexation books do not include any entries for articles dealing with homosexuality. That is because until 1955, any homosexuality-related news coverage was framed using "sex crimes," "sex deviance," "illness," or "employee security" news themes and was subsequently indexed under these themes by the newspapers' archivists. In *The Lavender Scare*, David Johnson's (2004) study of the persecution of lesbians and gay men in the federal government during the McCarthy era, Johnson recounts the problems with "homosexual invisibility" he encountered while researching his book. He maintains that most newspapers during the 1950s used coded language to report on homosexuality. In other words, news reports alluded to homosexuality without actually mentioning it. Although the existence of homosexuality was acknowledged, it was often reported on with a vagueness that made it necessary to read between the lines of the article. Johnson states, "When not referred to directly as homosexuals or sex perverts, such persons were often called 'moral weaklings,' 'sexual misfits,' 'moral risks' (with regard to employment in the federal government), 'misfits,' 'undesirables' or 'persons with unusual morals.'" (p. 7). The absence of direct references to homosexuality in some news media may falsely suggest that homosexuality, therefore, was not named. However, most major newspapers, such as the *New York Times* and the *Los Angeles Times*, and current affair magazines *Time* and *Newsweek* were straightforward when it came to reporting on homosexuality. For example, in one 1950 *Los Angeles Times* article titled "Congress Hears 5000 Perverts Infest Capital," it was reported that, according to the head of the Washington Vice Squad, there were "about 5,000 homosexuals in the capital" and that "three out of four of them work for the government." Another *Los Angeles Times* journalist reported on the firing of "16 homosexuals and 5 other persons" in an article titled "State Department Fires 16 as Homosexuals" (1953).

The Homosexual Criminal

During the 1940s and 1950s, engaging in sodomy or other perceived homosexual activities was illegal in all U.S. states, even if those activities took place between consenting adults. The criminalization of homosexuality was emphasized by its inclusion in articles dealing with sex crimes such as rape or child molestation. In an October 1949 *Newsweek* article, "Queer People," one journalist wrote: "The sex pervert, whether a homosexual, an exhibitionist, or even a dangerous sadist, is too often regarded merely as a 'queer' person who never hurts anyone but himself." However, the journalist continued, often the homosexual is a danger to society as well. He delineated the different types of "sex perverts" that exist in society: the rapist, the pedophile, the sadist, and the homosexual. It may be clear to most of us why a rapist, a sadist, or a pedophile constitutes a risk to society, but both the journalist and the medical expert he cited in his article, criminal psychiatrist Dr. J. Paul de River, fail to explain why homosexuals are included in this category—what risk they are to society. Media scholar Edward Alwood (1996) maintains that the fear of homosexuals was largely influenced by a fear of child molesters. In *Straight News*, his study of lesbians and gay men in the news media, Alwood discusses a 1954 editorial published in the *Miami Herald.* The editorial comments on an ongoing police investigation of several attacks on small children in Miami. According to the editorial, the police had focused their police investigation on a cluster of gay bars dubbed "Powder Puff Lane." The editorial read, in part: "The rapists and molesters are mental incompetents; they are killers per se, with uncontrollable passions." However, Alwood states, "[it] failed to explain why gay men would be prime suspects for molesting a young girl" (p. 16).

Indeed, the *Miami Herald* was not the only paper guilty of such oversight. In fact, most journalists failed to explain what threat, other than that of being a potential rapist, a pedophile, or a security risk, the homosexual was to society.

Historians often suggest that the condemnation of homosexuality is rooted in the Judeo-Christian tradition, which views homosexuality as a Biblical sin. Although this explains why homosexuality was perceived as sinful and immoral, it fails to justify the inclusion of the homosexual in the category of "sex criminals," other than that sadism, rape, and pedophilia also were considered immoral and illegal. The perception of homosexuality as a threat to society can be understood within a sociological context by looking at the power dimensions involved. Such an approach would argue that homosexuality is illegal and a sex perversion because it is not heterosexuality. Should homosexuality be accepted as a legitimate sexual category, then heterosexuality loses its privileged position in society. Therefore, the "natural abnormality" of homosexuality, as defined against heterosexuality, allows medical experts and the media, or heterosexuals in general, to "other" it, or to criminalize it, without having to provide any moral, legal, or political justification as to its alleged threat to society. For example, one could compare the "othering" of homosexuality with racist policies of the past that justified the mistreatment of African Americans because of their nonwhiteness, which then becomes symbolic of inferiority. "Othering" allows the dominant groups in society to perceive nonconformist groups as a threat to social stability, without having to explain why. In the United States, the investments in heterosexuality (the rewards attached to being heterosexual) are so immense that any effort is made to reinforce social heteronormativity, especially because most people do not wish to share or lose their social privilege. For example, present-day debates surrounding lesbian and gay marriage serve a purpose similar to the criminalization of sodomy: Both perpetuate heteronormativity. Thus, whenever efforts are made to "other" particular groups in society, further investigations are warranted into the political and economic investments that are safeguarded by such efforts.

Although it was taken for granted that homosexuality was illegal, not all media treated homosexuality as something fundamental or biological. Some articles quoted medical experts who believed that homosexuality was a biological or hereditary trait, and other journalists cited studies that suggested that sex perversions, such as homosexuality, were learned behaviors and treatable through medicine or therapy. A *New York Times* article by Dr. Edward Strecker (1953) recounts a letter he received from a desperate boy who does not know what to do with his sexual attractions to other boys. Strecker explains the boy's sexual feelings as the result of too much motherly devotion. Because of the boy's closeness to his mother, he had inadvertently adopted her aversion toward sex. Thus, he explains, the boy's "normal masculine instincts" developed into "female patterns he learned to sympathize with and admire." However, Dr. Strecker believed the boy's condition was treatable due to his young age. Not everyone believed in the effectiveness of treatment programs for homosexuals, though. For example, a 1953 *Time* magazine article discussing California's Sex-Psychopath Law, which provided psychiatric treatment for convicted offenders, suggests that most sex offenders rarely repeat their offense once out on parole, "except for homosexuals," thus suggesting that homosexuality as sexual preference was inherent (yet still deviant) to some humans. It is interesting to see how, despite a 50-year time gap, medical debates still surround the issue of treatment programs for sex criminals and homosexuals. An example would be the controversy surrounding medical programs that allow for voluntary castration and hormone therapy for convicted child molesters and rapists. Simon LeVay's (1996) discussion of research into homosexuality provides a good overview of studies that have been conducted throughout the 20th century into the alleged biological origins of homosexuality.

The bulk of articles published during the 1940s and early 1950s reporting on homosexuality consisted of editorials or opinion pieces written by medical experts and published in the medical sections of newspapers and magazines. As mentioned previously, these articles lacked contextualization. In other words, the journalists failed to ask why homosexuality was perceived as a sex perversion and why it was illegal. This lack of contextualization can be explained by two factors: the field of journalism during this time period and its notions of newsworthiness, and the lack of homosexual visibility prior to the 1940s. Alwood (1996) makes an important observation when he questions the three fundamentals of news reporting: neutrality, objectivity, and autonomy. His skepticism about these three fundamentals is influenced by the idea that reality is socially constructed and that, therefore, news also is socially constructed. The very nature of news and news reporting—the media frames used by news reporters to represent "reality"—makes it impossible for the news media and news reporters to be neutral and objective.

Particularly during the 1940s and 1950s, gender, race, and heteronormativity greatly influenced the ways in which news was reported to the public. At this time, most reporters and news editors were male, white, and middle class. Although these characteristics do not necessarily prevent an individual from being sympathetic to a cause, they do color that individual's perception of reality and how he interprets and reports on particular situations and what he considers to be newsworthy. For example, the overrepresentation of news coverage of crimes committed by nonwhites, particularly if they involve a white victim, often is linked to the absence of ethnic minority journalists and news editors in the newsrooms. Thus, race plays a large factor in the construction of news. However, given the homophobic climate in society during the 1950s, the presence of openly lesbian or gay journalists or news editors alone may not have changed the framing of homosexuality. At the time, homophobia was such a widespread and accepted social practice that reporting on homosexuality outside the traditional frames would most likely get the journalist fired. Furthermore, it was not until the mid-1950s, when the Mattachine Society was founded, that lesbian and gay rights activists started to lobby the media by staging protests and questioning medical reports on homosexuality, and thus a larger diversity of available images became available. Prior to the founding of the Mattachine Society, homosexuality was relatively hidden, and few individuals would dare to come out in the national news media. Even in the larger cities, where, according to historian George Chauncey (1994), lesbians and gay men lived quite openly, there was no (national) organization of lesbians and gay men that had the actual ability to lobby the media.

The founding of the Mattachine Society in 1950, by political activist Harry Hay, was one of the first attempts of lesbians and gay men to organize themselves politically around issues of civil rights. Initially, the Mattachine Society analyzed homosexuality through a framework of Marxist ideology and saw homosexuals as an oppressed cultural minority. The Mattachine Society set out to radically redefine what it meant to be gay in U.S. society—they advocated a 1950s version of "gay pride"—and set up a program for cultural and political liberation. Despite this rather progressive political and ideological platform, however, the Mattachine is predominantly remembered for its perceived conservatism and accommodation politics. As discussed earlier, Sen. Joseph McCarthy's widely publicized hunt for communists and "sex perverts" in the government had created a distrust of all communists and homosexuals—not just those in the government. A moral panic, a widespread fear out of proportion to the actual threat, spread like a wildfire through society, creating an atmosphere in which anyone at anytime could be reported to the federal authorities for alleged communist sympathies and be subpoenaed to appear before the House Un-American Activities Committee, which investigated claims of possible subversion. Being investigated by the House Un-American Activities Committee had potential life-threatening consequences. Apart from the risk of being imprisoned, once convicted of treason, one could even receive the death penalty—a fate undergone by Ethel and Julius Rosenberg, who were executed in 1953 for conspiracy to aid the Soviet Union. Since many of the Mattachine Society's founding members were or had been affiliated with left-wing political organizations, the conservative members of the organization urged a more passive and conservative approach to avoid government scrutiny. Giving in to growing pressures of a more moderate political direction based on accommodation politics, in May 1953, the founding members resigned from the board. The new board members of the Mattachine Society did not believe that a minority lesbian and gay culture existed, and rather than mobilizing lesbians and gay men and advocating social change, they opted for accommodation politics; for example, by inviting medical professionals to speak to group meetings who believed that homosexuality was an illness but supported homosexuality equality. Gradually, the Mattachine Society lost most of its members to more radical lesbian and gay organizations that emerged after the Stonewall Riots in 1969 in New York, and ultimately, it disappeared from the political landscape. Despite the criticism that the Mattachine Society received for its assimilation politics, scholars such as John D'Emilio (1983) agree that the Mattachine laid the foundation for the so-called lesbian and gay liberation organizations of the post-Stonewall era.

Homosexuality as National Security Risk

Homophobia in society in general, and in the newsroom in particular, may have contributed to the journalist's perception of newsworthiness and to the ways in which homosexuality was framed. This homophobic climate was not caused merely by the early medicalization of homosexuality but also resulted from the politicization of homosexuality: 1950s communism. The 1950s were a time of political unrest. Not only had the Soviet Union detonated its first atomic bomb, but communism had spread to countries such as China and, in 1959, Cuba. To maintain social stability, explanations were needed to explain the spread of communism in the world and to reassure the American public that the United States still was the most powerful nation in the world. In 1950, Sen. McCarthy found such an explanation by claiming that "subversives" had infiltrated the federal government and were disclosing secret information on nuclear weapons. Undersecretary of State John Puerifory suggested that in addition to closet communists, Washington was rife with sex perverts, constituting a "homosexual underground" that was abetting the communist conspiracy. Numerous reports of this "pervert peril" were published in the spring of 1950, and in June 1950, the Senate ordered a full-scale investigation of the claims.

From 1947 until the mid-1950s, based on McCarthy's recommendations, more than 1,700 individuals were denied employment in the federal government because of their alleged homosexuality or affiliations with homosexuals. McCarthy justified the necessity for the exclusion of lesbians and gay men from federal government by claiming that "those who engage in overt acts of perversion lack the emotional stability of normal persons"(S. Doc. No. 241, 1950). Therefore, McCarthy reasoned, given the stigmatization associated with homosexuality, most homosexuals would not be able to withstand the pressures of blackmail. In a 1962 *Los Angeles Times* article, journalist Henry Taylor agreed, writing that "The homosexual is the enemy's marked man." Taylor added, "Every nation's agents and intelligence service, including [those of the United States], concentrate on homosexuals if they can find such a target." Because homosexuals were considered to be weak of character, it was argued that they would betray their government first rather than be exposed as "sex perverts." Finally, Taylor justifies McCarthy's exclusion of lesbians and gay men from the federal government by pointing to the tendency for homosexuals to shield each other. "Testimony shows tragic cover-ups of security violations and entanglements buried within what practically amounts to cells of homosexuals," he concludes. However, as Johnson (2004) argues, "the constant pairing of 'Communists and queers' led many to see them as indistinguishable threats. Evidence that one group had infiltrated the government was seen as confirmation of charges that the other had as well." McCarthy and Taylor's perceptions of gay men as potential subversives reflects the way most media reports during the 1950s represented homosexual men: as physically and morally weak, feminine, and "lesser men" than "normal" heterosexuals, particularly than those men employed by the federal government, who were considered to be more masculine and of higher moral standards than any other in society. Of course, McCarthy's difficulty in weeding out homosexuals from the federal government negates the notion of gay men's visible effeminacy. Noticeably, however, most of the gay stereotypical beliefs held by McCarthy and his followers are still being used in today's entertainment media.

There are few mentions of lesbians in the media's coverage of homosexuality during the 1950s, even after Kinsey's controversial publication of *Sexual Behavior in the Human Female* in 1953. However, it has to be noted that Kinsey's findings in this book, unlike those in its male counterpart, revealed little shocking data with regard to same-sex sexual encounters between women. Although terms such as "homosexuals" or "sex perverts" were not always used in overtly gendered ways, indirectly it was made clear that homosexuals, or at least those society had to worry about, predominantly were male. Of course, lesbians have existed throughout the 20th century. However, in a patriarchal society, men are not necessarily threatened by women. In fact, the perception of male homosexuals as feminine and weak suggests that most journalists and society in general did not regard femininity highly. Therefore, in a society in which men competed for power, one can imagine that men felt more easily threatened by other men being "deviant" rather than by women. Although nowadays many more heterosexual men feel more comfortable with male homosexuality, the fact remains that most hate crimes are committed by other men, not women.

McCarthyism, Homosexuality, and the Media

At the beginning of this chapter, the double-edged sword of media stereotypes for minority groups was mentioned. This brief overview of news coverage of homosexuality during the 1950s shows that stereotypes abounded: Homosexuals were portrayed as white men who were easily distinguishable by their femininity and their moral and physical weakness. These stereotypes suggest that homosexuality was not only a religious sin or medical deviation, as it was portrayed in the media prior to the 1950s, but also reflective of bad citizenship. In other words, the claims that homosexuals were susceptible to treason due to their sexuality suggests that, by definition, homosexuals did not make good citizens. This condemnation provided two important functions: It justified the marginalization of homosexuality and equated socially responsible citizenship with heterosexuality. The news media played an active role in the negative portrayal of homosexuals, as they often failed to question politicians' negative statements on homosexuality and perpetuated the idea that homosexuality was a sex perversion. Still, as negative an impact as such coverage must have had on the self-esteem and self-acceptance of homosexual women and men, the visibility—the acknowledgment that homosexuality existed—contributed to the beginning of the lesbian and gay rights movement.

Invisibility in the media denies minorities a voice, and by lack of representation, allows their further marginalization. At the same time, however, when minorities are represented, stereotypes are used to guard investments made in the social status quo. Stereotypes differentiate between "us" and "them" and are often used to "other" undesirable groups. *Will and Grace*'s Will and Jack are nonthreatening television characters because their mannerisms and interests are so different from those of most heterosexual men. Still, as Susan Douglas argues, those stereotypes are an important part of lesbian and gay rights activism as, without them, there would not be any.

❖ DISCUSSION QUESTIONS

1. Do the media have a social responsibility when it comes to fairly portraying minority groups? Why? What does this suggest about the social power and function of the media?

2. Why did Senator McCarthy include homosexuals in his list of "subversives"? Do you believe this inclusion was justified?

3. Do you believe that homosexuality, generally, is better perceived by society nowadays? Why? On what observations do you base this conclusion?

❖ HOMEWORK ASSIGNMENTS

1. Do your own content analysis of lesbian and gay representation in the news media. Find three newspaper or news magazine articles dealing with homosexuality during the 1950s. Critically discuss how the journalists "frame" (portray) homosexuality. Pay particular attention to the type of language they use to describe homosexuality. Who gets to speak in these articles?

2. Write a historical essay on the changing social perception of homosexuality, based on interviews with lesbian or gay senior citizens. In their experiences, in what ways have public perceptions of homosexuality changed since the 1950s? How did they experience the oppressive climate of the 1950s?

❖ NOTE

1. Joshua Gamson's (1998) study of daytime tabloid talk shows, *Freaks Talk Back,* is a good example of this "visibility leads to social liberation" premise. Gamson suggests that nonheterosexual guests on tabloid talk shows such as *Ricki Lake, Jerry Springer,* or *Maury* are often used as part of the entertainment value of the show—they become so-called sideshow acts, or "freaks." He does

not suggest that the shows' hosts deliberately set out to portray their guests as freaks. In fact, often the hosts and the audience are quite sympathetic to the guests' life stories. Rather, Gamson says, their entertainment value is an inherent consequence of "the field" of the tabloid talk show business—of the business's practices and customs. The concept of "the field" was first introduced by French sociologist Pierre Bourdieu. Bourdieu argues that in, for example, the field of journalism, many practices and traditions cannot be changed without changing journalism itself—what journalism stands for. In other words, television ratings—which are coupled with advertising revenue—dominate the talk show business, and freaks often generate competitive ratings. Therefore, in the Nielsen ratings–dominated world of daytime talk shows, most network executives believe that programs need freaks to make it into the next season. Although it is difficult to find merit in being portrayed as a freak on national television, Gamson maintains that often the guests know for what purpose they are on the show, but that they choose to see it as an agency, and they use this agency to let their voices be heard. He agrees that the guests' appearances in the talk show circuit do often lead to tensions with other members of the gay, lesbian, bisexual, and transgender community, as these do not wish to be associated with stereotypical representations of their sexual identities. Such tensions, however, are inevitable when marginalized groups become visible, as witnessed in the often heated assimilation debates that have divided ethnic minority groups in society. Still, Gamson suggests that if it were not for the tabloid talk shows, many of these shows' guests never would have had the opportunity to talk back to society—even if their voices are constrained by the field of the tabloid talk show.

❖ REFERENCES

Alwood, E. (1996). *Straight news: Gays, lesbians and the news media.* New York: Columbia University Press.

Bérubé, A. (1990). *Coming out under fire: The history of gay men and women in World War Two.* New York: Free Press.

Chauncey, G. (1994). *Gay New York: Gender, urban culture and the making of the gay male world, 1890-1940.* New York: Basic Books.

Congress hears 5000 perverts infest capital. (1950, March 29). *Los Angeles Times,* p. 28.

Crime in California. (1953, March 2). *Time,* p. 48.

D'Emilio, J. (1983). *Sexual politics, sexual communities: The making of a homosexual minority in the United States 1940-1970.* Chicago: University of Chicago Press.

Douglas, S. J. (1994). *Where the girls are: Growing up female with the mass media.* New York: Times Books.

Gamson, J. (1998). *Freaks talk back: Tabloid talk shows and sexual nonconformity.* Chicago: University of Chicago Press.

Gross, L. (2001). *Up from invisibility: Lesbians, gay men, and the media in America.* New York: Columbia University Press.

Johnson, D. K. (2004). *The lavender scare: The Cold War persecution of gays and lesbians in the federal government.* Chicago: University of Chicago Press.

Kinsey, A. C., Pomeroy, W. B., Martin, C. E., & Gebhard, P. H. (1948). *Sexual behavior in the human male.* Philadelphia: W. B. Saunders.

Kinsey, A. C., Pomeroy, W. B., Martin, C. E., & Gebhard, P. H. (1953). *Sexual behavior in the human female.* Philadelphia: W. B. Saunders.

LeVay, Simon. (1996). *The use and abuse of research into homosexuality.* Cambridge, MA: MIT Press.

Queer people. (1949, October 10). *Newsweek*, p. 52.

Russo, V. (1981). *The celluloid closet: Homosexuality in the movies.* New York: Harper and Rowe.

State Department fires 16 as homosexuals. (1953, March 14). *Los Angeles Times*, p. 5.

Strecker, E. (1953, March). Sex and your child's happiness. *The New York Times*, p. H7.

Taylor, H. (1962, March 14). Problems of deviates in the State Department is not easy to solve. *Los Angeles Times*, p. A5.

S. Doc. No. 241 (1950).

❖ ADDITIONAL RESOURCES

Gross, L., & Woods, J. D. (Eds.). (1999). *The Columbia reader on lesbians and gay men in media, society, & politics.* New York: Columbia University Press.

Marcus, E. (2002). *Making gay history: The half-century fight for lesbian and gay equal rights.* New York: Harper Collins.

McGarry, M., & Wasserman, F. (1998). *Becoming visible: An illustrated history of lesbian and gay life in twentieth-century America.* New York: Penguin Studio.

Sara Jane Moore's attempted assasination of President Gerald Ford is foiled by Oliver Sipple.

4

The Oliver Sipple Story

A Case Study in Homophobia

Rodger Streitmatter

❖ ❖ ❖

About 1:00 on the afternoon of September 22, 1975, Oliver Sipple was taking a walk through downtown San Francisco, as he did virtually every day, when he noticed a group of people gathering around Union Square. When he asked someone what they were all waiting for, Sipple learned that President Gerald Ford was scheduled to make a campaign appearance at the site later that afternoon. The Vietnam veteran decided to join the crowd (Cooney, 1975; del Olmo & Lembke, 1975).

"I stood there 2½ hours to see what Gerry Ford looked like," Sipple later said. "He's the President and he's done a lot for the vets" (del Olmo & Lembke, 1975, p. A3). Sipple had completed two tours of duty with the Marine Corps in Southeast Asia before being injured twice, including once in the head, and being sent home on full disability (Morain, 1989; Murphy, 1975).

Unbeknown to Sipple, for much of the time that he was waiting to see the President, he was standing just a few feet from a would-be assassin named Sara Jane Moore. The desperately lonely woman, the media later reported, planned to shoot the president in the hope that her action would gain her favor with a group of political radicals that she was trying to join.[1]

When Sipple saw the president, smiling and waving to his admirers, come out the front door of the St. Francis Hotel across the street about 3:30 p.m., he also noticed Moore pulling a pistol out of her purse. "When the President came out, I started to applaud," Sipple later said. "Then I looked up and a woman had a chrome revolver in her hand. I seen [sic] a gun and I took a dive for it" (del Olmo & Lembke, 1975, p. A3).

Sipple had no idea that lunging for that revolver would not only change his life but, at the same time, set in motion a bleak moment in the relationship between the media and homosexuality.

Sipple's story provides a compelling case study of the power of the widespread homophobia that was pervasive in this country in the mid-1970s. The Stonewall Rebellion in 1969 had launched the militant phase of the gay rights movement, helping to spawn efforts that led to such advancements as, in 1973, the American Psychiatric Association declaring that homosexuality was no longer considered a mental illness and, in 1975, the U.S. Civil Rights Commission dropping its ban against civilian gay men and lesbians working for the federal government.

The events that unfolded in the wake of Sipple's heroic act 6 years after the Stonewall Rebellion vividly demonstrate, however, that the long-standing loathing of homosexuals continued to dominate the American psyche.

❖ OLIVER SIPPLE: HERO

On that fateful day in the early fall of 1975, the brawny 33-year-old Sipple easily overpowered the 45-year-old woman who was taking aim at the president, knocking away the .38 caliber revolver as she fired and causing the bullet to lodge in a nearby building. Within a matter of moments, Ford was whisked away to safety, Moore was taken into custody, and Sipple was being lauded as a national hero.

The *San Francisco Chronicle* took the lead, with a front-page photo and story about Sipple the day after the shooting, praising him as a "battle-taut ex-Marine" whose "heroic lunge" had saved the president's life. The paper also described Sipple as "deeply moved and proud of what he had done" and went on to characterize him as a humble man. "Leave out that Marine stuff," the *Chronicle* reporter quoted Sipple as saying. "I'm no hero or nothing." The paper did, of course, include information about Sipple's military service, because that detail enhanced the flattering profile of him as a patriotic American. "I went in [the Marine Corps] to fight for my country in Vietnam," one quote read, "because I believe in my country" (Cooney, 1975, p. A1).

The *Los Angeles Times* gave the public still more details about Sipple's personal life. "He is unmarried and unemployed, supporting himself with pension benefits he is paid as a result of service-connected disabilities," the paper reported. Sipple—known to his friends as "Billy," a nickname derived from his middle name, Wellington—had grown up in Detroit, the *Times* continued, and had moved to San Francisco only a year earlier (del Olmo & Lembke, 1975).

At the same time that the newspapers were probing for details to flesh out their portrait of a reluctant hero, Sipple was doing everything he could to avoid public attention—a fact that only added to the media's image of him as a modest man. "He was so reluctant to let anyone know what he did," the *Chronicle* reported, "that he called radio and television stations and begged them not to mention his name or where he lived" (Cooney, 1975, p. A1).

Despite Sipple's efforts, the particulars of his life became headline news across the country. The newsworthiness of the story was heightened by the fact that another woman, Lynette "Squeaky" Fromme, had attempted to shoot Ford as he had exited a Sacramento hotel a mere 3 weeks earlier. In the first instance, Secret Service personnel had overpowered the would-be assassin, ultimately discovering that the gun she had pointed at Ford was empty. On this second occasion, the story was even more compelling, because a civilian had come to the president's rescue, and the revolver he had knocked to the ground still contained five live rounds.[2]

The myriad news reports and commentary pieces were unrestrained in their praise for the combat veteran. The lead editorial in the *Los Angeles Times* seemed to speak for all right-thinking Americans when it stated point blank: "The nation has reason to be grateful to Oliver Sipple" ("The shock," 1975, p. B6).

Oliver Sipple: Homosexual

Two days after the assassination attempt, the coverage took a dramatic turn when *San Francisco Chronicle* columnist Herb Caen reported that Sipple was, in fact, a particular kind of hero that the American public was not accustomed to reading about: a *homosexual* hero. Caen wrote: "'Bill' Sipple, the ex-Marine who grabbed Sara Jane Moore's arm just as her gun was fired and thereby may have saved the President's life, was the center of midnight attention at the Red Lantern, a Golden Gate Ave. bar he favors" (Caen, 1975, p. 33).

San Franciscans who read Caen's column knew that Golden Gate Avenue bars catered to homosexuals and therefore logically concluded that Sipple was gay. Neither readers nor Sipple knew it at the time, but Harvey Milk had tipped off Caen to the story. Milk, a long-time friend of Sipple, was running for the San Francisco Board of Supervisors that fall and simultaneously trying to educate the public in regard to the fact that gay men do not all wear dresses and high heels. Milk saw Billy Sipple—not only a hero, but also a former athlete, Marine, and combat veteran—as the perfect vehicle to communicate that message to the American people (Shilts, 1982).

Harvey Milk, a savvy politician who would soon become the first openly gay person elected to political office in a major American city, recognized that he could use Sipple to advance his gay rights agenda as well as his own political career.[3] After initially breaking the story about Sipple's sexuality by feeding the information to the *Chronicle* columnist, Milk pointed out to a *Los Angeles Times* reporter that Ford had not thanked Sipple for having saved his life. Milk then went on to accuse the White House of purposely trying to distance itself from the hero because of his homosexuality (Lembke, 1975b, p. A3).

That accusation propelled the *Times* reporter to contact the White House for a response and then write: "In Washington, Press Secretary Ron Nessen announced today that President Ford plans to personally thank 'all the people involved' in his security when a shot was fired at him in San Francisco." The story also reported that Nessen characterized the suggestion that Ford had hesitated to thank Sipple because of his sexuality as "ludicrous." It is unclear whether or not Milk's accusation contributed to the president's decision to thank Sipple—3 days had elapsed between the attempted assassination and the announcement that Sipple would be thanked—but there is no question that Milk had succeeded in making the story more controversial, thereby increasing both its news value and the prominence that editors gave it (Lembke, 1975a).

Another news story that immediately preceded the Sipple incident added to its newsworthiness. The attempted assassination had occurred

2 weeks to the day after the cover of *Time*, the country's largest weekly news magazine, had showcased an openly gay man on its cover for the first time. The subject was Leonard Matlovich, and the high-profile photo showed the Air Force sergeant in a dark blue uniform with a cluster of military medals and ribbons prominently displayed next to the headline: "I AM A HOMOSEXUAL." The story inside reported that Matlovich was being thrown out of the military, despite a spotless record of service, because of the long-standing ban on homosexuals (Leo, 1975, pp. 1, 32–43).

In the context of the Matlovich story, it was not surprising that newspapers across the country published articles about the sexuality of the country's newest hero. Some of the pieces appeared on page 1, and virtually all of them were accompanied by a photograph of Sipple—editors knew people wanted to see exactly what a gay hero looked like. Many headlines contained the word "hero" as well as either "gay" or "homosexual," a linguistic pairing that American newspaper readers had never been exposed to before. The *Chicago Sun-Times* announced: "Homosexual Hero in Ford Shooting" (Lembke, 1975d, p. A5), and the *Des Moines Register* opted for "Hero Member of S.F. Gay Community" (Lembke, 1975c, p. A15).

Oliver Sipple: Victim

At the same time that Milk was transforming Billy Sipple into a poster boy for breaking gay stereotypes and the titans of American journalism were using him as fodder for the front page, the man at the center of the story was desperately trying to maintain his privacy. He failed.

A person who was more knowledgeable about how to deal with an onslaught of unwanted media attention might have refused to grant interviews to the reporters who asked to talk to him, but Sipple naively thought that, if he asked politely, the journalists would accommodate him—they had portrayed him, after all, as a national hero—and not publish a story. Instead, each reporter listened to Sipple's request, and then asked *the* question.

When a *Los Angeles Times* reporter asked Sipple if he was gay, he responded: "I don't think I have to answer that question." When the reporter inquired a second time, Sipple said: "If I were homosexual or not, it doesn't make me less of a man than I am." After the persistent reporter preceded his third query by pointing out that the positive ramifications of a national hero being gay would be enormous, Sipple—not the most articulate of speakers—replied: "Yeah, well, they are enormous to me, too. I'm an ex-Marine. I was with a very decorated unit, and they are very enormous to me, too, and I have to think of a lot of dead people also, and the uniform that I once wore." The *Times* printed all three responses (Lembke, 1975b, p. A3).

Other reporters were soon beating a path to the door of Sipple's apartment as well. He told one from the *San Francisco Examiner:* "Homosexuality has nothing to do with this. The President's life was in danger and I did what I could" (Wood, 1975, p. A1) and another from the *New York Times:* "My sexual orientation has nothing at all to do with saving the President's life" (Fosburgh, 1975, p. A16). After several interviews and the consequent stories, Sipple went into hiding by moving to a friend's apartment.

As it became clear that Sipple was unwilling to provide the kind of details the reporters craved to add texture to their stories, they turned to a more talkative contact within the gay community. Milk not only confirmed Sipple's sexuality but added that the powerfully built man had participated in local Gay Pride parades and gay rights demonstrations (Fosburgh, 1975; Lembke, 1975b; Wood, 1975).

Sipple would have preferred that no stories whatsoever had been written about him, but the ones that he regretted the most were those that appeared in the Detroit newspapers. He had left his hometown and moved to San Francisco, widely known as the country's gay Mecca, to live openly as a gay man. Sipple had never told any of his relatives about his homosexuality, making only brief visits back home for Christmas and family events.

After Sipple was catapulted into the national spotlight, reporters from Detroit's two major dailies, the *News* and the *Free Press,* made a beeline for George and Ethyl Sipple's modest home in the southwest section of town.

When the first of the reporters sat down in Ethyl Sipple's living room to chat, she was bursting with parental pride. "I'm a very fortunate mother to have a son like Oliver," she said. "We're all very proud of him." Her husband, a retired autoworker, was too shy to talk to the press, she said, "But he shares the pride we all feel. He just doesn't want any limelight." Ethyl Sipple went on to talk about her son's successes as a Boy Scout and a high school football player. The proud mother's only negative comment came when she said that she had talked with her son by telephone for an hour after the shooting incident and had asked him if he had heard from Ford. "He said he hadn't heard a word," she said. "I don't think that's right. I think Oliver should get a telegram or something" (Michelmore, 1975, p. A3).

After the revelation that Oliver Sipple was gay, newspaper stories documented that his mother's feelings had changed radically.

"No wonder the President didn't send him a note," she said in a second interview. Other of her statements in the page 1 story reaffirmed the bitterness that Ethyl Sipple, after learning of his homosexuality, now felt toward her son. Looking at the recent photos of him that had appeared in the press, she said: "He's put on some weight," and of how the revelations regarding her son's sexual orientation had affected her own life, she grumbled: "I won't be able to walk down the street without somebody saying something" (Lembke, 1975a, p. A3).

The details that Oliver Sipple's mother now provided about her son's early life also created a starkly different—and decidedly negative—profile of him. "He skipped school a lot," she said. "He quit when he was in the 11th grade." After dropping out of high school, she continued, he had worked briefly in a factory and as a traveling salesman before joining the Marines to avoid being drafted. He was discharged and placed on disability not only because of his physical injuries, she volunteered, but also because of "mental adjustment problems" (Murphy, 1975, p. A1).

It was not just what Ethyl Sipple told reporters that propelled her son to take his next step, however, but also what she did. For when the young man telephoned home to try to mend fences with his parents by talking to them directly about his homosexuality, his mother said she had no interest in talking to him ever again. Then she hung up (Lembke, 1975a).

Milk, when Sipple approached his media-savvy friend for advice, urged the besieged hero to call a lawyer. Milk recommended John Wahl, who had handled other cases involving the San Francisco gay community (Morain, 1989).

Oliver Sipple: Plaintiff

Wahl's first piece of advice to his new client was to stop allowing the media to set the agenda and, instead, to take the offensive. The media-savvy attorney then organized a press conference, calling the various news outlets that had been following the story and assuring them that Sipple would be making a major announcement. Assuming that Sipple was finally going to talk openly about his sexuality, the reporters eagerly arrived at Wahl's law office for the session.

Rather than caving into the journalists' incessant demands for details about his personal life, however, Sipple read a prepared statement that was dramatic and newsworthy—but not what the reporters had been expecting: "My sexuality is a part of my private life, and has no bearing on my response to the act of a person seeking to take the life of another. I am first and foremost a human being who enjoys and respects life. I feel that a person's worth is determined by how he or she responds to the world in which he lives, not on how, or with whom, a private life is shared" (Lembke, 1975a, p. A3; Murphy, 1975, p. A1).

Far more articulate than Sipple's previous comments to the press, the statement clearly had been crafted by Wahl, who also had prepared his own remarks for the press: "It's very unfortunate that the man who saves the life of the Chief Executive of the United States is rewarded by having his family relationships broken up." Sipple's attorney then stated that his client would not answer any more questions from reporters because they already had put him "through his own private hell" (Lembke, 1975a, p. A3; Murphy, 1975, p. A1).

That comment led Wahl into his blockbuster announcement: He was preparing to file an invasion of privacy suit for Sipple against many of the very news organizations that the reporters at the press conference represented (Lembke, 1975a; Murphy, 1975).

Five days later, on September 30, 1975, Wahl filed a lawsuit that demanded a total of $15 million from seven newspapers. Because of "publication of personal and private facts" about the plaintiff's life, the suit alleged, Sipple's family had learned about his homosexual orientation for the first time. This revelation had resulted in "great mental anguish, embarrassment, and humiliation" for the plaintiff, according to the suit, because it had caused his parents and his seven brothers and sisters to cut off all contact with him. The lawsuit also added that, because Sipple's family had abandoned him and because of "the pressure of this whole business which has messed up his life," he was now being treated at a local veterans' hospital ("Ford hero sues," 1975, p. A4; "Man in Ford case," 1975, p. A20).

The only journalist specifically named in the lawsuit was columnist Herb Caen, the first to allude to Sipple's sexuality in print. In addition to the *San Francisco Chronicle,* the suit named the *Los Angeles Times* and five newspapers that had, through the news service operated by the *Times,* reprinted the story that had appeared in the Los Angeles paper—the *Chicago Sun-Times, Denver Post, Des Moines Register, Indianapolis Star,* and *San Antonio Express* ("Man in Ford case," 1975).

As is typical in the wake of such a legal action, the newspapers named in the suit kept their stories short and buried them on inside pages. The *Los Angeles Times,* for example, relegated news of the suit to a single paragraph in a column of news briefs on page A2—with no headline ("News in brief," 1975, p. A2).

The *New York Times,* on the other hand, devoted considerable attention to the latest development surrounding Sipple. The country's newspaper of record published not only a full news story about the lawsuit but also a lengthy commentary piece about the ethical issues that were emerging because of the Sipple news coverage. The article was written by the nationally known columnist William Safire and ranks as the first of numerous thought pieces that would speak to those issues over the course of the next quarter century. Safire's column began by reprinting an excerpt from the president's thank-you letter to Sipple: "'You acted quickly and without fear for your own safety. By doing so, you helped to avert danger to me and to others in the crowd. You have my heartfelt appreciation.'" Safire's piece continued: "But by doing his duty as a citizen, Mr. Sipple stepped into the white circle of pitiless publicity," and "Mr. Sipple is guilty of committing heroism in public and is trying to hold on to the last shreds of the privacy that was stripped from him as a consequence of his selfless act" (Safire, 1975, p. A31).

Oliver Sipple: Loser

Safire's sentiments not withstanding, the American legal system consistently ruled against Sipple. Indeed, in the half dozen court rulings and appeals that stretched over the next 9 years, not a single judge sided with the plaintiff, who lost in each and every instance.[4]

The newspapers' successful argument that Sipple's privacy had not, in fact, been invaded was aided considerably by the statements that Milk had made to reporters after the shooting. It was that material that provided the defense attorneys with questions they could ask Sipple to show that he had made his sexuality public, at least in the city where he was living, long before the newspapers had begun to report it. During one courtroom appearance, for example, an attorney stated: "He [Sipple] acknowledged in a deposition that at least 100 to 500 people in San Francisco knew he was homosexual." The attorneys representing the newspapers also argued persuasively that Sipple's sexual orientation was, without question, newsworthy. "There was a stereo-type of gays at the time as sissies," one defense lawyer said. "And here was an ex-Marine who heroically hit Moore's arm. That doesn't sound like a sissy" ("Gay hero's suit," 1980, p. A7).

The final decision in Sipple's prolonged legal efforts came in 1984, when the California Supreme Court denied his petition for a hearing to overturn a lower court ruling.[5]

At the same time that Sipple was suffering multiple defeats in the legal arena, he was also experiencing continued setbacks in his personal life. The gulf that separated Sipple from his parents was made poignantly clear in 1979 when Ethyl Sipple died and George Sipple ordered his estranged son, through another of his children, *not* to attend the funeral. In fact, after Oliver Sipple's parents learned about his sexuality, the man never saw either one of them again (Morain, 1989).

By the time Sipple's legal battle finally ended, he had become a pathetic figure. Doctors at the veterans' hospital diagnosed him as a paranoid schizophrenic and an alcoholic. "I have a lot of stress," Sipple admitted in one deposition, "and I take it out on booze." The problems that had plagued him before his fame clearly mushroomed in severity after it. Lonely and despondent, he damaged his health not only by drinking too much alcohol but also by eating too many rich foods. The 5'11" Sipple ballooned from the 224 pounds he weighed at the time of the Ford incident to 300 pounds a few months later, leading to heart problems that required that he have a pacemaker implanted in his chest. Reporters noted that Sipple, once described as a handsome man with thick blond hair and a square jaw, no longer paid attention to his appearance (Morain, 1989).

Sipple, turning away from gay activism because of the role it had played in the unwanted publicity he had received, no longer attended public events of any kind. Instead, he spent his days as a recluse, staying inside his rundown apartment, which one newspaper would later describe as looking

> like a junk store gone to seed. Mementos of value only to their owner were arranged in no order. Bad paintings covered chipped plaster. His most prized possession, the framed letter of appreciation from President Ford, hung on one wall. (Morain, 1989, p. E1)

After the lawsuit failed, Sipple no longer went out of his apartment in daylight, leaving only at night, when he wandered from one bar to the next. When the bourbon got him talking, bartenders later said, Sipple would boast about his heroism, inflating his military rank to that of a Marine colonel, when, in reality, he was discharged as a private first class. He also complained of shadowy figures following him (Morain, 1989; "Tragic heroes," 1996).

Although Sipple lived on a veteran's pension, he never stopped being generous, the bartenders said. Whenever someone in a bar asked him for a donation to charity or a few dollars to help a derelict in the rundown section of the Tenderloin district where he lived, Sipple opened his wallet without hesitation (Morain, 1989).

Sometime around the middle of January 1989, Sipple turned on his television set and lay down on his bed, half-gallon bottles of cheap bourbon and 7-Up within arm's reach. Although he died later that night, 2 weeks would pass before an investigator for the San Francisco District Attorney, dispatched by a bartender who had become concerned when he had not seen Sipple for several days, discovered his body (Morain, 1989).

Several newspapers marked the passing of the 47-year-old man with obituaries that recounted his story and quoted some of the people who had played roles in it. The investigator who found Sipple's body said: "People shouldn't die like that, alone." Attorney John Wahl said: "The guy died in pain, with a bottle by his bed. That's pain. That's need for anesthetic." When one reporter asked Caen if he had any regrets about having alluded to Sipple's sexual orientation in print 14 years earlier, the columnist responded that he did not: "It was a good item. Members of the gay community wanted it published to show they weren't all a bunch of wimps" (Morain, 1989, p. E1).[6]

Fewer than 30 people attended Oliver Sipple's funeral before his body was buried in a cemetery south of San Francisco. The combat veteran's final wish had been that he be buried at Arlington National Cemetery outside the nation's capital, but his attorney was told that Sipple did not qualify for that honor (Morain, 1989).

❖ THE POWER OF HOMOPHOBIA

The Oliver Sipple story is tragic. Heroes deserve to be treated with respect, dignity, and appreciation. However, the deed at the center of this poignant narrative ultimately brought such enormous quantities of pain and emotional suffering to a decent man that the shame and the anguish that he experienced led to his early death.

The Sipple incident has been referred to, in passing, in a major motion picture[7] and in a prime-time television program.[8] Several law review articles[9] and more than a dozen books and commentary pieces have also mentioned the perplexing ethical dimensions of the case,[10] although none of these references has extended beyond a few paragraphs.[11]

Because this chapter provides an extensive look at the Sipple tragedy and is being written from the vantage point of 30 years after the events at its heart took place, it seems appropriate to reflect on what this sobering case study tells students who are interested in how journalism treats gay men and lesbians.

Central to such a critical examination is a discussion of who or what caused the pain and suffering that Sipple was forced to endure.

It is tempting to point the finger of blame either at the newspapers that published the articles that led to the hero's torment or at one or more of the people who were involved in the activities that were part of this unfortunate footnote in American history. In fact, neither the news outlets nor any of those individuals deserves to wear the mantle of culprit.

As the nation's legal system repeatedly determined, the newspapers were fully justified in reporting Sipple's homosexuality because their articles were both accurate and newsworthy. And among those persons who may at first seem to have behaved reprehensibly, neither Ethyl and George Sipple nor Herb Caen nor Harvey Milk caused the sorrows that the national hero later suffered. All of these men and women were merely acting out the roles that were forced on them by the real villain in this regrettable case study: homophobia.

The fear and hatred of homosexuality has often caused people to feel uncomfortable with or repulsed by gay persons and their sexual activities. This concept can include the belief that having same-sex desires is abnormal or despicable and that, therefore, it is fully acceptable to harbor negative feelings toward members of this minority group and to discriminate against them. Homophobia has often resulted in verbal and physical attacks against gay men or lesbians. In addition, internalized homophobia may result in emotional anguish that is enormously damaging to the well-being of the gay person.[12]

It was the widespread loathing of homosexuals rampant in American society in 1975 that caused Ethyl and George Sipple to abandon their son, as indefensible as that act may seem. Likewise, it was the culture's stereotyping of gay men as weak and ineffectual, a repercussion of homophobia, that caused Caen and the other journalists of the era to characterize the juxtaposition of Sipple's homosexuality and national heroism as an important story—which, in the context of the widespread perceptions of gay people at the time, it most certainly was. Although it is difficult to justify Milk publicly disclosing sensitive information about a friend without first receiving that person's permission, the political activist's ultimate motive of educating newspaper readers about the realities of homosexuality is not only understandable but, in regard to his attempt to expand the human rights of a segment of the population that was suffering from discriminatory treatment, highly commendable.

In the three decades that have passed since that September afternoon when an ex-Marine instinctively knocked away a .38 caliber revolver that he saw was being aimed at the president of the United States, much has changed vis-à-vis treatment of and attitudes toward homosexuals. Openly gay men and women are now serving in the U.S. Congress,[13] for example, and other individuals with same-sex desires are being embraced by television and motion picture audiences via television programs such as *Will & Grace*,[14] *The Ellen DeGeneres Show*,[15] and *Queer Eye for the Straight Guy*,[16] as well as major motion pictures such as *The Birdcage*[17] and *My Best Friend's Wedding*.[18] In the area of legal rights, gay men and lesbians are allowed to adopt children, in most states,[19] and to perform sexual acts with other consenting adults without fear of arrest.[20] In broader terms, although gay people face the very real possibility of being physically attacked because of their sexual orientation, and whether they are allowed to marry or participate in civil unions is very much a matter of public and political debate, there is no question that they are no longer misunderstood, demonized, or discriminated against to the degree that they once were.

The Oliver Sipple case study provides students of the American media—and especially those with a particular interest in news coverage of gay men and lesbians—with a compelling example of the harmful effects that homophobia once had on the life of a national hero.

❖ NOTES

1. Moore later pleaded guilty to the assassination attempt and is currently serving a life term in federal prison.

2. The Fromme assassination attempt had taken place on September 5, 1975. Fromme was a disciple of mass murderer Charles Manson.

3. Milk was elected to the San Francisco Board of Supervisors on November 8, 1977. Milk and San Francisco Mayor George Moscone were assassinated by Dan White, the only member of the San Francisco Board of Supervisors to vote against the city's gay rights law, on November 27, 1978.

4. On the court cases, see "Hero's humiliation" (1977), "Hero in Sara Moore case" (1978), "Gay hero's suit" (1980), "Man who saved" (1980), Carlsen (1984), and "Homosexual is rebuffed" (1984).

5. The California Supreme Court denied Sipple's petition on June 21, 1984; see "Homosexual is rebuffed" (1984).

6. For obituaries about Sipple, see "Hero who foiled" (1989), "Hurt by war" (1989), and "Oliver W. Sipple" (1989).

7. *Absence of Malice,* released in 1981 by Columbia Motion Pictures and starring Academy Award winners Sally Field and Paul Newman, tells the fictitious story of a young journalist whose reckless reporting propels a source to commit suicide because she, a Catholic, is described in an article as having had an abortion. The Sipple incident is referred to in a conversation that occurs midway through the film when the reporter's editor attempts to console her by saying, "Look, people get caught up in things. Remember the woman in San Francisco a few years ago who took a shot at Ford? And the guy in the crowd grabbed her arm and saved the president's life—he was a hero. It turns out he was also gay. That's news, right? Now the whole country knows that, too."

8. In May 1990, the NBC drama *L.A. Law* aired an episode featuring a heroic police officer whose homosexuality was publicly exposed. On the character being modeled after Sipple, see Gross (1993), p. 66.

9. See Elwood (1992), Grant (1991), Moretti (1993), Pollack (1992), and Wick (1991).

10. See, for example, Abrams (1977); Cohen and Elliott (1997), p. 39; Elliott (1989); Friendly (1990); Goodwin and Smith (1994), pp. 255–256; Gross (1993), pp. 2, 64, 66; Howe (1999); Johansson and Percy (1994), pp. 127–128, 202, 284, 307; Mohr (1992), pp. 15–16, 38–39; Rodman (2001), p. 413; Shilts (1982), especially pp. 121–123; Siegel (2002), pp. 187–188; and "Tragic heroes" (1996), p. 17.

11. The longest of the references was in Goodwin and Smith (1994), which consisted of four paragraphs.

12. On homophobia, see, for example, Krinsky (2000).

13. The openly gay members of Congress are Rep. Tammy Baldwin (D-Wisconsin), Rep. Barney Frank (D-Massachusetts), and Rep. Jim Kolbe (R-Arizona).

14. *Will & Grace* premiered in September 1998 on NBC and has become one of the most-watched situation comedies on prime-time television.

15. *The Ellen DeGeneres Show* is a daytime talk show that premiered in 2003 and airs nationally on NBC. Ellen DeGeneres publicly acknowledged her

homosexuality in 1997 at the same time that the character she played on the ABC situation comedy *Ellen* acknowledged that she was a lesbian as well.

16. *Queer Eye for the Straight Guy* is a reality television program that airs on the Bravo cable channel and occasionally on Bravo's corporate sibling, NBC. On the makeover program, five openly gay men help a style-deficient straight man by reworking his wardrobe, teaching him to cook and choose wine, redecorating his home, giving him grooming advice, and counseling him on culture.

17. *The Birdcage* was released in 1996 by MGM Studios. One of the film's two leading characters was played by Nathan Lane, who has publicly acknowledged his homosexuality.

18. *My Best Friend's Wedding* was released in 1997 by TriStar Pictures. One of the film's leading characters was played by Rupert Everett, who has publicly acknowledged his homosexuality.

19. Florida is the only state in the nation with a complete ban on adoption by gay men or lesbians. The law was passed in 1977 after a campaign led by beauty queen Anita Bryant and has repeatedly been challenged, without success, since that time.

20. On June 26, 2003, the U.S. Supreme Court, with its ruling in the case *Lawrence v. Texas*, struck down all laws that prohibit sex between consenting gay adults.

❖ DISCUSSION QUESTIONS

1. If a gay ex-Marine were to knock the gun from the hand of a would-be presidential assassin today, how would you expect the news coverage of that event to differ from the coverage that followed the Oliver Sipple incident in 1975? Would the gay person's sexuality be a major aspect of the coverage?

2. If you were a news reporter assigned to cover a gay ex-Marine knocking the gun from the hand of a would-be presidential assassin today, would you ask the person's permission before reporting his or her sexuality? If he or she asked you not to publish that information, would you abide by his or her wishes?

3. Did the various individuals involved in the Oliver Sipple case study—such as newspaper columnist Herb Caen, political activist Harvey Milk, and Sipple's parents—act laudably?

4. Are you surprised about any of the specific aspects of the Oliver Sipple case study from thirty years ago?

❖ HOMEWORK ASSIGNMENTS

1. Conduct a survey of journalism students, asking them under what circumstances would they "out" a person as gay or lesbian in a news article.

2. Analyze how various news outlets handled the "coming out" of various public figures—from entertainment figures to government officials—over the past few years.

❖ REFERENCES

Abrams, F. (1977, August 21). The press, privacy and the Constitution. *New York Times*, p. F11.

Caen, H. (1975, September 24). In this corner. *San Francisco Chronicle*, p. 33.

Carlsen, W. (1984, April 14). Ford assassination case privacy ruling. *San Francisco Chronicle*, p. A2.

Cohen, E., & Elliott, D. (Eds.). (1997). *Journalism ethics: A reference handbook.* Santa Barbara, CA: ABC-CLIO.

Cooney, W. (1975, September 23). Ex-marine probably saved Ford. *San Francisco Chronicle*, p. A1.

del Olmo, F., & Lembke, D. (1975, September 23). Ex-marine deflects weapon as woman shoots. *Los Angeles Times*, p. A3.

Elliott, E. (1989, March 26). Reluctant hero. *St. Petersburg Times*, p. D1.

Elwood, J. (1992). Outing, privacy, and the First Amendment. *Yale Law Journal*, 102, 747–776.

Ford hero sues over news stories. (1975, October 1). *San Francisco Chronicle*, p. A4.

Fosburgh, L. (1975, September 26). Homosexual controversy erupts. *New York Times*, p. A16.

Friendly, F. (1990, April 8). Gays, privacy and a free press. *Washington Post*, p. B7.

Gay hero's suit on privacy is killed. (1980, April 24). *San Francisco Chronicle*, p. A7.

Goodwin, G., & Smith, R. (1994). *Groping for ethics in journalism* (3rd ed.). Ames: Iowa University Press.

Grant, J. (1991). "Outing," privacy, and freedom of the press: Sexual orientation's challenge to the Supreme Court's categorical jurisprudence. *Cornell Law Review, 77*, 103–141.

Gross, L. (1993). *Contested closets: The politics and ethics of outing.* Minneapolis: University of Minnesota Press.

Hero in Sara Moore case appeals. (1978, August 9). *San Francisco Chronicle*, p. A2.

Hero's humiliation. (1977, April 24). *New York Times*, p. A41.

Hero who foiled attack on Ford. (1989, February 6). *Chicago Tribune*, p. B7.

Homosexual is rebuffed in suit of newspapers. (1984, June 23). *New York Times*, p. A6.

Howe, K. (1999, April 15). A delicate balancing act. *San Francisco Chronicle*, p. A1.

Hurt by war and unwanted publicity, veteran who saved Ford dies alone. (1989, February 5). *Atlanta Journal Constitution*, p. A6.

Johansson, W., & Percy, W. (1994). *Outing: Shattering the conspiracy of silence.* New York: Harrington Park/Haworth.

Krinsky, C. (2000). Homophobia. In G. Haggerty (Ed.), *Gay histories and cultures: An encyclopedia* (pp. 447–449). New York: Garland.

Lawrence v. Texas, 539 U.S. 558 (2003).

Lembke, D. (1975a, September 26). Ford to thank S.F. man who deflected gun. *Los Angeles Times*, p. A3.

Lembke, D. (1975b, September 25). Hero in Ford shooting active among S.F. gays. *Los Angeles Times*, p. A3.

Lembke, D. (1975c, September 25). Hero member of S.F. gay community. *Des Moines Register*, p. A15.

Lembke, D. (1975d, September 25). Homosexual hero in Ford shooting. *Chicago Sun-Times*, p. A5.

Leo, J. (1975, September 8). Gays on the march. *Time*, pp. 1, 32–43.

Man in Ford case sues newspapers. (1975, October 1). *New York Times*, p. A20.

Man who saved Ford loses suit. (1980, April 25). *New York Times*, p. A18.

Michelmore, B. (1975, September 26). Ford should thank hero, mom says. *Detroit Free Press*, p. A3.

Mohr, R. (1992). *Gay ideas: Outing and other controversies.* Boston: Beacon.

Morain, D. (1989, February 13). Private lives. *Los Angeles Times*, p. E1.

Moretti, B. (1993). Outing: Justifiable or unwarranted invasion of privacy? The private facts tort as a remedy for disclosures of sexual orientation. *Cardozo Arts and Entertainment Law Journal, 11*, 857–890.

Murphy, P. (1975, September 26). Ford hero's mother has misgivings. *Detroit News*, p. A1.

News in brief: The state. (1975, October 1). *Los Angeles Times*, p. A2.

Oliver W. Sipple: Ex-marine thwarted shooting of Ford. (1989, February 6). *Los Angeles Times*, p. A24.

Pollack, D. (1992). Forced out of the closet: Sexual orientation and the legal dilemma of "outing." *University of Miami Law Review, 46*, 711–750.

Rodman, G. (2001). *Making sense of media: An introduction to mass communication.* Boston: Allyn and Bacon.

Safire, W. (1975, September 29). Big week for gays. *New York Times*, p. A31.

Shilts, R. (1982). *Mayor of Castro Street: The life and times of Harvey Milk.* New York: St. Martin's.

The shock: What to do? (1975, September 24). *Los Angeles Times*, p. B6.

Siegel, P. (2002). *Communication Law in America*. Boston: Allyn and Bacon.

Tragic heroes. (1996, August 19). *Time*, p. 17.

Wick, R. (1991). Out of the closet and into the headlines: "Outing" and the private facts tort. *Georgetown Law Journal, 80,* 413–433.

Wood, J. (1975, September 24). He saved Ford's life—period. *San Francisco Examiner,* p. A1.

❖ ADDITIONAL RESOURCES

www.gaytoday.com/garchive/viewpoint/092401vi.htm

www.lambda.net/~maximum/sipple.html

www.randomhouse.com/features/americancentury/imperialpres.html

5

"Publications of a Dangerous Tendency"

John C. Watson

❖ ❖ ❖

This intriguing notice appeared on the front page of a Kentucky newspaper in the summer of 2004: "It has come to the editor's attention that the *Herald Leader* neglected to cover the Civil Rights Movement. We regret the omission" (Blackford & Minch, 2004, p. A1). The *Clarion-Ledger*, a Mississippi newspaper, made a similar confession in the 1990s and revealed that it had published propaganda about the human rights struggle of African Americans in hopes of suppressing and killing the movement (Dao, 2004).

Suppression in a variety of forms has similarly dogged the human rights struggle of homosexuals for centuries, but when the Stonewall Rebellion became the emblematic event of the gay rights movement in 1969, press coverage in New York City was not suppressed. Rather, it teetered on the edge of propaganda, as the public was informed of a violent response to a police raid on the Stonewall Inn, a gay club. A headline in the *New York Daily News* derisively announced: "Homo Nest Raided, Queen Bees Are Stinging Mad" (Lisker, 1969, p. 1). Conversely,

The Village Voice sympathetically reported the incident under the headline: "Gay Power Comes to Sheridan Square" (Truscott, 1969, p. 1).

The mass media have played strikingly similar roles in advancing or suppressing the human rights campaigns of African Americans, homosexuals, and other disenfranchised groups in the United States. Social and political movements have faltered during their earliest days when the forces arrayed against them were able to stifle the media-aided public dialogue about the troubling issues they raised and thereby deny them a place on the public agenda. The gay rights movement and the 20th-century Civil Rights movement of African Americans are indebted to the First Amendment as applied in two major U.S. Supreme Court rulings that repudiated censorship and empowered the movements to achieve major triumphs at pivotal points in their historic struggles. A common rationale offered to justify denying the two movements access to the media was that they were transmitting "ideas of a dangerous tendency"—ideas that challenged the established social order.

This chapter explores how the First Amendment helped defeat efforts to keep the press from circulating information about the human rights and Civil Rights movements of African Americans and homosexuals.

❖ MEDIA AS MARKETPLACES OF IDEAS

Because the American public relies on news coverage for information about important issues—and even to learn which issues are important—the press plays a major role in setting the public's agenda. Information is so often the engine that drives democratic change in the United States that the First Amendment was written to keep information flowing freely. The First Amendment creates and protects a theoretical marketplace of ideas as a means of allowing an informed citizenry to change its political and social institutions peacefully through democratic processes. Ideas must be free to enter the marketplace so their weaknesses and strengths can become evident through comparison and competition. The public, informed by the interchange of ideas, will then choose and democratically adopt the best of them, according to the theory.

This marketplace was operational during the first stage of the African American Civil Rights movement, when the primary mission was to abolish slavery. It was fostered in no small measure during the

19th century by abolitionists' use of the mails to broaden circulation of newspapers, pamphlets, and novels that sought to convince the American public of the evils of human bondage and persuade them to end it. "The hope was that free speech would expose slavery as immoral, impractical, and inconsistent with the self-interest of the majority of Southerners," observed William T. Mayton (1994, p. 397), a scholar of 19th-century free-press issues. Indicative of this hope was the practice of abolitionist William Lloyd Garrison of Massachusetts. He routinely mailed his newspaper, *The Liberator*, to editors of Southern and other proslavery newspapers who would reprint his antislavery tirades and include their own counterarguments nearby. These papers would be mailed back to Garrison and he would publish excerpts of the slavery commentary with another rejoinder (Streitmatter, 1997). Southern writer Hilton R. Helper (1969), who lived through the period, was convinced that the slavery issue could have been settled democratically by the competition of ideas instead of through the cataclysmic clash of arms that was the Civil War. "Give us fair play, secure to us the right of discussion, the freedom of speech and we will settle the difficulty at the ballot box," he pleaded (p. 7).

Access to the mail was virtually indispensable to the free press during the 19th century. President Andrew Jackson once said of the postal service: "Through its agency we have secured to ourselves the full enjoyment of the blessings of a free press" (Richardson, 1904, p. 61). The great bulk of American newspapers during this period did not have an extensive network of correspondents throughout the country. They relied on articles culled from papers mailed from distant locales (McGill, 2003). "Well into the nineteenth century, most newspaper editors received out-of-town news by exchanging newspapers with each other," according to legal scholar Michael T. Gibson (1986, p. 263). Federal lawmakers recognized how vital this practice was to the American republic and enacted the Postal Act of 1792, which allowed editors to make these exchanges through the mail free of charge. Newspapers accounted for 70% of mail volume in the United States in the 19th century and clearly were the foremost medium supplying the marketplace of ideas.

Closing the Mail to Abolitionists

Abolitionists based in the northeastern states relied heavily on the postal service during the 1830s to circulate their newspapers and tracts throughout the country. Their couriers were attacked physically and verbally by opponents in the North and the South. In the latter region, these messages suffered official sanctions, because they were considered "publications of a dangerous tendency." Indeed, that was the terminology used by President Andrew Jackson in 1835 when he publicly asked Congress to pass laws barring abolitionist publications from the mail (*Congressional Globe*, 1835, p. 36).

Congress found the proposed legislation would violate the First Amendment and rejected it. A counterproposal by South Carolina Senator John C. Calhoun acknowledged the Constitutional infirmity of Jackson's suggestion but supported its purpose. At a time when the First Amendment limited only the federal government, Calhoun sought to reserve to the individual states this power to censor the mail. His proposal failed to carry, but it nonetheless became the *de facto* practice in the South (Eaton, 1951). By the late 1830s, abolitionist writings were being plucked from the mail as a matter of course by Southern postmasters.

Mayton and Helper's contention that the South might eventually have been able to solve the slavery problem peacefully had the issue remained in free debate relies on the fact that the debate had been under way in Dixie for decades before it was shut down. Indeed, as Williamson (1984) has observed, "There were more antislavery societies in the South in the 1820s than there were in the North" (p. 14). For long periods, the slavery issue remained such a focal point of Southern discourse that Williamson also characterized it as "a difficulty susceptible to solution" (p. 13). In Virginia, for example, legislative talks to end slavery were quite common and seemed to be headed toward abolishing that peculiar institution before the 1830s. As late as 1831, Virginia Governor John Floyd wrote in his diary: "Before I leave this Government I will have contrived to have a law passed gradually abolishing slavery in this state" (Ambler, 1918, p. 170). Floyd's vow was prompted by a slave uprising led by Nat Turner in Southampton County that killed approximately 60 white men, women, and children, slave owners and non–slave owners alike. The uprising effectively ended all debate about abolition in Virginia. If that debate had not ended, according to Williamson, the commonwealth might not have joined the secession of slave-holding states, and perhaps there would have been no Civil War. Virginia was crucial to the Confederacy's ability to wage a prolonged war (Foote, 1958; McPherson, 1988; Potter, 1976).

Turner's uprising and the fear of more slave violence caused massive suppression in the Southern marketplace of ideas. "The Turner insurrection and its sequel marked the last time that slavery was seriously challenged in Dixie. . . . And organized antislavery action would become an exclusively Northern phenomenon," Williamson wrote (1984, p. 16). After Turner, according to Southern historian Eaton (1951), "The subject that was most dangerous to discuss in the Old South was the eradication of slavery" (p. 162). As a result, Northern abolitionists relied heavily on the written word and the mail to circulate their message of freedom. The great bulk of these mailings were sent directly to elected Southern officials and policy makers in the hope of keeping the prospect of emancipation on the political agenda. Some of the more vociferous mailings, however, were intended for the slaves themselves and blatantly called for violent insurrection as a means to freedom. Such calls to violence were rejected by the American Anti-Slavery Society, the largest abolitionist group. Nonetheless, many Southerners assumed any call for abolition would eventually reach the slaves and incite them to violence, according to Curtis (1995). This caused terror in many Southern communities because black slaves drastically outnumbered whites. In some regions, the ratio of blacks to whites was 50 to 1.

Abolitionists conducted a concerted campaign against slavery by deluging the South with written vitriolic attacks on the system and demanding immediate manumission. The American Anti-Slavery Society placed more than a million newspapers and tracts in the mail in 1835 (Fowler, 1977). This prompted widespread mail censorship in the South. The case of Charleston, SC Postmaster Alfred Huger was pivotal. Huger's post office received a huge shipment of abolitionist writings that year and was surrounded by a mob of irate South Carolinians who wanted the materials burned. Huger resisted the mob but dutifully separated the offending materials from the other mail and placed them in one sack. That night, the post office was broken into and only that sack was taken, Fowler reported. Charleston subsequently formed a committee that passed a resolution that claimed the U.S. Constitution prohibited the conversion of the Post Office "into an instrument for the dissemination of incendiary publications" (Fowler, 1977, p. 26). The quoted section of the resolution is remarkable for its similarity to a statement made by a U.S. Supreme Court justice more than a century later as he complained about allowing homosexual-themed magazines to be circulated by mail (*Manual Enterprises v. Day*, 1962, p. 519).

During this mail onslaught, *The Liberator* emerged as one of the most strident voices of abolition. Printed in Boston and distributed in the South, it demanded immediate freedom for every slave in the United States and condemned the immorality of slaveholders (Cooper, 1983). Many abolitionists used personal invective that "produced a harsh and violent reaction in the North as well as the South. Indeed, anti-abolition incidents were probably more numerous in the North than in the South" (Curtis, 1995, p. 800). The widespread official suppression of the abolitionist message that occurred in the South did not materialize in the North, however. The Southern response was widespread and nearly manic because, according to Cooper, the Southern man considered these to be attacks on his honor and not mere social or political discourse. Note the tone of the following excerpt from a letter South Carolina Postmaster Huger sent to his counterpart in New York, where many of the abolitionist papers were mailed: "let the question of Slavery be decided elsewhere than in the P.O. where the Post Master himself is a Slave holder, and cannot believe it sinful without convicting his own soul & his own ancestors for five generations" (Fowler, 1977, p. 27). This letter indicates that when slavery was under abolitionist attack, considerations of moral and political philosophy became virtually irrelevant to the Southern man because honor was his most prized possession. It was essential to his liberty. Without it, he was no better than a slave.

In addition to prompting censorship of the mail, widespread circulation of abolitionist newspapers and pamphlets caused Southern states to outlaw the teaching of reading to slaves for fear that they could thereby be incited to insurrection. The penalties ranged from a year in prison and a public whipping for a first offense to "death without benefit of clergy" for a second offense (Eaton, 1951, p. 24). The fact that Nat Turner had been able to read abolitionist rants and news reports about the slavery debates was cited often as justification for these laws, but some of the legislation existed before the Turner uprising (Savage, 1938). Virginians complained that even newspaper articles reporting debates about the legitimacy of slavery could cause slaves to rebel and should be suppressed (Curtis, 1995, p. 798). As a result, Southerners instituted a system that would have censored all communications in the mass media to such an extent that the entire Southern population, whites and blacks, would be limited to "reading only ideas acceptable for circulation among slaves" (Curtis, 1995, p. 108). This denigration of the messages deemed suitable for public consumption precisely parallels what U.S. postal officials did to periodicals with homosexual themes more than a century later.

These "incendiary" publications transformed the Jeffersonian liberal Southern society into a closed and repressive community (Eaton, 1951). As a result, "the Virginia Legislature passed in 1836 the most intolerant law that was ever placed on its statute books" (Eaton, 1951, p. 127). It became a felony to dispute the right to own slaves, advocate the end of slavery, or urge slaves to rebel. "To enforce these provisions postmasters and justices of the peace were given inquisitorial power over the mails and offenders against these laws could be arrested by any free white person" (Eaton, 1951, p. 44). These laws were never challenged on federal Constitutional grounds; a fact Eaton (1951) called a "striking example of the nonassertion of Federal power." Federal authority to stop the Southern censorship had been on the books since 1782, and Congress passed legislation in 1836 that allowed the criminal prosecution of any postmaster who unlawfully detained mail. There is no record, however, of federal law being invoked to stop the widespread interdiction of abolitionist mail. U.S. Postmaster General Amos Kendall officially informed the Southern postmasters that they had no legal authority to pull abolitionist publications from the mail, according to Fowler (1977). At the same time, Kendall indicated that they would not face federal prosecution if they excluded incendiary writings about slavery. "We owe an obligation to the laws, but a higher one to the communities in which we live, and if the *former* be perverted to destroy the *latter* it is patriotism to disregard them" (Fowler, 1977, p. 28).

In accord with local public sentiment and state legislation that forbade the circulation of written material with "bad tendencies," Southern postmasters purged the mail of incendiary matter as well as more placidly reasoned discussions of the slavery issue. "Southern postmasters simply assumed the authority to refuse delivery of antislavery publications" (Mayton, 1994, p. 400). With the federal policy so weak, allowing or conducting mail censorship became the rational choice for Southern postmasters, especially when the state and federal consequences were compared: Federal law imposed a penalty of only 6 months in jail for hindering the mails, but a Maryland law, for example, imposed a penalty of 10 to 20 years imprisonment for delivering antislavery publications. In North Carolina, the penalty was death.

As a result of widespread interdiction, the opportunity was lost to test and peaceably determine the worth of slavery in the marketplace of ideas. By 1860, the schism between slaveholding and free states was firmly established. Fowler (1977) surmised that "abolitionists' insistence on sending incendiary literature through the mails in spite of state laws was one factor that led to the Civil War" (p. 41). Mayton (1994) similarly concluded: "One of the causes of the impending dissolution was thought to be an abridgment of speech that had established the North and South as separate intellectual environments" (p. 398).

Closing the Mail to Homosexual Messages

More than a century later, postal interdiction of "publications of a dangerous tendency" was still practiced in the United States, but it was not limited to the South. Suppression was imposed throughout the country wherever a publication that sought to explore homosexuality or communicate among homosexuals entered the mail delivery system. Los Angeles Postmaster Otto K. Olesen precipitated the landmark homosexual press rights decision, *One, Inc. v. Olesen,* when in 1954 he banned the delivery of an edition of a publication unabashedly titled *ONE–The Homosexual Magazine.* American homosexuals' fight for equal Constitutional rights began as a result of that decision, according to journalist-historians Murdoch and Price (2001). Homosexual subject matter, whether verbal or pictorial, was restricted from the mail, but not because the majority of society feared it would incite a Nat Turner–like violent uprising by this largely hidden and powerless minority. Nonetheless, a Post Office lawyer claimed during oral argument before the Supreme Court that this material might well incite its homosexual recipients to commit illegal lustful acts because they were more susceptible to sexual influences than heterosexuals (Friedman, 1970). Postal officials found the concept of homosexuality morally repugnant and perfunctorily deemed communication about it to be obscene. For more than a century, these postal restrictions were maintained in accord with the latest manifestation of the Comstock Act, a federal law named for legendary American censor Anthony Comstock. Congress passed the first law specifically prohibiting the transmission of obscenity through the mail in 1865, but it acquired teeth with the imposition of criminal penalties in 1873 by the enactment of the Comstock Act.

Despite an abundance of state and federal legislation against obscenity and dictum in a Supreme Court ruling in 1941 that said obscenity was not protected by the First Amendment (*Chaplinsky v. New Hampshire,* 1942), the court did not define obscenity until 1957 in the case of

Roth v. United States (1957). *Roth* deemed a communication obscene if it (a) primarily appealed to the prurient interest in a patently offensive manner and (b) had no redeeming social value. The *Roth* decision also reaffirmed that the First Amendment did not protect obscenity and that purveyors of obscenity could be criminally prosecuted. The ruling also unequivocally outlawed the Hicklin Test, which postal authorities had been using for decades to exclude many types of sexual communications. The Hicklin Test was developed in the courts of England in the 19th century and found any communication obscene if it was deemed to have a tendency to deprave or corrupt any person who might perceive it.

Nonetheless, when the Los Angeles postmaster determined several years later that *ONE* magazine was obscene and therefore not mailable under federal law, he was applying a version of the Hicklin Test. Two federal courts found the postmaster's action legal. One of them, the U.S. Ninth Circuit Court of Appeals, wrote: "Our ultimate conclusion as to whether the magazine is mailable or not must be based on the effect or impact that the wording of the various articles in the magazine have upon the reader" (*One, Inc. v. Olesen*, 1957, p. 775).

Postal censors in the antebellum South similarly had found justification for their actions in the potentially dangerous effect that mail-borne abolitionist writings might have on the slaves who read them. Just as Southern mail handlers apparently decided they would not risk converting customarily docile slaves into rebellious, murdering Nat Turners, 20th-century postal officials decided they would not risk exposing "normal" people to materials that could undermine their sexual orientation or affront their morals, or that might inflame homosexuals to commit illegal acts. Postal officials' reluctance to expose the public to these 20th-century "publications of a dangerous tendency" was based on the same rationale used a century earlier. Just as the latter had censored the mail so that it was safe for slaves to read without producing harmful effects, federal postal officials of the mid–20th century censored mail so it would be safe for children and others susceptible to the harmful effects of homosexual-themed communications. This was the rationale of the discredited Hicklin Test.

To explain the harmful effect of *ONE* magazine, the appeals court reviewed an article titled "Sappho Remembered," the story of a young woman who leaves her male childhood sweetheart to live with a woman. The court described the article as "nothing more than cheap pornography calculated to promote lesbianism" (*One, Inc. v. Olesen*, 1957, p. 777). A *ONE* poem about homosexual activity among British lords was similarly found obscene because it "pertains to sexual matters of such a vulgar and indecent nature that it tends to arouse feelings of disgust and revulsion. It is dirty, vulgar and offensive to the moral senses" (p. 777). Attorneys for the magazine claimed its owners had been denied equal protection of the law by the postal officials' use of a biased definition that equated homosexuality with obscenity, but the appeals court disagreed.

When that ruling was appealed to the U.S. Supreme Court, it was overturned (*One, Inc. v. Olesen*, 1958). Although this was an unprecedented victory for an openly homosexual publication, there was considerable uncertainty about what the ruling actually meant, because it said very little. It is not unusual for Supreme Court rulings to run from 20 to 75 pages. The entire text of the ruling in *One v. Olesen* was one sentence and a fragment: "The petition for writ of certiorari is granted and the judgment of the United States Court of Appeals for the Ninth Circuit is reversed. Roth v. United States, 354 U.S. 476." Some scholars of jurisprudence found significance in the fact that the opinion in *ONE* was delivered the same day as the opinion in *Sunshine Book Co. v. Summerfield* (1958) and was verbally identical. The Sunshine Book Company was before the high court because it published nudist photo magazines. Postal authorities found its February 1955 edition of *Sunshine and Health* magazine and the January–February 1955 edition of *Sun Magazine* obscene and therefore unmailable. The Supreme Court overturned the finding.

The message of the court's combined release of the rulings may have been that mere nudity without depictions of explicit sexual conduct was not obscene—or that the Post Office had no legal authority to act as a censor—or that homosexual themes and subject matter, as featured in *ONE*, were not inherently obscene. The uncertainty did not end until 1962, when the court decided *Manual Enterprises v. Day* (1962), a landmark case that challenged postal interdiction of magazines that featured nudity in association with homosexuality. Manual Enterprises published three homosexual magazines, *Grecian Guild Pictorial*, *MANual*, and *Trim*, which were filled with photographs of nude men and were mailed to newsstands across the country. Postal officials in Virginia seized 405 copies of these magazines in 1960 and determined that they were obscene and therefore unmailable. The company took the matter to the Supreme Court.

The court's rulings in *Manual Enterprises v. Day* (1962), although fragmented, dispelled some confusion about the central points of law established in *Sunshine Book Co. v. Summerfield* (1958) and *ONE v. Olesen* (1958). Justice John M. Harlan, who wrote the 6-1 decision, stated early on: "Of course not every portrayal of male or female nudity is obscene" (p. 490). A concurring opinion by Justice William Brennan, which was joined by two more justices, said postal officials did not have the legal authority from Congress to judge obscenity. Brennan wrote:

> The provisions . . . would have to be far more explicit for us to assume that Congress made such a radical departure from our traditions and undertook to clothe the Postmaster General with the power to supervise the tastes of the reading public of the country. (p. 519)

Until the *Manual Enterprises v. Day* (1962) ruling, postal authorities had a long-standing policy of excluding from the mail materials featuring nudity in association with homosexuality. Nudity in a heterosexual context, however, was not automatically proscribed. This discriminatory practice was defended by Arthur E. Summerfield, who was the U.S. postmaster general and respondent in *Sunshine Book v. Summerfield*. He referred to nudist magazines and "so-called art studies," which were the primary content of the magazines at issue in *Manual Enterprises v. Day* (1962), as "the most troublesome and potentially the most serious" types of obscene material found in the mail (Summerfield, 1960, p. 140). Summerfield also claimed a causal link from "the commercialized spread of obscenity to the increase in juvenile delinquency and other crimes." He claimed "Psychiatrists have pointed out that a perfectly healthy child, exposed continually to the depravities of smutty material can be turned into an immoral and distorted creature, if not an outright pervert" (p. 143).

One of the types of "perversion" Summerfield referred to was homosexuality. Implicit in the Post Office's arguments made at judicial and administrative hearings to exclude material from the mail was the assertion that these materials could cause a young heterosexual to become a homosexual and that homosexuals could be incited by these materials to go on sexual rampages. Just as the 19th-century Southern postal censors sought to cleanse the mail of material that was not "suitable" for slaves, the 20th-century censors sought to excise material unsuitable for homosexuals. In *Manual Enterprises v. Day* (1962), the

Supreme Court found that postal officials and the lower courts had woven these justifications into their definition of obscenity, which was at odds with the definition the court crafted in *Roth v. United States* (1957). "In the Post Office they have changed this [*Roth*] definition or this test of obscenity that this court has laid down, to one in which material is obscene if it would appeal to the prurient interest of a homosexual," attorney Stanley Dietz told the court during oral argument on behalf of Manual Enterprises (Friedman, 1970, pp. 90–91).

The conflicting definition was not allowed to survive. The court said the lower courts had relied solely and incorrectly on the part of the *Roth v. United States* (1957) definition that deemed material obscene if it appealed to the prurient interest. The court said the material also must be patently offensive. If the two requirements were not conjoined, the popular heterosexual men's magazines *Playboy* and *Esquire*, which were mailable, would be legally obscene. Although Harlan claimed the court did not have to address the question of whether a magazine's appeal to the prurient homosexual interest was relevant to determining whether it was obscene, in practical effect it did address and dispose of that issue. When the court made the legal and factual determination that the magazines' sexually suggestive photographs of nude and seminude men were clearly intended to titillate other men but were not patently offensive, it indicated that homosexual themes and appeals did not render communication obscene per se. The court had acknowledged that homosexuals have the same right to sexual communication as the majority heterosexual population. Dietz had raised the issue during oral argument. "If we so-called normal people . . . are entitled to have our pin-up, then why shouldn't the second class citizen, the homosexual group . . . be allowed to have their pin-up?" (*Manual Enterprises v. Day*, 1962, p. 93).

Scholars have cited the *Manual Enterprises v. Day* (1962) ruling as pivotal in the development of the lesbian and gay rights movement because it laid the "groundwork for the growth of a national gay press" (Hunter, 1993, p. 1701). Some homosexual publications had avoided the mail for fear of the postal censors and criminal prosecution. A Los Angeles–based lesbian journal titled *Vice Versa*, for example, was published by Lisa Ben in 1947, but she would not place it in the mail for fear of prosecution, according to Eskridge (1997, pp. 757–758). The message sent by the court in *Manual Enterprises v. Day* (1962) encouraged the production and widespread circulation of many more homosexual publications, from highbrow to porn, and that phenomenon gave this once-hidden group a public identity and status as a minority group, according to Eskridge. "Homophile publications . . . were the first evidence many gay people had that they were not accidental monsters," he wrote (p. 708). Eskridge concluded that homosexual newspapers helped displace the bars as the local center of gay subculture.

This sense of homosexual consciousness coalesced into a movement, a cultural presence, and a political power largely as a result of the lifting of restrictions on the homosexual press. One of the understated but most important demands made by the lawyer representing Manual Enterprises was that homosexuals be treated just as heterosexuals are, without discrimination and with the full protection of the Constitution. Officially, the court did not directly address any issue of homosexual discrimination until 1996 in the case of *Romer v. Evans* (1996), but arguably it did so indirectly in *Manual Enterprises v. Day* (1962). *Romer v. Evans* (1996), in an admittedly imprecise comparison, was to the gay rights movement what *Brown v. Board of Education of Topeka* (1954) was to the Civil Rights movement, in that both rulings found discrimination against a minority group to be unlawful. *Manual Enterprises v. Day* (1962) also can be credited with bringing the curtain down on the U.S. Postal Service's long role as a federal censor and for putting homosexual rights on the Supreme Court's civil rights agenda.

Muffling Their Rising Voices

As the resurrected Civil Rights movement began to develop momentum during the 1950s and early 1960s, Southern officials reacted much as their predecessors had a century earlier by trying to suppress media discourse about the abolitionist stage of the movement. The targeted media in the 20th century were newspapers and television, which had outstripped the mail as primary information sources for the public. The movement's mission had evolved from freeing the slaves to winning for their descendants the same panoply of human rights exercised by other Americans. News coverage was an integral part of the movement, as indicated by civil rights activist James Farmer's explanation of the purpose of the "freedom rides" through the segregated South: "We figured that the government would have to respond if we created a situation that was headline news all over the world, and affected the nation's image abroad" (Garrow, 1988, p. 156). Similarly, journalist-author Anthony Lewis, in his book *Make No Law,* reported an Alabama newspaper editorial's complaint that the South was libeled daily by Northern news coverage and "subjected to more calumnies than it had been 'in the days of the New England fanatical abolitionists'" (Lewis, 1991, p. 84). This hostility to print and broadcast commentary on the movement was apparently deep-seated and widespread in the South and prompted retaliatory suppression in the guise of libel lawsuits. Lawsuits became instruments of censorship after the Alabama attorney general consulted with the governor and gave the tactic his imprimatur, according to documents filed with the U.S. Supreme Court by four civil rights activists who became defendants in the most famous of these lawsuits. This was the landmark *New York Times v. Sullivan* (1964) case, and African-American clergymen Ralph D. Abernathy, Fred L. Shuttlesworth, S. S. Seay, Sr., and J. E. Lowery were named codefendants with the *New York Times* newspaper.

Montgomery, AL's Public Safety Commissioner L. B. Sullivan filed the lawsuits against the newspaper and the clergymen because the paper published an ad that bore the activists' names and made some minor misstatements about how Alabama officials had treated the African-American civil rights protestors. The ad solicited contributions to support the Civil Rights movement and its embattled leader, the Rev. Martin Luther King, Jr. Most of the text recounted the travails of King and his college student followers as they staged peaceful protests throughout the South. Printed in large type at the top of the ad were the words: "Heed Their Rising Voices," a phrase taken from a March 19, 1960 *New York Times* editorial supporting the movement. Sullivan's court papers said he sued as a result of false claims of "rampant, vicious, terroristic and criminal police action in Montgomery Alabama, to a nationwide public." Lewis, however, surmised that "Commissioner Sullivan's real target was the role of the American press as an agent of democratic change" (Lewis, 1991, p. 42). The four activist ministers also were targets, and they were used as pawns to keep the lawsuit in state courts, away from federal interference. The four ministers were among 16 people listed as supporters of the ad's message, but none of the others was sued. The four were the only residents of Alabama. If any of the others had been sued, the initial trial could have been moved to federal court, because out-of-state defendants can invoke federal diversity jurisdiction. Sullivan did not want to take that risk. "Mr. Sullivan deliberately joined the four ministers as a means of destroying diversity in the case," explained Fred D. Gray, the ministers' attorney (Gray, 1992, p. 1226).

Other Southern officials adopted the libel lawsuit tactic. As Lewis (1991) noted, by 1964, lawsuits seeking nearly $300 million in libel damages had been filed against newspapers, television networks, and the distributors of pamphlets that addressed civil rights issues in the South. Among these was a suit against the CBS television network for reporting on the difficulties African Americans faced when trying to register to vote in Montgomery. Another suit targeted two African-American ministers who distributed a pamphlet telling how a Birmingham police chief shot an African-American man in the back and permanently paralyzed him. *Times* reporter Harrison E. Salisbury was not only sued for millions of dollars by Alabama officials in Birmingham and Bessemer, he was also indicted on 42 criminal libel charges in Jefferson County.

Sullivan's complaints about factual errors in the ad were valid, but the basic gist of the ad was correct. For example, the ad claimed King had been arrested by Alabama officials seven times, but it was actually only four; the ad claimed police officers had surrounded the campus of Alabama State College, but the officers did not completely encircle the campus, although large numbers of them were dispatched about the campus; the ad claimed the cafeteria had been closed to starve the student protestors, but it was actually closed for other reasons.

Sullivan prevailed at trial and on the defendants' appeal to the Alabama Supreme Court. Alabama libel law allowed the imposition of strict liability and permitted government officials to claim their reputations were impugned by false reports of bad acts attributed to those they supervised. The Alabama Supreme Court's ruling relied on prior U.S. Supreme Court pronouncements that libel was not protected by the First or Fourteenth Amendments. As the *Times'* lawyers sought a hearing before the U.S. Supreme Court, Sullivan's lawyers tried to persuade the court not to think of their case as part of a wave of lawsuits against the press as the *Times* and civil liberties groups had requested, but to weigh its merits alone. A brief filed by the American Civil Liberties Union said:

> The trial of this action was not brought to right a wrong against [Sullivan] but to carry out the recommendation of the state of Alabama ... to punish the Negro clergymen and the newspaper that printed the publication and to prevent that newspaper and other newspapers who hear of the judgment from making similar publications in the future. (American Civil Liberties Union, 1964, pp. 36–37)

Ultimately, the nation's highest court decreed that libel was protected by the First and Fourteenth Amendments, and the justices were convinced of a concerted Southern effort to use libel law to suppress the press. The latter realization underscored the necessity of extending Constitutional protection for the press. Justice William Brennan, who wrote the decision, indicated that the Alabama courts' application of libel law functioned in a manner reminiscent of the embarrassing Sedition Act of 1798 by penalizing the public for criticizing government. That application would upend the basic American democratic principle that government officials are subordinate to the people and should be subject to criticism and receptive to the people's grievances. Brennan wrote:

The present advertisement, as an expression of grievance and protest on one of the major public issues of our time, would seem clearly to qualify for the constitutional protection. The question is whether it forfeits that protection by the falsity of some of its factual statements and by its alleged defamation of respondent. (New York Times v. Sullivan, 1964, p. 271)

The court's answer was expressed best earlier in the opinion, with the observation that "libel can claim no talismanic immunity from constitutional limitations" (*New York Times v. Sullivan*, 1964, p. 269). The court also crafted a rule that prevents government officials from winning libel suits based on criticism of their job performance unless they can prove actual malice. That means officials have to prove the libel was published with knowledge that it was false or with a reckless disregard for whether it was false.

Through *New York Times v. Sullivan* (1964), the court articulated the important role the press must play in the American democratic system that makes the public superior to the officials they elect. It also established protective rules and guiding principles that have been bulwarks against government censorship in every area of communication.

❖ CONCLUSION

Press freedom is correlated to the peaceful progress of the homosexual and African-American human rights movements in the United States. Opponents of the movements sought to hobble them by suppressing public discourse related to them. When these restrictive efforts succeeded, as in the first stage of the Civil Rights movement, spearheaded by the abolitionist press in the 19th century, the rights issues were decided by a civil war that nearly destroyed the American democratic experiment. A century later, the Civil Rights movement was revived, the gay rights movement arose, and both achieved considerable measures of success as efforts to restrict mainstream and nontraditional press discourse related to them were thwarted by Supreme Court rulings. The court protected the freedom of the press and allowed the rights issues to continue toward resolution through public discourse and subsequent political action. The crucial role that an unfettered marketplace of ideas plays in fostering peaceful social and political change was affirmed in these cases. Court rulings not only maintained press freedom but expanded and strengthened it to provide greater guarantees of liberty, to the ultimate benefit of the country as a whole and to other minority voices that may seek to be heard in the future. These rulings substantially bolstered the First Amendment's procedural and substantive protection of the press. They opened the door to greater diversity in the news and entertainment media and affirmed the American principle that a minority population is entitled to the same rights as the majority.

The fundamental tenets of the expanded marketplace of ideas theory are supported by this limited comparison of successful and failed efforts to suppress the press in conjunction with two human rights movements. Similar consequences arguably accrue when the marketplace of ideas is suppressed, not only by external forces, but by the press itself. This latter situation was raised by the Kerner Report's condemnation of the American news media in the aftermath of the urban riots of the 1960s (National Advisory Commission on Civil Disorders, 1988). Chapter 15 of the report claimed that the uprisings were partially attributable to the news media's failure to report on the longstanding problems afflicting African American communities. In this instance, the doors to the marketplace had been closed from within, through negligence, indifference, or rancor, according to the report, and may have contributed to the ensuing violence.

❖ DISCUSSION QUESTIONS

1. How many similarities other than those given in this chapter do you recognize in the two rights movements?

2. How have the entertainment media, particularly television programs, music, and movies, assisted or hindered rights movements by their depictions of minority groups?

❖ HOMEWORK ASSIGNMENTS

1. Analyze how African Americans and gay men and lesbians are presented in the news media today by auditing coverage of these two communities in a newspaper, magazine, or newscast over a specific period of time. How are the two movements being served by the presentations?

2. Examine the media treatments of African Americans passing for white and homosexuals who remain closeted by analyzing media coverage of such incidents. What are the similarities and differences?

❖ REFERENCES

Ambler, C. H. (1918). *The life and diary of John Floyd, governor of Virginia: An apostle of secession*. Richmond, VA: Richmond Press.

American Civil Liberties Union. (1964). New York Times Co. v. Sullivan [Brief No. 39].

Blackford, L., & Minch, L. (2004, July 4). Front page news—back page coverage. *Lexington Herald Leader*, p. A1.

Brown v. Board of Education of Topeka, 347 U.S. 483 (1954).

Chaplinsky v. New Hampshire, 315 U.S. 568 (1942).

Congressional Globe, 24th Congress, 1st Session, 36 (1835).

Cooper, W. J. (1983). *Liberty and slavery: Southern politics to 1860*. New York: Alfred A. Knopf.

Curtis, M. K. (1995). The curious history of attempts to suppress antislavery speech, press, and petition in 1835-37. *Northwestern University Law Review, 89*, 785–870.

Dao, J. (2004, July 13). 40 years later, civil rights makes page 1. *New York Times*, p. A1.

Eaton, C. (1951). *Freedom of thought in the old South*. New York: P. Smith.

Eskridge, W. N. (1997). Privacy jurisprudence and the apartheid of the closet. *Florida State University Law Review, 24*, 703–838.

Foote, S. (1958). *The Civil War: A narrative*. New York: Random House.

Fowler, D. G. (1977). *Unmailable: Congress and the Post Office*. Athens: University of Georgia Press.

Friedman, L. (1970). *The complete oral arguments before the Supreme Court in the major obscenity cases.* New York: Chelsea House.

Garrow, D. J. (1988). *Bearing the cross.* New York: Vintage Books.

Gibson, M. T. (1986). The supreme court and freedom of expression from 1791 to 1917. *Fordham Law Review, 55,* 263–333.

Gray, F. D. (1992). The Sullivan case: A direct product of the civil rights movement. *Case Western Reserve Law Review, 42,* 1223–1228.

Helper, H. R. (1969). *The impending crisis of the South: How to meet it.* Miami, FL: Mnemosyne.

Hunter, N. D. (1993). Identity, speech, and equality. *Virginia Law Review, 79,* 1695–1719.

Lewis, A. (1991). *Make no law.* New York: Random House.

Lisker, J. (1969, July 6). Homo nest raided, queen bees are stinging mad. *New York Daily News,* p. 1.

Manual Enterprises v. Day, 370 U.S. 478 (1962).

Mayton, W. T. (1994). Buying-up speech: Active government and the terms of the first and fourteenth amendments. *William and Mary Bill of Rights Journal, 3,* 373–418.

McGill, M. L. (2003). *American literature and the culture of reprinting 1843–1853.* Philadelphia: University of Pennsylvania Press.

McPherson, J. (1988). *Battle cry freedom: The Civil War era.* New York: Oxford University Press.

Murdoch, J., & Price, D. (2001). *Courting justice: Gay men and lesbians v. the Supreme Court.* New York: Basic Books.

National Advisory Commission on Civil Disorders. (1988). *The Kerner report: The 1968 report of the National Advisory Commission on Civil Disorders.* New York: Pantheon.

New York Times Co. v. Sullivan, 376 U.S. 254 (1964).

One, Inc. v. Olesen, 241 F.2d 772 (1957).

One, Inc. v. Olesen, 355 U.S. 371 (1958).

Potter, D. M. (1976). *The impending crisis.* New York: Harper and Row.

Richardson, J. D. (1904). *A compilation of the messages and papers of the presidents* (Vol. 2). Washington, DC: Bureau of National Literature and Art.

Romer v. Evans, 517 U.S. 620 (1996).

Roth v. United States, 354 U.S. 476 (1957).

Savage, W. S. (1938). *The controversy over the distribution of abolition literature 1830-1860.* New York: Negro Universities Press.

Streitmatter, R. (1997). *Mightier than the sword.* Boulder, CO: Westview Press.

Summerfield, A. E. (1960). *U.S. mail: The story of the United States Postal Service.* New York: Holt, Rinehart and Winston.

Sunshine Book Co. v. Summerfield, 355 U.S. 372 (1958).

Truscott, L. (1969, July 3). Gay power comes to Sheridan Square. *The Village Voice,* p.1.

Williamson, J. (1984). *The crucible of race.* New York: Oxford University Press.

❖ ADDITIONAL RESOURCES

Altman, D. (1971). *Homosexual: Oppression and liberation.* New York: Outerbridge and Dienstfry.

Columbia Free Press. (2004). The *Free Press:* Speaking truth to power. Retrieved April 22, 2005, from http://www.freepress.org/index2.php

D'Emilio, J. (1983). *Sexual politics, sexual communities.* Chicago: University of Chicago Press.

Educational Broadcasting Corporation. (2005). African American world. Retrieved April 22, 2005, from the Public Broadcasting System Web site: http://www.pbs.org/wnet/aaworld/index.html

Entman, R., & Rojecki, A. (2000). *The black image in the white mind: Media and race in America.* Chicago: University of Chicago Press.

Fuller, W. E. (1980). *The American mail, enlarger of the common life.* Chicago: University of Chicago Press.

Gross, L. P., & Woods, J. D. (1999). *The Columbia reader on lesbians and gay men in media, society, and politics.* New York: Columbia University Press.

Human Rights Campaign: Working for Lesbian, Gay, Bisexual and Transgender Equal Rights. (2005). Retrieved April 22, 2005, from http://www.hrc.org

Johnson, P., & Keith, M. C. (2001). *Queer airwaves: The story of gay and lesbian broadcasting.* Armonk, NY: M. E. Sharpe.

Newkirk, P. (2000). *Within the veil: Black journalists, white media.* New York: New York University Press.

Seeing black: The funky, alternative site for black reviews, news & voice. (2004). Retrieved April 22, 2005, from http://www.seeingblack.com

Somerville, S. (2000). *Queering the color line: Race and the invention of homosexuality in American culture.* Durham, NC: Duke University Press.

Streitmatter, R. (1995). *Unspeakable: The rise of the gay and lesbian press in America.* Boston: Faber and Faber.

Streitmatter, R. (2001). *Voices of revolution.* New York: Columbia University Press.

Streitmatter, R., & Watson, J. C. (2002). Herman Lynn Womack: Pornographer as first amendment pioneer. *Journalism History, 28*(2), 56–65.

Sumner, C. (1900). *Charles Sumner: His complete works* (Vol. 6). Boston: Lee and Shepard.

Mass media's depiction of AIDS influences the way society reacts and responds to information about the disease and to those who have contracted it.

SOURCE: Dean Lance. www.deanlance.com. Reprinted with permission of the artist.

6

Framing the AIDS Epidemic

*From "Homo"genous
Deviance to Widespread Panic*

Jamel Santa Cruze Bell

❖ ❖ ❖

M edia are a critical part of the social landscape that help shape audience perceptions and facilitate public discourse and debate by defining acceptable parameters for discussion. As the most commonly shared source of information, media serve as sense-makers to the world and are the primary presenters of ideology for large audience consumption (Collins, 2004). Controversial social issues and concerns frequently become conventional and mainstream and are represented in various media contexts (Hart, 1999). Issues surrounding sex and sexuality are prevalent examples of this, especially as modern sexuality is policed primarily by media representations. These representations are fundamental to society's knowledge and perceived understanding of diseases such as acquired immune deficiency syndrome (AIDS), a growing epidemic and social phenomenon. Much as with the intersection of media and the politics of the day, AIDS does not exist apart from the practices that conceptualize it, represent it, and respond to it (Piontek, 1992).

The AIDS epidemic has presented American society with perhaps its greatest public health and social challenge of the 20th and 21st centuries. Given the significant role media play in conveying medical information (Brodie, Hamel, Brady, Kates, & Altman, 2004), most of what people know about AIDS is derived from the media (Radford, 1996). This is especially the case for young people, who identify media as their top source of information regarding sexual health issues (Tannen, 2003).

This chapter chronicles the way AIDS has been portrayed in the media, beginning with the onset of the epidemic in the early 1980s and extending to today's depictions. This chapter begins with a discussion about the roots of AIDS, what it is, and how it is transmitted. It then discusses the evolution of media coverage and depictions of AIDS and the implications of those depictions for specific groups and society in general.

❖   A SHORT HISTORY OF AIDS

AIDS emerged as a health threat in American society in 1981. The disease was initially portrayed by media, religious leaders, and even politicians as the unfortunate consequence of sexual deviance brought on by the sexual revolution and, consequently, the transgressive behavior of homosexual men (Grmek, 1990). The positive strides achieved by gay men in the 1970s and early 1980s suffered major setbacks as AIDS was inextricably linked to the community and their lifestyle "choice." First, a group of homosexual, white men were diagnosed with a rare cancer called Kaposi's sarcoma. The cases of Kaposi's sarcoma, also called "gay cancer," were followed by a more widespread disease called pneumocystis carinii, which several homosexual men contracted. During this time, the "condition" was referred to as GRID, which stood for gay-related immune deficiency. It was believed that the newly emerging disease was a result of the homosexual lifestyle. The Centers for Disease Control (CDC) in Atlanta first wrote about the disease in 1981 in the weekly report that it distributed nationally to doctors and hospitals. The disease became known as AIDS after the CDC adopted the term in 1982 (Gross, 2001). Two other risk groups, intravenous drug users and Haitians, were later identified, along with hemophiliacs, who were known as the first "innocent victims" of AIDS (Gross, 2001).

The AIDS panic began to spread once it was suggested that the disease was not limited to the aforementioned risk groups but was a nondiscriminatory disease that could infect anyone in the general population, including children, straight men, and women. By the early 1990s, AIDS was considered the country's most urgent health problem, and the number of infected people was on the rise (Rogers, Singer, & Imperio, 1993). As public perceptions, policies, and medical advancements have evolved and changed, so too have the demographics of Americans being diagnosed with AIDS. There was such a rapid increase in AIDS diagnoses among minorities between 1991 and 1996 that AIDS emerged as the leading cause of death for 25- to 44-year-old African American men and African American women in that same age group during that time (Pickle, Quinn, & Brown, 2002). By 1999, AIDS was one of the leading causes of death for all 25- to 44-year-old adults in America (Hart, 1999). Currently, the number of infections grows by about 40,000 each year (Lehrman, 2004). Cases of AIDS resulting from heterosexual transmission of the human immunodeficiency virus (HIV) are on the rise, with women and adolescents comprising a significant percentage of these cases; nonetheless, the HIV continues to grow fastest in poor communities of color (Lehrman, 2004). African Americans, Latinos, and women are disproportionately affected by the disease and represent the majority of the new HIV cases (Brodie et al., 2004; UNAIDS, 2004).

Transmitting AIDS

AIDS is the collection of symptoms and infections linked to the most severe and advanced stages of HIV (UNAIDS, 2004). AIDS is not generally transmitted through water, nonsexual contact, or by breathing the same air as an infected person. The exchange of bodily fluids, such as blood and semen, is necessary for the transmission of the virus, which may progress to AIDS. Specific ways of contracting the virus include anal and vaginal sexual intercourse, receiving transfusions from infected blood, and sharing needles; infected pregnant women may pass the virus to their fetuses (Levitt & Rosenthal, 1999). Although AIDS has been a serious malady for particular societal groups, such as gay men and African Americans, there is no identifiable demographic of people who are more at risk than any other due to their specific demographic categorization. It is risky behavioral choices and actions that put people at risk for contracting HIV.

❖ FRAMING AIDS

Media framing involves selection and salience. It is an issue of power that functions to define the context of an occurrence, highlighting distinguishable elements and controlling how those elements are interpreted. Reese (2003) describes framing as an exercise of power, particularly as it affects people's understanding of media's posture and their relationship with the social and political world. In other words, media framing is a socialization strategy that has powerful implications for the way people react and act toward social issues and events. Thus, media frames affect the way one understands and perceives social reality (Baylor, 1996; Entman, 1993; Hertog & McLeod, 2003; Jamieson & Waldman, 2003; McQuail, 2000). "The media's frame helps determine whether people notice, understand, or remember a problem, and how they evaluate and choose to respond to it" (Pickle et al., 2002, p. 430). A metaphoric description of framing relates to the frame of a picture. The purpose of this type of frame is to highlight particular elements of a picture and hide others by establishing a clearly delineated border. Entire people or events can be lost or hidden as the frame functions as a guide for the recipient's eyes and attention. In short, the frame only allows an observer to focus on and ultimately see what is purposefully selected and shown within its boundaries. The observer may then assume that whatever is hidden from view is of little importance or value.

In the context of AIDS, framing refers to the way in which mainstream media package and disseminate information about the epidemic. Because structural and institutional norms influence the process of framing, mass media's depiction of AIDS influences the way society reacts and responds to information about the disease and to those who have contracted it. Diseases are given meaning and carry certain attributions in the media (Clarke, 1992). "Frames give us particular renditions of events and issues that, in time, define what is normal or legitimate and what is deviant" (Bardhan, 2001, p. 287). The media, according to Gross (2001), "are likely to be most powerful in cultivating images of events and groups about which we have little firsthand opportunity for learning" (p. 11). Media played a pivotal role in shaping people's perceptions of those who were HIV-positive and those who acquired AIDS by locating the disease in the deviant and mysterious homosexual lifestyle. According to Bardhan (2001), AIDS coverage has historically fallen within the following frames: (a) victimization, (b) deviance and abnormality, (c) blame attribution, and (d) power of modern medicine to develop a miracle cure.

Early Coverage

HIV/AIDS became a significant sociopolitical issue in the early 1980s. Early mainstream media coverage was scant, and little attention was paid to the new virus (Alwood, 1996; Gross, 2001; Hertog, Finnegan, & Kahn, 1994). Mainstream media took its cues from the political leadership, whose first response was an attempt to regulate gay men's sexual behaviors and to contain the disease. There was little government effort and support offered to expand research efforts, to enhance health-care provisions, or to provide educational and preventive services (Levitt & Rosenthal, 1999). This government reticence was fought by nongovernmental AIDS service organizations, which played a vital role in the creation of support and educational services. AIDS was generally viewed as a disease afflicting the isolated world of homosexuals, who, because of their perverse and immoral lifestyle, were responsible for their own illness (Alwood, 1996). The first mention of then-unknown disease in the American mainstream media appeared in a June 4, 1981, *Los Angeles Times* article that resulted from the CDC's weekly report to doctors and hospitals and discussed the mysterious disease that would later be called AIDS (Alwood, 1996).[1]

Although mainstream media largely ignored the epidemic or viewed it primarily as a threat to the "general population" if it spread beyond deviant "risk groups" (Gross, 2001), the gay press covered the new and deadly disease—even when mainstream media refused. Consequently, the gay press played a pivotal role in publicizing the devastating effects of the disease on the community.

When the mainstream media did cover AIDS during this era, they were ambiguous in their descriptions of how the disease was transmitted, for fear of offending the readers, viewers, or advertisers (Lander, 1988). This strategic ambiguity resulted in the use of terms about contracting the disease that were unfamiliar to many readers and viewers, yet the link to the already stigmatized gay male and his deviant lifestyle remained clear (Piontek, 1992). The *us versus them* dichotomy was prevalent, which set the stage for AIDS to be depicted in the media as "gay plague, the price paid for anal intercourse," or "the disease that turns fruits into vegetables" (Treichler, 1999, p. 32–33). AIDS was framed as a universal problem perpetuated by gay men (Altman, 1986; Netzhammer & Shamp, 1994), or *them*. Epstein (1995) compares the three stages in the American and Australian media's construction of AIDS. She characterizes the initial reports about the epidemic by the marking of people with AIDS as "other," accompanied by the vilification of homosexuality. "AIDS disrupts comfortable boundaries of gender, race, sexuality, and nationality" (Bardhan, 2001, p. 283). "It questions the parameters of homosexuality and heterosexuality, and it renders permeable the superficially concocted dichotomy between the 'healthy us' and the 'diseased other'" (p. 284). Although scant, 100% of the news media coverage about AIDS in 1981 focused on gay men (Brodie et al., 2004). Much of the early 1980s coverage relied on Bardhan's (2001) deviance and abnormality frame; it observed the more sensational aspects of the disease, such as the fears it generated in the population at large or its connections to gay sexual behavior (Levitt & Rosenthal, 1999).

Media coverage, according to Albert (1986), focused on the "deviant characters of the victims rather than the problematic aspects of the illness itself" (Albert, 1986, p. 135). Early media portrayals of AIDS were like moral tales linked to sexual promiscuity or deviance, and thus morality became a common way to avoid the disease.

> AIDS provided society and the media with a double-edged opportunity and challenge, the truly frightening specter of a deadly disease that could be associated with sexual permissiveness, showing up among a group the media have consistently defined as being outside the mainstream. (Gross, 2001, p. 95)

Constructing AIDS in this way provided a false sense of security to the general population and reinforced the "badness" of homosexuality. As a result of the concentrated effort by media to locate and isolate the disease solely in the homosexual community, Fumento (1993) says, the press deliberately misled the public about the likelihood of a hetero-sexual AIDS epidemic.

There was a dramatic rise in media coverage in the latter half of the 1980s. According to Bardhan (2001), "The event that finally spilled the virus into the mainstream was the 1985 revelation that Hollywood star Rock Hudson was living with AIDS" (p. 290). The subsequent death of Rock Hudson, one of the first well-known celebrities to die from AIDS, signaled what Bird (1996) called a turning point in national conscious-ness about AIDS. During the last half of 1985, NBC broadcast more than 200 stories about AIDS, which was more than three times the number of stories the network had aired over the previous 4 years (Gross, 2001). The news about Hudson also encouraged the first men-tion of AIDS by President Ronald Reagan (Alwood, 1996).

In 1986 through 1987, the media coverage more than doubled from that in the previous year, and the major stories that began to surface on several mainstream stations focused on AIDS as a possible threat to the "general public" (Bardhan, 2001; Bird, 1996; Rogers et al., 1993). This increased coverage represented the changing perception of AIDS in American society from a disease infecting isolated and marginalized groups of people to one contracted by people of varying demograph-ics. Mainstream media also began to use explicit language when discussing AIDS instead of the safe and cautious language used through-out the early 1980s. The dramatic increase in the quantity and focus of coverage also represented a shift in the newsworthiness of AIDS. Throughout the late 1980s and early 1990s, coverage of AIDS waned drastically. *Accidental* AIDS victims, such as those who contracted the disease as a result of a blood transfusion, were the media makers that kept AIDS at the forefront of mainstream media coverage. This cover-age, in turn, led to legislation and changes in public policy.[2]

Although television, according to Pilipp and Shull (1993), hesi-tantly became a mouthpiece for reporting and responding to the AIDS epidemic, it began to acknowledge the disease in the mid-1980s by creating prime-time movies and plots that addressed the issue. For example, in 1985, NBC took note of the significance of the epidemic by airing *An Early Frost*, its first made-for-TV prime-time movie about a young man with AIDS. By the late 1980s, the subject of AIDS was work-ing its way into individual episodes of many prime-time television shows (Netzhammer & Shamp, 1994). The challenge with the shows and prime-time movies such as *An Early Frost* was the manner in which AIDS and AIDS victims were depicted. These prime-time images explicitly or implicitly perpetuated the false image of AIDS as a homosexual disease by focusing the plot around homosexual, white males (Netzhammer & Shamp, 1994).

In addition to reinforcing the link between gay men and AIDS, the shows deemphasized the experiences of the infected person (Pilipp & Shull, 1993). "In order to appeal [to] rather than appall the populace, TV must resort to cautious and sensible treatment of the AIDS threat" (p. 20). This caution and sensibility meant that the emphasis was placed not on the AIDS victim, but on the experiences and reactions of those around the victim. The trials of the victim were essentially ignored, and the focal point became the challenges of acceptance experienced by family and friends or the unfortunate circumstances that the victim's illness forced his loved ones to deal with (Clarke, 1992).

> The person with AIDS was portrayed as a diseased person, as morally repugnant, hopelessly doomed, and isolated from potentially significant sources of emotional support such as lovers and family members. . . . They [media] focus on sexual practices, drug use, the fear of contagion, and the uncertainty about the causes of the contagion. (p. 117)

The homosexual community responded to these skewed depictions, in part, by establishing the Gay and Lesbian Alliance Against Defamation, or GLAAD, to address mainstream media's handling of AIDS-related stories. As the 1980s drew to a close, the demographics of AIDS victims continued to shift dramatically, and the mediated construction of AIDS as an isolated disease contracted by gay men was being reframed. Mainstream media began to broaden the scope of the disease to heterosexuals, creating widespread fear.

AIDS Can Happen to *Us* Too

Although media coverage of AIDS increased dramatically after the death of Rock Hudson, there was still not much focus on AIDS as a universal epidemic that infected heterosexuals. It took a National Basketball Association (NBA) icon and a world-renowned tennis player to encourage another shift in media coverage of HIV and AIDS. In 1991, Earvin (Magic) Johnson publicly announced his HIV-positive status (as a result of promiscuous heterosexual contact) and subsequently retired from the NBA. This was a significant historical signpost, because

Johnson was considered a prominent role model for youth at the time (Rogers et al., 1993), and his HIV status helped to place HIV/AIDS within a heterosexual context. That same year, national tennis star Arthur Ashe announced that he contracted AIDS from a blood transfusion years before. These two announcements forced media to cover AIDS as a nondiscriminatory epidemic and forced people to perceive the threat of AIDS as universal.

AIDS had gone from being virtually ignored by the mainstream media, to being depicted as an isolated, homosexual disease, to finally being framed as a widespread epidemic. Consequently, mainstream media coverage became concerned with reducing widespread public panic (Pickle et al., 2002). The epidemic was "mainstreamed" by emphasizing the threat to the "general population," or normal people in society. Fumento (1993) notes headlines from mainstream newspapers early as 1986 (after Rock Hudson's death) that illustrate this shift from AIDS as the disease infecting the *other* to one infecting *normal* people. A *Newsweek* headline, according to Fumento, read, "AIDS is not *their* disease but *ours*." Similarly, a *U.S. News & World Report* headline read, "The disease of them is suddenly the disease of us." Fumento also includes a headline from *USA Today* that read, "Cases Rising Fast Among Heterosexuals." As the coverage increased, the public began to show more outward displays of support by wearing red ribbons, creating quilts that celebrated AIDS victims, and organizing fundraising and commemorative events for AIDS research (Levitt & Rosenthal, 1999).

Media reporting at this stage also included the promotion of sexual morality, including abstinence and use of prophylactics as a form of protection against the disease. Various media outlets, including the music genre, incorporated warning messages to listeners about the dangers of AIDS. Media such as music may have been a more informative medium, because the artists, unlike the news media, used common and familiar terminology to discuss and describe the ways in which AIDS was transmitted and the ways to guard against contracting the disease. For example, rap artists such as Ice Cube, who mentions AIDS several times on his 1991 album *Death Certificate,* were not concerned about offending listeners with explicit lyrics.

For a portion of the 1990s, HIV/AIDS was an ongoing story for the mainstream media and society at large, but this was also the decade when AIDS coverage steadily declined and was no longer a newsroom attention-getter. The coverage became routine and more reactive than proactive (Bardhan, 2001; Epstein, 1995). Coverage was only revived by celebrity stories, scandal, or innovative biomedical treatment procedures (Bardhan, 2001). AIDS reporting over the past few years has evolved to include mostly medical research and public health measures (Pickle et al., 2002).

Recent Media Coverage

"Ever since the *New York Times* Magazine declared 'The End of AIDS: The Twilight of an Epidemic' in 1996, media coverage of AIDS has steadily declined" (Brodie et al., 2004, p. 24)—this, despite the fact that the number of AIDS cases continues to grow, especially among minority groups. Few prime-time shows now include AIDS plots, and the news media only cover AIDS when a promising new treatment or possible cure is being researched. AIDS has fallen so far from the mainstream media and public agenda that when Vice President Dick Cheney was asked during the 2004 vice-presidential debate about his and President George Bush's plans to address AIDS, the number-one killer of African-American women, he said that he was unaware that AIDS was such a prevalent issue with that subgroup.

Despite all this, the late 1990s did represent a significant shift in media framing of the disease. In fact, framing of the disease as a global threat increased significantly. AIDS is now framed as a global pandemic. Roughly 90% of those living with HIV and AIDS currently live in Third World regions, specifically South Africa, South and Southeast Asia, and Latin America (UNAIDS, 2004). As Brodie et al. (2004) explain, it is customary news practice to shift the way an epidemic is covered once it becomes a global issue. Recent coverage has shifted to HIV/AIDS in Africa, which is the hardest hit region, representing nearly 66% of the people living with HIV or some 30 million cases (UNAIDS, 2004; West, 2004). The decline and change in media coverage of AIDS over time coincides with a change in the nature of HIV/AIDS in the United States, from a death sentence to a chronic disease that more people live with and manage (Brodie et al., 2004). Additionally, some cable networks have created AIDS prevention campaigns with catchy themes to target specific subgroups. An example of this is Black Entertainment Television's (BET) *Rap It Up* campaign, created to persuade young viewers to employ and embrace safer sex options.

Media initially ignored the changing demographics of the epidemic, including the increasing number of reported cases of AIDS resulting from heterosexual transmission of HIV (Hart, 1999). In many ways, media continue to ignore this fact. The portrayal of AIDS on American television and news programs has remained virtually unchanged, perpetuating the connection between AIDS and homosexuality (Hart, 1999). The groups affected most by AIDS—racial minorities, youth, and women—are seldom depicted by the media as the disease's most vulnerable and susceptible targets. In 1996, the number of African Americans who tested positive for HIV surpassed that of whites, and that gap has continued to widen. Today, African Americans account for 50% of all new infections every year (37% of the total number of infections), yet only 3% of media stories focused on U.S. minorities (Brodie et al., 2004; Wright, 2004). In 2000 and 2002, only 2% of the AIDS news stories focused on African Americans, and during that same time, Latinos, Asians, and American Indians were excluded from coverage and discussion about AIDS altogether. There is a similar pattern of media coverage of women, who represented 50% of the people infected with HIV in 2002, up from 41% in 1997 (UNAIDS, 2004).

These depictions are problematic, because they reinforce and legitimize the notion that AIDS is primarily a gay disease, thereby diminishing the magnitude and complexity of the epidemic. In other words, mainstream media continue to protect heterosexist ideologies through the misrepresentation of AIDS as a disease that is the consequence of the deviant homosexual; the unprotected and reckless heterosexual encounter, of course, seldom has the same outcome. Furthermore, only rarely are there discussions about the sociopolitical implications of AIDS and the health and treatment inequities that exist in many poor communities where the incidence of AIDS continue to rise.

❖ CONCLUSION

What began as a mysterious form of cancer in a few homosexual men in 1981 has become one of the most serious health problems in our nation's history. Media influenced the direction of the AIDS epidemic by controlling the dissemination of information about the disease. Although Haitians, intravenous drug users, and hemophiliacs were also among the first identified victims, mainstream media coverage focused on and blamed the origination and spread of the disease on the transgressive lifestyle of homosexual men. Initial media coverage about AIDS focused on the dichotomous relationship between the healthy, moral *us* and the diseased, immoral *them*. Coverage of AIDS in the news and entertainment genres has, in some ways, evolved, but the dominant frames that have emerged about AIDS over time carry significant implications for public attitude, cultural interpretation, and policy outcomes (Entman, 1991). Who mainstream media chooses to depict, or omit, during discussions about AIDS is also critical to policy decisions and public perception. This is an important consideration, given the recent numbers that show that the majority of new AIDS cases are found in poor communities and among racial minorities, particularly African Americans. One significant difference in the coverage is the broadening of focus to a more global perspective. This shift in the media frame makes sense, given the prevalence of AIDS in other countries, such as South Africa.

❖ DISCUSSION QUESTIONS

1. Media depictions of AIDS cannot be separated from the political landscape. Why was the "AIDS as a homosexual plague" frame so prominent and so consistently reinforced in the early 1980s? What patterns, if any, did this AIDS frame share with frames for other sociopolitical events and issues of that time?

2. Should mass media be expected to shoulder the responsibility for providing continuous education to individuals, the public, and the government about AIDS? Why or why not?

3. What is the range of implications that may result due to the lack of coverage of racial minority sources and characters in AIDS-focused media stories and programs?

❖ HOMEWORK ASSIGNMENT

1. Watch the movie *An Early Frost* and then analyze, in 2 or 3 pages, the manner in which the AIDS victim is depicted.

2. Use the Internet and your library's newspaper archives to locate three of the most recent newspaper articles about the AIDS epidemic. Read each article and write a 2- or 3-page paper discussing the purpose and information in each of the articles. How is the AIDS epidemic framed in the articles?

3. Use the Internet and your library's newspaper archives to study how ethnic media, particularly the African-American press and Hispanic-serving newspapers, have covered the AIDS crisis in their communities. Write a 2- or 3-page paper discussing the number of articles published, the prominence of their placement, and how AIDS was framed.

❖ NOTES

1. Alwood (1996) provides an in-depth description of the manner in which the *Los Angeles Times* and other widely circulated newspapers of the time began covering the AIDS epidemic. His discussion will allow for a comparison and contrasting of the papers that may also speak to the question of liberal versus conservative media.

2. Larry Gross (2001), in *Up From Invisibility*, provides a thorough discussion of the legislation that stemmed from increased media coverage of accidental AIDS victims. Gross discusses young hemophiliac and AIDS victim Ryan White and the Ryan White Act, as well as legislation sponsored by North Carolina senator Jesse Helms that required health-care professionals to reveal their HIV status.

❖ REFERENCES

Albert, E. (1986). Acquired immune deficiency syndrome: The victim and the press. *Studies in Communication, 3*, 135–158.

Altman, D. (1986). *AIDS in the mind of America*. Garden City, NJ: Anchor.

Alwood, E. (1996). *Straight news: Gays, lesbians, and the news media*. New York: Columbia University Press.

Bardhan, N. (2001). Transnational AIDS-HIV news narrative: A critical exploration of overarching frames. *Mass Communication and Society, 4*(3), 283–310.

Baylor, T. (1996). Media framing of movement protest: The case of American Indian protest. *Social Science Journal, 33*(3), 241–256.

Bird, S. E. (1996). CJ's revenge: Media, folklore, and the cultural construction of AIDS. *Critical Studies in Mass Communication, 13*, 44–58.

Brodie, M., Hamel, E., Brady, L. A., Kates, J., & Altman, D. E. (2004). AIDS at 21: Media coverage of the HIV epidemic 1981–2002. *Columbia Journalism Review, 42*(6), S1–S8.

Clarke, J. N. (1992). Cancer, heart disease, and AIDS: What do the media tell us about these diseases? *Health Communication, 4*(2), 105–120.

Collins, P. H. (2004). *Black sexual politics: African Americans, gender, and the new racism.* New York: Routledge.

Entman, R. M. (1993). Framing: Toward a clarification of a fractured paradigm. *Journal of Communication, 43*(4), 51–58.

Epstein, S. (1995). Moral threats and dangerous desires: AIDS in the news media. *Sociology, 29*(1), 190–192.

Fumento, M. (1993). Media, AIDS, and truth. *National Review, 45*(12), 45–48.

Grmek, M. D. (1990). *History of AIDS: Emergence and origin of a modern pandemic.* Princeton, NJ: Princeton University Press.

Gross, L. (2001). *Up from invisibility: Lesbians, gay men, and the media in America.* New York: Columbia University Press.

Hart, K. R. (1999). Retrograde representation: The lone gay white male dying of AIDS on Beverly Hills, 90210. *Journal of Men's Studies, 7*(2), 201–213.

Hertog, J. K., Finnegan, J. R., & Kahn, E. (1994). Media coverage of AIDS, cancer, and sexually transmitted diseases: A test of the public arenas model. *Journalism Quarterly, 71,* 291–304.

Hertog, J. K., & McLeod, D. M. (2003). A multiperspectival approach to framing analysis: A field guide. In S. D. Reese, O. H. Gandy, & A. E. Grant (Eds.), *Framing public life: Perspectives on media and our understanding of the social world* (pp. 139–162). Mahwah, NJ: Erlbaum.

Jamieson, K. H., & Waldman, P. (2003). *The press effect: Politicians, journalists, and the stories that shape the political world.* New York: Oxford University Press.

Lander, E. (1988). AIDS coverage: Ethical and legal issues facing the media today. *Journal of Mass Media Ethics, 5*(2), 66–72.

Lehrman, S. (2004, March). AIDS coverage has been lost in recent years. *Quill, 92*(2), 24–25.

Levitt, M., & Rosenthal, D. B. (1999). The third wave: A symposium on AIDS politics and policy in the United States in the 1990s. *Policy Studies Journal, 27*(4), 783–796.

McQuail, D. (2000). *Mass communication theory* (4th ed.). Thousand Oaks, CA: Sage.

Netzhammer, E. C., & Shamp, S. A. (1994). Guilt by association: Homosexuality and AIDS on prime-time television. In R. J. Ringer (Ed.), *Queer words, queer images: Communication and the construction of homosexuality* (pp. 91–106). New York: New York University Press.

Pickle, K., Quinn, S. C., & Brown, J. D. (2002). HIV/AIDS coverage in black newspapers, 1991–1996: Implications for health communication and health education. *Journal of Health Communication, 7*(5), 427–445.

Pilipp, F., & Shull, C. (1993). TV movies of the first decade of AIDS. *Journal of Popular Film and Television, 21*(1), 19–27.

Piontek, T. (1992). Unsafe representations: Cultural criticism in the age of AIDS. *Journal for Theoretical Studies in Media and Culture, 15*(1), 128–153.

Radford, T. (1996). Influence and power of the media. *Lancet, 347*(9014), 1533–1536.

Reese, S. D. (2003). Framing public life: A bridging model for media research. In S. D. Reese, O. H. Gandy, & A. E. Grant (Eds.), *Framing public life: Perspectives on media and our understanding of the social world* (pp. 7–31). Mahwah, NJ: Erlbaum.

Rogers, T. F., Singer, E., & Imperio, J. (1993). The polls: Poll trends, AIDS. *Public Opinion Quarterly, 57*, 92–114.

Tannen, T. (2003). Media giant and foundation team up to fight HIV/AIDS: International campaign will use advertisements and plotlines to raise awareness. *Lancet, 361*(9367), 1440–1442.

Treichler, P. (1999). *How to have theory in an epidemic: Cultural chronicles of AIDS.* Durham, NC: Duke University Press.

UNAIDS. (2004). 2004 report on the global AIDS epidemic. Retrieved May 27, 2005, from http://www.unaids.org.

West, C. (2004). *Democracy matters: Winning the fight against imperialism.* New York: Penguin Press.

Wright, K. (2004). AIDS: Hiding in plain sight. *Columbia Journalism Review, 42*(6), 5–6.

❖ ADDITIONAL RESOURCES

AIDS media center: Global AIDS resource for the media. (n.d.). Retrieved April 23, 2005, from http://www.aidsmedia.org

Gitlin, T. (1980). *The whole world is watching: Mass media in the making and unmaking of the new left.* Berkeley: University of California Press.

International Marketing Council of South Africa. (n.d.). HIV/AIDS in South Africa. Retrieved April 23, 2005, from http://www.southafrica.info/ess_info/sa_glance/health/aids.htm

Kinsella, J. (1989). *Covering the plague: AIDS and the American media.* New Brunswick, NJ: Rutgers University Press.

Miller, D. (1998). *The circuit of mass communication: Media strategies, representation and audience reception in the AIDS crisis.* London: Sage.

Myrick, R. (1998). AIDS discourse: A critical reading of mainstream press surveillance of marginal identity. *Journal of Homosexuality, 35*(1), 75–94.

Shevory, T. C. (2004). *Notorious H.I.V.: The media spectacle of Nushawn Williams.* Minneapolis: University of Minnesota Press.

United Nations. (2005). UNAIDS: Joint United Nations Programme on HIV/AIDS. Retrieved April 23, 2005, from http://www.unaids.org

With Jorgensen's transformation from a man into a woman in 1953, the public was
introduced to a new word and a new concept: transsexual.

7

Transgender Images in the Media

Willow Arune

❖   ❖   ❖

In May 1950, a man stood on the decks of the ocean liner Stockholm watching the New York City skyline fade from view. There was nothing unusual about the slightly built blond former Army clerk who was sailing off to visit his ancestral homeland of Denmark. His family had come to see him off; no newspaper or radio station covered his departure, because there was nothing newsworthy about him. That would change, however, in a little more than 2 years.

That young man, George Jorgensen, Jr., became Christine Jorgensen in December 1952 after undergoing hormone therapy and surgery. A small private letter home passed on to a friend and then to the media sparked an onslaught of publicity even before she left the hospital. Led by the *New York Daily News*, Jorgensen was besieged by reporters. In fact, within 2 weeks after the story first broke, *Newsweek* reported that the wire services had carried more than 50,000 words about her. That number skyrocketed with her very public return to

New York City on February 13, 1953. Reporters crowded the airport and covered her every move for months.[1]

"GI Becomes Blonde Beauty," "MDs Rule Chris 100% Woman," "Christine Banned," "Ex GI Turned Woman Flying Home for Yule," "AMA Asks for Report on Change," "Christine 'By George!,'" and "New Woman Is Happy," read some of the headlines. (See Meyerowitz, 2002, and Rudacille, 2005). Jorgensen's transformation from a man into a woman became the leading story in the United States in 1953. With that, the public was introduced to a new word and a new concept: transsexual.

❖ EARLY HISTORY: PRE–WORLD WAR II

Although men who act like women and women who behave like men have been noted throughout history and in many cultures around the world, until the late 1800s there had been no effort made to classify or study such people. Some infants were born with "ambiguous genitalia," often part male, part female, and called hermaphrodites. Those who were clearly men or women but behaved as the other in their societies either went unnoticed or were given a designated role in their culture. In many North American Indian tribes, the berdache was a special person, a "gifted one." For the Thais, a katoey was the temple performer. India gave hirjras a special role in the birth of new baby boys. In most cases, these people were treated differently than "normal" men or women.

Magnus Hirschfeld was the first to study those whom we now call homosexuals in the early part of the 20th century. He noted some who appeared much different in some aspects. Although homosexual men were interested sexually in other men, some men were apparently trying to be women, full- or part-time. They dressed in women's clothing and attempted to be women in Berlin clubs and bars. Others even lived as women for much or all of their lives. Without attempting to divide these in any manner, Hirschfeld called them both "transvestites" (Meyerowitz, 2002, pp. 16–35; Rudacille, 2005).[2]

Havelock Ellis, in England, studied the same group and attempted to give the "condition" a new name—eonism—but the label *transvestite* seemed to prevail (Grosskurth, 1980, pp. 378–380; see also Meyerowitz, 2002, pp. 26–27). Concurrently, in Paris and Vienna, the new study of endocrinology was moving toward the discovery of male and female hormones. The concept emerged that male and female differed in body secretions. It was noted that in animals, injections of one or the other could radically change behavior—a male rat that was injected with female hormones would begin to act like a female, and vice versa. Hormones became the possible answer to the mystery of the sexes (Meyerowitz, 2002, pp. 16–17; Rudacille, 2005, pp. 39–44). Hirschfeld had by then established his clinic in Berlin, which was to last until the Nazi book burnings of the 1930s. Certainly, an Institute for Sexual Science, especially one run by a Jewish doctor, would not be tolerated by the brownshirts.

In the late 1920s, an ideal candidate emerged for potentially groundbreaking surgery. Lillie Elbe, who became known as "The Danish Girl," was born a man but had a distinctly feminine appearance. He became a renowned Danish painter and eventually married an American woman. In an evolving series of conversations with his wife, who used Lillie as a model for her paintings, Elbe's feminine side emerged and took root. Whereas most wives would shun a man who thought he was a female, Elbe's wife was more accepting, and together they sought out Hirschfeld. The first "sex reassignment surgery" took place in Wiemar Germany in 1931. A team of doctors completed the operations in several stages; Elbe was to die shortly after she received transplanted ovaries (current operations make no attempt to provide reproductive capacity, as the problems of rejection, allegedly the cause of Elbe's death, remain).

Elbe's operation became a book in 1933—*Man Into Woman*, by Neils Hoyer. A well-regarded 2001 novel titled *The Danish Girl*, by David Ebershoff, also chronicled her life. As it turns out, Elbe was born with internal female reproductive organs, discovered during one of her several operations. In present-day terminology, Lile was not a "transsexual" (a person of one sex becoming a person of the other) but rather "intersexed" (a person born with ambiguous genitalia and some attributes of both sexes, formerly known as hermaphrodites).

❖ POST–WORLD WAR II

The post–World War II era was a conservative time in the United States. Women, who had been encouraged to work outside of the home—in factories and offices—to keep the American economy strong while the majority of "working age" men were fighting in World War II, were now being cajoled back into the home to serve as homemakers upon the soldiers' return. Besides (re)placing women in the home, the postwar era saw the establishment of the "Iron Curtain." This curtain demarcated areas that subscribed to communist ideologies (and were either parts of or allies with the Soviet Union), on one side, and areas that were allies of the United States, on the other. Nations on both sides of the curtain were testing nuclear bombs, and tensions were running high. School children practiced "duck-and-cover" bomb drills, crouching under their desks or filing out of classrooms to school basements, in case bombers or missiles were detected.

It was during this time that Sen. Joseph McCarthy had Capitol Hill and the United States on the watch for a "homosexual underground" that was abetting the "communist conspiracy." Gay men were seen as security risks and summarily terminated from jobs. Some were even arrested, to be charged with "buggery" or other crimes or sent to asylums. McCarthy's chief aide, Roy Cohn (himself a closeted gay man), ignited a media frenzy with his efforts to hunt down the "pervert" and "commie" peril.

In this conservative society, a small magazine is credited with coining the word "transsexual." Dr. D. A. Cauldwell published *Sexology*, one of the few publications of the era that presented an objective view of sexuality (Meyerowitz, 2002, pp. 41–45). In a series of articles, Cauldwell explored, in a negative manner, men who wanted to be women, and called them "transsexuals" (that some women might wish to be men was not considered, nor would it be for many years). Cauldwell continued to oppose sex reassignment surgery, claiming that to do otherwise would give way to "fantastic hopes." Accepting that a person who was born a man could never fully be a woman, he denounced "tales of magic cures and magical accomplishments of surgery" (Meyerowitz, 2002, pp. 44–45). Unlike Benjamin, he could not see that partial solutions would serve.

❖ THE "TRANSSEXUAL" EMERGES

It was in the midst of this era that Jorgensen made her debut. Dr. Harry Benjamin, a German-born New York City endocrinologist and student of Hirschfeld, popularized the word *transsexual*. He went on to establish an association that developed the "Benjamin Standards of Care"— a set of medical recommendations—to ensure proper treatment for this "condition" (Meyerowitz, 2002, pp. 45–48, 102–111).[3] Modified over the years, these standards are used today as guidelines by doctors, psychiatrists, psychologists, plastic surgeons, and endocrinologists who treat transsexual patients. Benjamin would eventually write a book titled *The Transsexual Phenomenon* in 1966.

Benjamin was not alone. Other American doctors, including Robert Stoller at the University of California, Los Angeles, and John Money and Richard Green at Johns Hopkins University Hospital in Baltimore, also were hard at work. Each would later write articles and books about the treatment of transsexuals that would change our views of gender and sexuality forever (e.g., Green & Money, 1968; Stoller, 1976). The publicity surrounding Jorgensen's return gave transsexuals in the United States hope that the medical community would hear their call for treatment similar to that Jorgensen had received in Denmark.

Shortly after World War II, operations were available for transsexuals in some countries, notably Tunisia. Eventually, thanks to the financial resources of a rich Texan female-to-male transsexual named Reed Erickson (Meyerowitz, 2002, pp. 209–226),[4] the presumed illegality and immorality of sex reassignment surgery was overcome. Although there had been reports of underground "black market" operations, the first legal and public operation took place at Johns Hopkins University Hospital in 1965. The patient was a young African American named Avon Williams (Ball, 2003, pp. 158–159).

Diagnostic and Statistical Manual of Mental Disorders

In 1973—the year that homosexuality was dropped from the *Diagnostic and Statistical Manual of Mental Disorders* (*DSM*) used by psychiatrists—"transsexuality" was added. In a later revision of the *DSM*, the name of the condition was changed to "gender identity dysphoria" (GID). It is still classed as a disorder today, despite objections from many in the transgender community.[5]

In countries of the world with state health programs, the listing in the *DSM* (and other classification systems) opens many doors. As a disorder, the recommended treatment for GID includes both hormone therapy and sex reassignment surgery. Canada, Britain, Sweden, France, Italy, and many other countries—even Iran—have state funding for the treatment of transsexuals. Still, it remains the only psychiatric disorder for which surgical intervention is part of the recommended treatment.

This is not the case in the United States. With few exceptions, treatment for GID is not covered by private insurance, and in fact may be specifically excluded. As such, transsexuals in the United States are generally opposed to the continued listing in *DSM,* as it represents a "stigma," a mental disorder that must be disclosed in certain situations. Their opposition is very understandable, given the continuing bias against transsexuals evidenced in our society.

❖ TRANSGENDER

Further confusion arose in the 1980s when Virginia Prince, a transvestite in Los Angeles, coined a new term—"transgendered." Initially, this was used to describe those individuals who did not want the operation for sex reassignment but did want to live at least part-time as the "opposite gender." Since the *DSM* demanded that a desire for sexual reassignment surgery was required to be diagnosed as transsexual or as having GID, the term *transgendered* initially referred to those who lived the life of the opposite sex but did not want genital surgery.

Because some transsexuals were unable to have surgery for economic or medical reasons, the gap between the two shrank and overlap followed. *Transgender* has morphed into an inclusive term for anyone who is "gender variant," who full- or part-time acts or behaves as the other sex. This includes heterosexual cross-dressers, she-males (restricted to the sex industry, with a male "bottom" and a female "top"), female impersonators, transvestites, and even transsexuals (but *only* if they agree to be so included). Politically volatile in the transgendered community, the inclusion of transsexuals and intersexed persons (both being those who need medical and sometimes psychiatric treatment or assistance) with others making a lifestyle choice is debated endlessly. The conflict between those who want support and those who want to have fun and party is divisive and has created hard feelings on both sides.

"On Demand"

Today, some transsexuals—mostly in the United States—want "surgery on demand." If you can pay for it, you can have it, without the need for psychiatric assessment and medical approvals. To a limited degree, this is possible outside of the United States, in places such as Thailand. It is also possible to obtain surgery inside U.S. borders through illegal operations or from doctors in private practice.

These are all sensitive issues, as is the name of the operation. For years it was known as "sex reassignment surgery," "gender reassignment surgery," or "gender confirmation surgery." It was most certainly not simply a "sex-change operation." This is a semantic minefield, and reporters should be aware of the controversies when covering any story concerning transsexuals or transgendered persons.

Legal and Biological Matters

In most states and countries, the legal gender or sex of a transsexual following surgery can be altered. For male-to-female transsexuals, this is usually a simple matter. In most cases, once the penis is eliminated and replaced with a vagina, the person is a woman, not a man. In some states, driver's licenses can be modified even before the operation.

All that changes for female-to-male transsexuals. The "top" operation for females is fairly straightforward and involves double mastectomies. Hormone treatment quickly gives patients lower voices, facial hair, and perhaps male-pattern baldness. The "bottom" operation is much more difficult and is often viewed as "experimental." In the case of a female-to-male transsexual, requirements for changes in birth certificates and driver's licenses vary.

Legally and socially, there is no doubt that the "change" can be complete. Biology raises political correctness issues, however. Medical professionals agree that the operations do not make a man into a woman or vice versa. No operation, for example, is able to restore reproductive abilities for the transsexual. Biologically, one remains as one was born. Science thus differs from legal and social norms.

To ensure that the patient is a transsexual, the generally required or accepted Standards of Care require a "real-life test" (RLT) (this involves living as a member of the desired sex or gender full-time for a certain time, from several months to 2 years) and taking hormone replacement treatment (HRT) with male or female hormones and blockers of "birth" hormones. In many cases, psychiatric assessment requires therapy over a long period of time before or during RLT and HRT. The concept behind this routine is fairly straightforward. As diagnosis of the disorder depends largely on the patient's own subjective presentation, RLT and HRT are presumed to "weed out" those who might not be actual transsexuals but some other type of trangendered person.

Treatment is thus a combination of several medical specialties: psychiatry first, although many psychiatrists do not accept the *DSM* treatment and will provide therapy to effect a "cure." Psychiatry is followed by endocrinology. Finally, there is plastic surgery. These are often combined with personality tests and appraisals, offerings of other options, interviews with those who have known the patient, and more. The road is long and hard and designed to be so. In effect, the medical position is to make it so difficult that only the real transsexuals will persevere to the final surgery. The classic view is that surgery is the last option, to be used only when all else fails and the patient still wants genital surgery.

Patients who think they are transsexual may come to different conclusions during treatment. They may accept one of the many trangendered lifestyles or simply return to their birth sex on a full-time basis.

Unless there are other complications, none of the other types of transgendered persons need or require medical intervention or psychiatric appraisal, any more than permission is needed to have a gay or lesbian lifestyle. You simply go out and do it.

As we move toward a more liberal application of the Standards of Care, to and including surgery on demand, the possibility of a person obtaining the operation without proper diagnosis grows. As of this writing, cases against surgeons and psychiatrists are under way in Australia and England.[6] With patients demanding more liberal access, legal issues are certain to arise more often.

Gender and *Sex*

Until the 1950s, gender and sex were deemed to be the same. One was born male (the sex) and was of the masculine gender, a man. John Money noted a distinction—that sex and gender did not necessarily coincide. From being a synonym for sex, gender (in English only—many other languages make no similar distinction) became the mental aspect ("between the ears") and sex became the physical ("between the legs"). This separation became one concept incorporated into the so-called first wave of feminism. Applied to transsexuals and, later, transgendered persons, it took off in a totally new direction, aided by a shift from essentialism to postmodernism.

Some transsexuals take the position that they are "trapped in the body" of the opposite sex; "a woman in a man's body" became a common phrase to apply. Certainly, this does convey the feelings associated with transsexuality. With a little jump, this morphed into the concept that one was born with a male or female brain. Some limited scientific work seemed to support this concept, but none of it was sufficient to prove the existence of different male and female brains. Indeed, many feminists would rebel at such a suggestion. Such an idea makes the mental "disorder" into a biological fact and a birth condition and thus adds fuel to the fire of those demanding that the *DSM* classification be deleted. A female brain in a male body would be similar to being intersexed—no mental condition, simply a matter of a little "problem" that could be surgically corrected.

Postmodernist Concepts

The next step was philosophical. Taking a leaf from Foucault and the postmodernists (More & Whittle, 1999), a transsexual could—and many did—claim to be both female and a woman, as both were social constructs that could be modified by the individual. Emerging from this concept was the notion that a female could have a penis or a vagina. If she had a penis, it could be dismissed as a birth defect and "cured" by an operation. The "biological imperative" was effectively eliminated.

Another group, initially more persuasive, sought answers in the "third gender" concept. Kate Bornstein (1994) gave voice and power to this theory in the 1990s. One need not be either male or female. That was merely a binary construct by society. Between those two poles was a fertile ground for variation—the "third gender" could take many forms. This concept was supported by the accepted anthropological view of apparent transsexuals in Southeast Asia and the Pacific. Under many names, anthropologists "discovered" or researched the existence of indigenous "third-gendered" peoples. Our society was seen to enforce a binary divide that was not natural, merely cultural (Herdt, 1996).

The Bottom Line

All that considered, we live in a society that generally views humans as divided into two sexes, male and female. Our society generally accepts that males become men and females, women. Concepts of transsexuals aside, that is how readers, listeners, and viewers will interpret anything written or produced concerning transsexuals or transgendered subjects. Legally, the line is firm—only a postoperative transsexual can change from a man to a woman or a woman to a man. In the English language, that leaves the journalist to sort everything out for the general public, including the use of the pronouns, such as "he" and "she."

Regardless of what is written, some will be offended. A fundamentalist Christian will be offended if you refer to someone as a "she" when the fundamentalist considers that person to be a "he"; a transgendered person who is biologically a "he" might be insulted if she is referred to as "he."

The Reason Why

Various concepts have been advanced as reasons for transsexuality specifically and transgendered behavior more generally.

Some argue for a difference in the brain itself, suggesting that male and female brains are inherently different. Science has yet to generally accept this proposition, and many feminists would recoil in horror at the mere idea. Janice Raymond, writing in the second wave of feminism in 1979, attacked transsexuals as pawns in a conspiracy by the paternalistic medico-psychiatric community to "take over" the radical lesbian movement then emerging. Her book had long-lasting effects in separating lesbians from transsexual women. Things have mellowed since that date so long ago, however. My own copy of Raymond's book was signed by her to me, a transsexual woman, as follows: "To Willow: Who, although we may not share the same solutions, share the quest for a better life and humanity for all." As years pass, dogmatic positions crumble or change, mellowing as we all do. Others have suggested that something ingested by the mother at a certain time of the pregnancy is the cause, at least in part. One possible substance is diethylstilbestrol (DES), given to pregnant women during the 1940s and 1950s (Rudacille, 2005, pp. 240–276).

Those are physical reasons advanced to present a biological reason, in contrast to the psychiatric model, which simply assumes a disorder, a "dysphoria."

At this time, the simple answer is actually the best. Simply, we do not know what causes the condition. Treatment is done "in the best interests of the patient" to secure a better "fit" into our binary society, in conformity with our society's perception of sex as either male or female. Although many transsexuals hold to one concept or another, there is no proof of any specific cause, and current treatment standards concentrate more on the result than the reason. The almost religious zeal of some transsexuals can be overwhelming, but the science remains missing.

There are those who are diagnosed as transsexual who do not go forward to surgery—it is certainly not a required treatment. Some might be tempted to say that those who do not have the surgery are not transsexuals, but it could be equally true that some have more control or more inhibitions or concerns or, perhaps, social constraints that weigh upon them. We simply do not know.

Still More Labels

There are often references to the terms *primary*, *secondary*, and *true* in reference to transsexuals. These dated terms are really not used outside of medical, psychiatric, or transsexual circles. *Primary* referred to those who enter transition at an early age (in their early 20s or younger); *secondary* covered the older ones (often older than 40); *true* was used in the 1950s to attempt to differentiate between transvestites and transsexuals. These terms should be avoided in the media and are very politically charged in transgendered circles.

Intersexed

One further variation is the "intersexed" people. Formerly called hermaphrodites, these are people born with ambiguous genitalia. The established medical practice was to perform "corrective" surgery at birth and not tell the child what was done. Nowadays, that process is under attack by those who have been subjected to it. Surgery should not be performed until the child is able to determine his or her "correct" sex, they say.

Gender Identity

Gender identity is central to a person's being. From an early age, people see themselves as boys or girls. This core identification is vastly different from "sexual orientation." One cannot assume, for example, that because a man is a cross-dresser (also known as a transvestite), that man is looking for a sexual relationship with a male. Indeed, most cross-dressers are heterosexual married men, and the major cross-dresser associations will not accept transsexuals for membership, preferring men who will be attending events with a partner—a female partner (Boyd, 2003, pp. 20–48).

It should also not be assumed that a transsexual woman is "straight" as a woman, as was required at one time, and still is in some cases, before surgery is approved. She may be, but she might also be lesbian, asexual, bisexual, or even omnisexual, pansexual, or any other type of sexuality.

❖ RESPONSIBLE REPORTING

Media coverage of transgendered persons has tended toward the sensational. To those in the transgendered community, media coverage is often seen as insensitive and prejudicial. Although the media has slowly learned to cover gay men, lesbians, and even swingers in neutral terms, coverage of the transsexual and transgendered often remains a source of snide humor and sensationalism.

Again, the myriad types of gender variance require different treatment. To a transsexual—who may have struggled all her life simply to be "normal" and accepted as part of her local community as a woman— the sudden glare of a media spotlight can be very upsetting, and potentially fatal, as violence against transgendered persons of all types is very high, as is the risk of suicide. Additionally, many believe that as a group, transsexuals have the highest suicide level of any known group, and this is largely attributed to the manner in which transsexuals are treated by our society. In discussing teen suicide, Gibson (n.d.) reports:

Transsexual youth are perhaps the most outcast of all young people and face a grave risk of suicidal feelings and behavior. Huxley and Brandon found that 53 percent of 72 transsexuals surveyed had made suicide attempts. Harry feels that "transsexuals may be at higher risk than homosexuals and much higher risk than the general population" to suicidal behavior. Transsexual youth believe they have a gender identity different from the sex they were born with. They often manifest this belief beginning in childhood through an expressed desire to be a person of the opposite gender, repudiation of their genitalia, gender nonconformity and cross dressing. These behaviors may subside by adolescence due to extreme pressures to conform to social expectations. Some transsexual youth, however, try to "pass" in junior high and high school as a person of the opposite sex or engage in increasingly pronounced behaviors that do not conform to gender expectations. These adaptations present serious internal and external conflicts for these youth.

All transsexuals are vulnerable to internalizing an extremely negative image of themselves. They experience tremendous internal conflict between this image and their persistent desire to become the person they believe they are. Heller notes that suicidal transsexuals tend to feel hopelessly trapped in their situation. These feelings may be particularly pronounced in young transsexuals who are forced to hide their identity. While wanting to change their sex, they are seldom able to do so and feel condemned to a Life they are convinced is a mistake. The *DSM-III* notes that transsexuals frequently experience "considerable anxiety and depression, which the individual may attribute to inability to live in the role of the desired sex." This depression combined with a poor self esteem can easily result in suicidal feelings and behavior in transsexual youth.

It can be akin to or worse than the sudden exposure of a closeted gay man by the media. He might lose his existing relationships, his job or career, his close family and friends. The transsexual person lacks even the minimal legal protection afforded to the gay man under human rights laws. Most human rights codes do offer protection to gay men and lesbians, preventing discrimination due to sexual orientation. "Gender identity" is only rarely included in protective laws, making the transsexual "fair game" for any aggressive and predatory journalist.

Perhaps the worst example of this is the "outing" of Caroline Cossey by the British press. A model who became a James Bond girl, Cossey had built up a successful life leading to marriage. Out of the blue came a call to her family, and then the story, with banner headlines. She was not the first or the last to be exposed in this manner. A remarkable contrast is the close-knit community where Aleshia Brevard was raised in the American South. Many attempts by the media to out her as transgendered were rebuffed; local residents simply refused to confirm the stories.

Although most journalists are now respectful of gay men and lesbians, they seemingly feel free to casually marginalize and ridicule any transsexual in their coverage. Transsexuals are sensitive to the anchor who smiles and changes voice when a report of transsexuality comes to the fore or the reporter who visibly changes demeanor when facing the cameras, or raises an eyebrow, or simply uses the expression "was dressed as a woman at the time." Transgendered or transsexual, anything is deemed "newsworthy." A notable recent example is the Kantaras matrimonial trial in Florida ("Transsexual custody battle," 2002). Disputes over custody are commonplace and rarely covered in the news, let alone shown in their entirety on Court TV. This case was different, for the husband was a female-to-male transsexual. This focuses the onus of "responsible reporting" clearly on the journalist.

Adding to this difficulty is the status of the transgendered person in our society. Discrimination causes many transsexuals to seek privacy. They wish simply to be known as women or men, as the case might be. Most members do not want publicity due to the probable consequences to their career or life.

Publicity or outing might well destroy a new life or career or may well eliminate the great personal gains made after a successful transition. Does the public need to know that a local politician or businessman likes to "dress up" on the weekends or that a respected teacher performs as another gender onstage Friday nights? What would represent simply another story to a journalist might have a large impact on the life of an otherwise "invisible" and successful transgendered person who is fully "passing" as a member of his or her target gender. Again, this raises an issue of responsible reporting for any journalist or editor.

Let's look at only a few examples. In California, a well-liked teacher was fired, without any hesitation, by the school board when she announced her transition. A few of the parents complained ("Why this boy," 2000). In a small town in British Columbia, parents rose up in anger when a transsexual female student was allowed to use the women's washroom (Armstrong, 2004). In most instances, transsexuals fight these battles on their own, for there is little support offered by the gay and lesbian communities. Indeed, on occasion the discrimination comes from those very communities (Nolan, 2000). Relationships with the Rainbow communities are tenuous at best. Many transsexuals do not consider themselves other than members of their target gender, and thus they are "heterosexual" if involved with a member of their birth gender; cross-dressers are mostly heterosexual. Transsexuals and transgendered persons feel abandoned by the Rainbow when their rights are excluded from new legislation (see Bronski, 2002). Writing of Sylvia Rivera's activism, Bronski states:

While her dream of a functioning political movement that fought for people of variant gender may have come true, many of the struggles remained the same. Only recently have many of the national leading gay and lesbian organizations even included "trans-gender" in their titles, and few have dealt with the myriad concerns, from discrimination to health care to violence, that are associated with people (drag queens, transsexuals, or intersexed people) who do not conform to accepted gender norms. The Human Rights Campaign has made a conscious decision not to include "transgender" as a protected category in the Employment Non-Discrimination Act that has appeared before Congress several times. Their reason is that, while the bill may have some chance to pass if it only covers sexual orientation, it has absolutely no chance if it includes gender issues.

The same problem exists with the SONDA—Sexual Orientation Non-Discrimation Act—bill that is before the New York House. Many New York–based civil rights groups feel that the inclusion of transgender concerns would be disastrous for the passage of the legislation.

Some gay men consider transsexual women to be gay men who simply did not know where to stop; feminist lesbians have denied entry to transsexual women (as in the Nixon case from Canada referenced earlier) or alleged that any transsexual woman is a pawn of the paternalistic medical and psychiatric establishment bent on taking over women's groups throughout America and reinforcing the gender binary, as Janice Raymond asserted—a concept which was in fact presented at the Nixon trial.

Here is a personal story that shows how deep the scar—and the fear—can be. During my transition, I received a call from a reporter who asked to do a story on me. As I had been "national news" for events unrelated to my transition, I accepted with some trepidation. Still, I thought the chance of educating some was worth the risk.

The article that appeared (July 20, 2000, in the *Vancouver Province*) covered two full pages of the newspaper. The result was all I had hoped for—letters and comments from "normal" people were very favorable, leading to other media appearances. However, I had broken the unwritten rules of the transsexual organization in my home city by being openly "out" and transsexual. A letter to the editor from another transsexual woman was insulting; a short time thereafter, an article and editorial appeared in the local transsexual magazine (the summer 2000 issue of *Zenith Digest*[7]) advising members to avoid me, even to not going for coffee with me. The reason? By being "out," I was known. To be seen with me was possibly to be taken as a transsexual person also— outed by association. No natal woman ever assumed this, but other transsexual women most certainly did.

There are the stories, repeated far too often for comfort, of those targeted and killed simply for being transsexual or transgendered (see, for example, the "Resources" section at http://www.gender.org/ remember/day/). In 2002, a 17-year-old transsexual woman, Gwen Araujo, was savagely murdered by three teenage boys, her body discarded in a shallow grave. One of the accused confessed. The other two pled not guilty to the crime, which received wide media coverage. The first trial ended with a mistrial, and the second has yet to start. Massive media coverage has been able to avoid too many mistakes by using the word "teen" to describe the victim (National Transgender Advocacy Coalition, 2002; see also the Gwen Araujo Web site at http://www .jaimesite.homestead.com/gwenaraujo.html).

A few years earlier, the brutal murder of a female-to-male transgendered person, Brandon Teena, in Nebraska had been covered in much the same sensational manner, but with far more errors in terminology. Her story was depicted in the movie *Boys Don't Cry*, which earned an Academy award for actress Hilary Swank, who played Brandon. Brandon was raped on Christmas Day and murdered, with two others, on New Year's Day, by the same perpetrators. Her rape was reported to the police, who ignored it. The movie showed the public what transgendered people had known for years—that even when they are victims, they are often ignored.

A Small Minority

Transvestites are said to outnumber transsexuals by at least 50 to 1; gay males outnumber transsexuals by about 900 to 1. In addition, these other two groups are composed entirely of males only; transsexuals are nearly evenly divided between male-to-female cases and female-to-male cases. (Conway, 2002)

Transsexuals themselves might number as many as 1 in every 30,000 people; other estimates range from 1 in 100,000 to as high as 1 in 10,000 (Conway, 2002).

The variations within the transgendered and transsexual community are difficult to understand. To an outsider, a transvestite looks the same as a transsexual, and a she-male can appear to be both. As we have seen, however, these actually are labels applied to different types of transgendered people. Within the transgendered community, these labels are very important. A responsible reporter must seek to understand the labels and what they imply before using them indiscriminately.

Using the term *she-male* for a transsexual woman would be considered highly offensive, for it implies that she is working "in the [sex] trade." It may be considered libelous. A person who is a cross-dresser who simply dresses as a member of the opposite sex during the weekend is more often than not a heterosexual male, married, very likely with children. He is not a transsexual, nor is he a she-male. A post-op transsexual person is definitely not a cross-dresser when dressed as a member of his or her new gender.

To avoid being offensive, a journalist can take two easy steps. First, when reporting on any transgendered person, become familiar with the labels and terms employed within the community. In many—but not all—cases, use of the terms *transgender* or *gender variant* or *dysphoric* might be acceptable to the person and to the community. Even there, those labels are often loaded words, and care should be taken. The answer starts with research. A good journalist should assume nothing. All details should be checked and verified. When writing a story, a journalist should remember that in this, as in all things, not all people will be pleased.

Of course, another way to be certain of the label to use is quite simple. Ask, do not assume. If, during an interview, a person appears to be a woman, it might be safe to assume she is a woman. Given the nature of the transgendered society, a quick question by the journalist will most often easily resolve any terminology issues.

Pronouns and Quotation Marks

"He" and "she"—seems simple, doesn't it? In most cases of reporting, it is, but not when covering the transgendered community.

As with the labels, the use of pronouns in any articles concerning transgendered persons raises issues of responsible reporting. Here we are concerned not only with the change from one sex or gender to another, but with the span of time over which the person has been, for example, visibly a man—and then a woman.

The *Associated Press Stylebook* offers recommendations and guidelines for covering transgendered people under the heading "Sex Changes." It says that journalists should

> use the pronoun preferred by the individuals who have acquired the physical characteristics (by hormone therapy, body modification, or surgery) of the opposite sex and present themselves in a way that does not correspond with their sex at birth. If that preference is not expressed, use the pronoun consistent with the way the individuals live publicly. ("'Changes' at the," 2000)

That certainly addresses some of the issues that arise, but not all. In cases of doubt, rather than proceed with erroneous assumptions, journalists can contact the Transgender Law and Policy Institute (http://www.transgenderlaw.org/) or local transsexual or transgendered groups.

A problem also exists with the use of quotation marks by inexperienced reporters, or those with a prejudice to proclaim. The use of quotations marks has become a method of editorializing, as in: "Sally declared that she was a 'woman' and asked us to use that term when speaking of her."

Verbally or in print, the quotation marks are an insidious way of calling into question the word used. Although this may be acceptable in certain circumstances, it is deemed highly offensive in regard to matters of sex and gender. The intent is to question the word within the quotation marks and call it into doubt. A responsible reporter would be better advised to avoid the use of quotation marks and follow appropriate usage.

Much the same comment could be made regarding the tone of voice and body language used by on-air reporters. The arched eyebrows, jocular expressions, and disbelieving eyes often say more than the words, just as they do in day-to-day conversation. This kind of editorializing is the role of a commentator, not a reporter or anchorperson.

Transgendered Persons in the Media Today

A local evening news broadcast over BCTV–Global Network in my home city (Vancouver) recently carried a story from Thailand, where the transgendered are more often encountered. The story concerned a Thai boxing champion, who was completing transgender surgery.

The first question is whether this was truly a story of interest to a North American community. The anchor, a well-established "personality," segued into the story from a major story and on his way to a commercial break. His demeanor told much about his opinion. His position was relaxed, and his voice was that of a person sharing a joke with a friend. The tension and seriousness that had been visible during the prior hard news story was gone. His voice added quotation marks to every pronoun, and he also used the term "transvestite," not "transsexual." The boxer has been featured in a Thai movie called *Beautiful Boxer*, concerning his rise as a boxer and his transition. That movie was empathetic, not derogatory, as this television broadcast had been.[8] Transgendered and transsexual people are all too familiar with that manner of reporting. *DaVinci's Inquest*, a crime series on normally sensitive Canadian TV, had an episode that dealt with the case of a murdered transsexual woman. From the "discovery" during the autopsy to the close, the pronoun "he" was always used. *ER* has shown doctors disregarding transgendered patients—but feeling bad about it afterward. On *Law & Order: Special Victims Unit*, a pre-op transsexual woman was gang-raped and beaten when placed in a male prison facility, an act done as expedient, as she was still "male," being preoperative. Rules that ensure safety have yet to be evolved in many jurisdictions. In the United Kingdom, police have instructions to isolate transsexuals from the rest of the male prison population. Transsexuals are good victims. A reality police show, *Cops*, dealt with the sex trade on Sunset Strip. The police depicted regularly bandied about terms such as "trannies," "transvestite," "transsexual" and worse. *Trannie* is a word much like *fag* or *nigger*. It may be permitted in conversation between members of the same group but is deemed an insult when applied to a transsexual by someone who is not transsexual. *Transvestite* is deemed a derogatory term when applied to a transsexual. Indiscriminate use of these three words, along with others, shows a lack of training in and understanding of minority relations. American cinema, too, has sensationalized transsexuals and transgendered persons by depicting them in a negative manner. *Dressed to Kill* (1980) featured Michael Caine as a transsexual murderer; "Buffalo Bill" of *Silence of the Lambs* (1991), based on the book of the same title by the reclusive Thomas Harris (no interview has ever been given), presented more of the same. Only in very recent times have movies such as *Different for Girls* (1996), *Boys Don't Cry* (1999), and *Normal* (2003) portrayed a more multidimensional and realistic view of transsexuals. While the Internet and the porn industry are crowded with sex ads for she-males and transsexuals, the more typical transgendered person feels justifiably denigrated when this very small portion of the community is taken to be representative of the whole. Continuous references to "trannie hookers," as on the TV program *Cops*, add to the misconceptions and stigma.

Even today the media has yet to fully recognize the transsexual and transgendered experience as part of our human diversity and mosaic. In the 50 years following Jorgensen's return to New York, much in the transgender communities has changed, thanks to new insights and understanding. The media-made frenzy of 1953 seems nearly unfathomable today, but journalists unfamiliar with the transgender community still employ judgmental phrasing and suggestive words, leading to sensationalist work. Innuendo and slurs are all too common in modern journalism. It is imperative that editors and producers work tirelessly to eradicate the prejudices of an earlier era.

It is not easy for any journalist or communications professional to accurately portray a section of our society that is so diverse, yet so small in number. Nonetheless, sensitivity to its existence and the differences that exist within it will help greatly in the depictions of this community.

❖ DISCUSSION QUESTIONS

1. A close friend announces that he or she is transsexual and has started hormone treatment under a doctor's care. What is your reaction? What do you think the reaction of some of your classmates might be? Your parents?

2. You are in the washroom at a fancy restaurant. Another person enters and is visibly not a man or woman, as you are. You leave quickly. Do you report this to the manager and staff? Tell all your companions at the table? Ignore the situation?

3. If you could change your sex for a week, would you do so? What differences would you expect to experience? What events would you want to experience?

4. Your neighbor, a married firefighter with two children who has coached your baseball team for years, announces he is transsexual and is entering transition to become a woman. How does

this affect your relationship with him? Do you believe he has a right to do this to his wife and family?

5. One of your favorite teachers in high school has just announced that he is becoming a she. Parents of his students are planning to demonstrate against this teacher. What steps do you take, if any?

❖ HOMEWORK ASSIGNMENTS

1. Check for news stories in your local newspaper or the Internet concerning transsexuals or trangendered people. Are the articles slanted in any manner? Is the reporter biased in his or her reporting? Write a paper analyzing these articles.

2. Write a feature story about a community center or other services that are available for transsexuals or transgendered people in your community. If none are available, write a story about why that is the case.

❖ NOTES

1. For the complete story of Christine Jorgensen, see her autobiography (Jorgensen, 2000) or chapter 2, "Ex-GI Becomes Blonde Beauty," in Meyerowitz (2002).
2. In particular, see Rudacille's (2005) chapter 2, "From Science to Justice."
3. The current and updated Standards of Care may be found online at http://www.altsex.org/transgender/benjamin.html.
4. A forthcoming book by Holly Devor will deal with Erikson's role in the early development of transsexual treatment in North America.
5. Information about GID as it appears in the fourth edition of the *DSM* may be found online at http://mshsanctuary.com/gender/dsm.htm.
6. In England, Charles Kane is suing his doctor; in Australia, a post-op named Fintch is suing those who diagnosed him. Both are now post-op transsexuals who have reverted to male roles in society and allege incorrect medical diagnosis led them to have surgery.
7. *Zenith Digest*, a newsletter of the Zenith Foundation, ceased publication with this issue, and the group later disbanded for lack of membership.
8. For more about this story, see http://www.beautifulboxer.com/ .

❖ REFERENCES

Armstrong, J. (2004, June 12). The body within: The body without. *Globe & Mail*, p. F1. Retrieved May 31, 2005, from the evalu8.org Web site: http://evalu8.org/staticpage?page=review&siteid=7950

Associated Press. (2005). *The Associated Press stylebook 2005*. Cambridge, MA: Perseus.

Ball, E. (2003). *Peninsula of lies*. New York: Simon & Schuster.

Benjamin, H. (1966). *The transsexual phenomenon*. New York: Erickson Press.

Bornstein, K. (1994). *The gender outlaw: Of men, women and the rest of us*. New York: Routledge.

Boyd, H. (2003). *My husband Betty*. Berkeley, CA: Thunder Mouth Press.

Bronski, M. (2002, April). Sylvia Rivera: 1951–2002. No longer on the back of the bumper. *Z Magazine*. Retrieved May 31, 2005, from http://www.zmag.org /Zmag/articles/april02bronski.htm

"Changes" at the Associated Press (AP). (2000). Retrieved May 31, 2005, from the University of Michigan Web site: http://ai.eecs.umich.edu/people/conway/TS/PuertoRicoAPstory.html

Conway, L. (2002, December 17). How frequently does transsexualism occur? Retrieved May 31, 2005, from the University of Michigan Web site: http://ai.eecs.umich.edu/people/conway/TS/TSprevalence.html

Ebershoff, D. (2001). *The Danish girl*. London: Penguin Books.

Founding Committee of the Harry Benjamin International Gender Dysphoria Association, Inc. (1990). Harry Benjamin standards of care for gender dysphoric persons. Retrieved April 26, 2005, from http://www.altsex .org/transgender/benjamin.html

Gibson, P. (n.d.). Gay male and lesbian suicide. Retrieved May 31, 2005, from the Lambda Web site: http://www.lambda.org/youth_suicide.htm

Green, R., & Money, J. (1968). *Transexualism and sex reassignment*. Baltimore, MD: Johns Hopkins University Press.

Grosskurth, P. (1980). *Havelock Ellis*. Toronto, ON: McClelland & Stewart.

Herdt, G. (Ed.). (1996). *Third sex, third gender: Beyond sexual dimorphism in culture and history*. New York: Zone Books.

Hoyer, N. (1933). *Man into woman: An authentic record of a change of sex*. New York: E. P. Dutton.

Jorgensen, C. (2000). *Christine Jorgensen: A personal autobiography*. San Francisco, CA: Cleis Press.

Meyerowitz, J. (2002). *How sex changed: A history of transsexuality in the United States*. Cambridge, MA: Harvard Press.

More, K., & Whittle, S. (Eds.). (1999). *Reclaiming genders: Transsexual grammars at the* fin de siècle. London: Cassell.

National Transgender Advocacy Coalition. (2002, October 19). Three men arraigned in death of transgendered teen. Retrieved May 31, 2005, from the Transgender Crossroads Web site: http://www.tgcrossroads.org/news/archive.asp?aid=423

Nolan, S. (2000, December 9). Fighting to do a woman's work. *Globe & Mail.* Retrieved May 31, 2005, from the Vancouver Rape Relief and Women's Shelter Web site: http://www.rapereliefshelter.bc.ca/issues/knixonglobe.html

Raymond, J. (1979). *The transsexual empire: The making of the she-male.* Boston: Beacon.

Rudacille, D. (2005). *The riddle of gender.* New York: Pantheon Books.

Stoller, R. (1976). *Sex and gender. Vol. 2. The transsexual experiment.* New York: Aronson.

Transsexual custody battle. (2002). Retrieved May 31, 2005, from the Court TV Web site: http://www.courttv.com/trials/kantaras/

Why this boy was raised as a girl (2000, February 9). Retrieved May 31, 2005, from the Oprah.com Web site: http://www.oprah.com/tows/pastshows/tows_2000/tows_past_20000209_c.jhtml

❖ ADDITIONAL RESOURCES

Bolin, A. (1988). *In search of Eve.* Westport, CT: Bergin & Garvey.

Boylan, J. F. (2003). *She's not there.* New York: Broadway Books.

Brown, M. L., & Rounsley, C. A. (1996). *True selves: Understanding transsexualism.* San Francisco: Jossey-Bass.

LeRoy, J. T. (2001). *Sarah (a novel).* New York: Bloomsbury.

Lewins, F. (1995). *Transsexualism in society.* Melbourne, Victoria: MacMillan.

Peters, J. A. (2004). *Luna (a novel).* New York: Little Brown.

Townsend, L. (2002). *Hidden in plain sight.* New York: Writers Club Press.

The political events of 1992 may have set the stage for later elections and the subsequent political polarized climate.

SOURCE: © Dean Lance www.deanlance.com. Reprinted with permission.

8

The "Moral" Right Versus the "Queer" Left

Claims-Making by Religious Conservatives and Gay Activists at the 1992 Republican Convention and Beyond

Thomas M. Conroy

Claims that "marriage is to be defined as between one man and one woman" are "socially constructed" expressions through which social actors can assert values or mark their world as somehow problematic, according to sociologists Malcolm Spector and John Kitsuse (1977; Kitsuse & Spector, 1973). Claims are thus the products of claims-makers, who go about attempting to either change or preserve social conditions and situations in terms of the ways they perceive them. The process of claims-making typically occurs over stages, as claimants attempt to define problems, identify solutions, address specific audiences, and mobilize a following, and then to engage in further activities in light of social developments or official policies that may occur.

Here, it also helps to consider the role of the mass media, an enterprise engaged in social reality "construction" in the sense that how it frames its coverage of topical events is selective and thus interpretive (Parenti, 1986). For example, the conflagration occurring in Los Angeles in April 1992 was largely termed "a riot," with all of the associated implications that such a term entails, by most public officials and thus by most of the mainstream media. It was only through a radical political and progressive framework, as, for instance in the reports of a variety of "alternative" news outlets (e.g., the *Village Voice, The Nation,* the *Pacifica News Network,* etc.) that the same event might have been alternately termed a "rebellion" or as a rational community response to police brutality. The selected frame then preserves, as documentation, a public record of the events, such that later actors can use the record as an information source and a guide to further action.[1] News media can be seen as offering several purposes, or functions, including providing important information to the public, conveying values, and helping to interpret ongoing events. News frames are thus normative and can either assist or hinder those who make claims. Therefore, the interpretation of or reaction to news media itself can become part of the claims-making process.

One rather compelling example of claims-making activities, along with the making of counter claims by an opposing side, can be found in the conflicts between religious and social or cultural conservatives (hereafter referred to as the "Religious Right," or simply as the "Right") on one side, and on the other side, gay rights activists and movements pressing toward the normalization of homosexuality. This controversy has also taken place within mass media, affecting everything from news coverage to popular culture and entertainment media. For example, one can recall the attention in the late 1990s paid to the comedian Ellen Degeneres, whose top-rated situation comedy *Ellen* was at the center of the media spotlight when both Ellen the actress and Ellen the character came out of the closet as a lesbian. Predictably, this event was immediately followed by heavy criticism by social conservatives complaining that (what they took to be the *elitist* liberal) media was promoting what they took to be a sinful, amoral lifestyle. In recent years, we have seen this conflict played out in a wide variety of issues, ranging from the AIDS crisis to treatment of gays[2] in the military to the ordination of gay men and lesbians within established religious groups to, most recently, the controversy over gay marriage, with this latter issue incorporated into 2004's political debates. Although opposition to gay marriage appears to be fairly widespread in the United States, it also appears that more Americans generally accept gay rights, although the range of acceptance also appears to reflect some fundamental cultural differences between more liberal urban and more conservative rural areas of the country. This range of acceptance of gays can also be found across various religious affiliations, although more conservative members of Christian (including both Protestant and Catholic), Jewish, Moslem, and other such faith groups tend to be morally opposed to homosexuality, seeing it as a sinful or disordered condition and a violation of basic morality. Many such groups also tend to see it as a "chosen lifestyle." It is therefore here, on the antipathy between gays and religious conservatives, that this chapter will focus, given that this conflict provides a central dynamic through which contemporary American politics are driven.

❖ THE 1992 PRESIDENTIAL ELECTION

There are some specific times and places in which to examine the politics of morality, as well as some possible meanings behind such politics, and so we can turn to recent political history, and specifically, the 1992 U.S. national election. It was in 1992 that George Herbert Walker Bush, a sitting president who was also a World War II hero, faced off against William Jefferson Clinton, a baby boomer who came of age in, and was thus associated in popular discourse with, the 1960s, and whose campaign theme was one of "change." In that sense, the 1992 election was, among other things, a full-fledged referendum on the social and cultural changes from the 1960s on, including the trend of the loosening or liberalizing of personal morality; conservatives were, from the late 1970s on, insisting on more absolute standards of right and wrong. The 1960s was also a significant period for the gay rights movement. It was, after all, in the late 1960s that the "Stonewall Riots" in New York City made visible a new movement, one expressing a demand for equal rights for homosexuals. As Eric Marcus (1992), in a history of the gay rights movement, points out, what next occurred is that by the early 1970s "the number of gay and lesbian organizations soared to nearly 400, ranging from politically oriented groups with names like Gay Liberation Front, to chapters of the gay Metropolitan Community Church" (p. 172). Marcus adds that

In San Francisco, New York, Los Angeles, and other large cities, protests against antigay discrimination became commonplace. These protests ranged from "kiss-ins" at restaurants that refused to serve gay customers to highly publicized applications by gay and lesbian couples for marriage licenses to on-air interruptions of national news programs that gay people accused of avoiding or distorting gay issues . . . Protestors demanded that local and national politicians address the issue of gay civil rights. They were so effective that, in 1972, Democratic presidential candidates spoke favorably of supporting national legislation to protect gay people from discrimination. And two openly gay delegates addressed the Democratic National Convention in Miami. (Marcus, 1992, p. 172)

Thus, in examining the 1992 convention, we view contrasting constructions of notions of "gayness" and political "morality." These then provide an ideal context for examining claims and counter claims-making activities; it might even be said that the (queer) left and (Christian) right continuously construct one another, or at least a version of one another, through such claims as those contained in this case and in related cases. However, this example is also ideal for revealing a complexity about the production of meanings in their social context.

Claims-Making at the National Republican Convention

By 1992, the Christian conservative influence within the national Republican Party had become particularly strong. Christian social activists, affiliated with the *Christian Coalition* and with other such organizations, now dominated the party organizations of a large number of states. This hegemony came about as particular churches (mainly Evangelical or fundamentalist) or church-based organizations converted their various resources into political capital. Christian conservatives had at their disposal the use of such resources as television broadcast facilities, programs, and networks; mailing lists; newsletters; pre-existent church networks; Bible schools and colleges; influence over local school boards; and a large pool of steady financial contributors. Most, if not all, of such resources could be readily directed toward politics, with church leaders legitimating this as part of a religious duty to preserve morality. Such religious-political organizations then garnered and developed various resources of their own, including devout followers willing to spend multiple hours in the nuts and bolts work of grassroots political organizing. The earlier mutuality of Ronald Reagan and Rev. Jerry Falwell, head of the "moral majority," in their political courtship with one another during 1980 was such that, by 1992, Christian conservatives were able to be influential in inserting into the Republican Party's platform such items as statements supporting the notion of "the traditional American family," child tax credits, school vouchers, prevention of AIDS through "marital fidelity, abstinence, and a drug-free lifestyle," opposition to including "sexual preference as a protected minority," opposition to "same sex marriages," opposition to adoption or the provision of foster care by same-sex couples, calls for a "national crusade against pornography," and opposition to abortion, among other themes (Rosenbaum, 1992).

In earlier decades, Christian conservatives tended to stick to religion and avoid active involvement in politics. In the first half of the 20th century, the Republican Party tended to be more moderate and to draw its base of support from liberal northeastern reformers, from industrialists, and from Western factions. In terms of religion, there was probably an overlap between the Republicans and mainline Protestant denominations. At the same time, Catholics tended to be found in urban, blue-collar occupations and tended to be members of ethnic minority groups, and these groups—along with the working classes of the rural South—tended to vote Democratic. However, starting in the 1960s with the Civil Rights movement and continuing with the "Reagan revolution" of the 1980s, the American electorate began a historic realignment. Although white Southern evangelicals supported the Democratic candidate Jimmy Carter in 1976 by a large margin (and in doing so, revealed the Christian Conservative voters to be a voting bloc), by 1980, this bloc (and the socially conservative South regionally) was becoming firmly aligned with the Republican Party.

Thus, with the moral conservatives now seemingly carrying the day (and generating controversy in the process), the spotlight tended also to shine on the ideological or issue-oriented opponents, many of which were located in, or perceived to be grounded in, the left end of the political spectrum and in the (ever more centrist) Democratic Party.

Among the leading opponents of the moral conservatives were such gay and lesbian organizations as the Gay and Lesbian Alliance Against Defamation (GLAAD), Human Rights Campaign, National Lesbian and Gay Task Force, and AIDS Action Council, all of which perceived that it was in their interest to oppose conservative attacks on their main concerns. Other opponents included feminist, women's, and pro-choice organizations such as the National Organization of Women, Planned Parenthood, and the National Abortion Rights Action League, who opposed the conservatives' calls for the banning and criminalization of abortion and who perceived religious conservatives as being opposed to the principle of gender inequality, as well as civil libertarian organizations, such as the American Civil Liberties Union (ACLU), People for the American Way, various anticensorship movements and organizations, and others, who expressed various concerns about free speech and the separation of church and state. Included in this latter category were such artists as the painter Andres Serrano; the photographer Robert Mapplethorpe; the performance artists Karen Finley, Tim Miller, and Wendy Hughes; and the filmmaker Todd Haynes; many of these (mostly openly gay) artists presented homoerotic or scatological themes and politically or culturally challenging works, which then got caught up in the crossfire between those on opposing sides of the cultural divide. The works of such artists—fodder for debates about the propriety of government funding, through the National Endowment of the Arts, for what was taken to be "morally decadent" art—indicated that the dialectic of leftist versus mainstream politics had become particularly oriented toward symbolic expression.

The Democratic Party was, by 1992, noticeably more open to the gay community than ever before (Gallagher & Bull, 1996). In part, this reflected a broader level of social acceptance of gays than in the past. In part, it also reflected the level of organization of the gay community, which now had the strength and ability to express itself as a political (i.e., voting and fund-raising) bloc. It also reflected a growing political association between the Democratic Party and the relatively gay-friendly entertainment industry; in particular, Hollywood. In 1992, AIDS was the primary issue, making for an increased gay visibility within the political process (Gallagher & Bull, 1996, p. 69), not to mention within entertainment and mass media. AIDS was also the issue that helped galvanize such protest groups as the AIDS Coalition to Unleash Power (ACT UP) and Queer Nation and that provided the backdrop against which such symbols as pink triangle displays, the

"Silence = Death" slogan, and "we're here, we're queer, get used to it!" street chants became ironically familiar. One of the reasons that gay organizations had for opposing President Bush was their perception that his AIDS policies (like Reagan's before him) were inadequate and discriminatory (Schulman, 1994). Thus, with gay politics intertwined with partisan politics, and with the high visibility of bands of flamboyant street activists seemingly flaunting more traditional standards of propriety, the Religious Right could and did react in a combination of moral and political terms; rhetorically, the Democrats were touted as the party that "condoned immorality." Religious conservatives also drew on the more controversial images of gay activists in their depictions of them, as, for instance, in the showing of "lewd" behavioral displays (i.e., campy "drag queens," thong-wearing bodybuilders, religious parody performers, etc.) at gay pride marches, shown repeatedly on Christian TV. Another such reaction by the Religious Right was its persistent sponsorship and organization of ballot initiatives, in such states as Oregon, Maine, and Colorado, denying lesbians and gay men the protection of civil rights laws. What was seen as a hate campaign by gay activists and other opponents of such initiatives was put forth by the sponsors as not hateful but, rather, dictated by a particular reading of scripture (in which homosexuality is considered "an abomination") and in response to a perception that lesbians and gay men were asking for "special rights."

Media Coverage of the Convention

Conservative ideology was fully on display, and well covered by news media as a major event, on the opening Monday night of the GOP convention, August 17, a night that featured both former candidate Pat Buchanan and former president Ronald Reagan as main speakers. Buchanan officially gave his endorsement to Bush but mainly touted his own culturally conservative views,[3] claiming to stand with Bush "for freedom of choice religious schools [sic] and we stand with him against the amoral idea that gay and lesbian couples should have the same standing in law as married men and women" (Berke, 1992). He referred to the United States as "God's country" and closed his speech with a call to his followers to "take back our cities, and take back our culture, and take back our country." News media reported that Buchanan's speech played very well to the assembled audience; *The New York Times*, for instance reported (Kolbert, 1992) on CBS's cutting away during Buchanan's speech and showing the reactions of such leading conservatives as Falwell and Phyllis Schlafly, "looking on approvingly," and of "groups of young men pumping their fists into the air in a militaristic show of approval." The *Washington Post* (Jordan, 1992) also reported the presence of signs reading "Family Rights Forever/ Gay Rights Never" that were waved during the various speeches, particularly Buchanan's and Pat Robertson's.

In fact, the mainstream media tended to present the story of the Republican convention in a mostly matter-of-fact way, lending it the credence and legitimacy by which its arguably reactionary views were presented as relatively mainstream. News organizations may have been split in editorial terms regarding supporting Bush or Clinton, but the very institutionalized system of news production and distribution guaranteed that, in terms of the conflict between conservative Republicans and gay objects of religiously filtered rhetoric, gays were likely to be seen as marginalized and outside of the mainstream. In that way, the media and the conservatives were partners. In fact, gay activists were often depicted as outsiders, present in Houston for the sake of disrupting events.

As such speech-making activities were occurring inside the Houston convention hall, news reports were issued about confrontations in Houston between Republican conservatives and anticonservative protesters, particularly those advocating gay rights. One report (Harris & Jenkins, 1992) noted the occurrence of planned disruptions by members of the gay advocacy group Queer Nation at a speech by Jerry Falwell given at an afternoon rally of the Virginia delegation. As Falwell was condemning abortion and homosexual rights, protesters interrupted with chants of "our family is dying of AIDS." The *Post* report described the protest, which was also sponsored by the National Gay and Lesbian Task Force, as "an angry row, with minor scuffling and several arrests" and as a "clash, captured by a phalanx of television cameras." Another report in the *Washington Post* ("AIDS activists clash," 1992) described a protest by the AIDS activist group ACT UP in which anywhere from 300 to 2,500 demonstrators burned an effigy of Bush and clashed with Houston police, who then made six arrests of demonstrators. According to the report, police attempted to prevent the protesters from moving into the official demonstration area, leading to clashes with the police and the arrests. Reports also indicate the interruption of Bush's Wednesday afternoon speech at a Republican National Committee luncheon by ACT UP protesters, who chanted,

"What about AIDS?"[4] In fact, throughout the 1992 political season, ACT UP had led or participated in numerous protest actions and addressed itself to candidates in both parties.

One detailed report, given in the Boston-based gay weekly newspaper *Bay Windows* (Malkin, 1992b), described a protest event occurring during Buchanan's speech in which "approximately 2,000 people marched outside the convention in a protest for gay and lesbian rights and increased leadership on AIDS." The article identified ACT-UP, the National Gay and Lesbian Task Force, and Queer Nation as being the main participants. However, as a gay media publication, it attempted to provide a bit more explanatory context, such as thorough quotations from various participants, who claimed:

"We hope to deliver a message to the government that we're tired of this. The government has done nothing to fight AIDS."

"This is our one chance before the election to come together and to tell George Bush he's a murderer. Hopefully, it will take some of the spin off of their convention."

"It looks to me that what we saw inside the convention hall from Pat Buchanan was being demonstrated in terms of physical violence against gay and lesbian people and people who are concerned about AIDS outside the convention hall. I think that these two things are very much connected . . . [and] inextricably tied and the president of the United States is responsible."

In other words, some of the gay activists may have been responding to what they perceived to be a delegitimizing form of hatred from within the convention hall.

As has been suggested, gay and lesbian groups and organizations had by 1992 attained a certain level of development vis-à-vis the larger political process. Although there were, perhaps, well-established gay civil rights organizations existing as far back as the early 1960s (see Marcus, 1992) and clearly identified gay districts—and accompanying local power bases—in the nation's major cities, it is also arguably the case that if any singular issue helped to define the gay rights movement as national (and even international) in scope and visibility, this issue was the AIDS virus, a virus for which gay males represented a high-risk demographic group in particular, beginning in the early 1980s. AIDS soon thereafter became linked in the public consciousness with homosexuality. In addition, we have clearly seen a widening, though gradual, level of cultural acceptance of gays, just as gays have become increasingly mainstreamed in terms of cultural representation; inevitably, however, this degree of acceptance has lead to a backlash by gay rights opponents, who are largely religiously based and who look to the political sphere as a place within which to express themselves. It should be noted, as well, that there are a variety of important tactical, generational, and ideological differences between mainstream gay rights organizations, such as GLAAD and the Human Rights Campaign, and nonmainstream militant groups, such as Queer Nation, just as there were, in the mid- to late 1960s, significant differences between the mainstream civil rights organizations and the more militant black power movement. One such difference between older and younger generations of gay activists is appropriation of the term "queer" by the latter as a term of self-affirmation, an act that eventually gave this formerly derogatory term a new set of much more positive connotations.[5]

News reports thus also underscored the expressive rallying of moral conservatives. The *Washington Post* described, for example, a "God and Country rally." Here, Pat Robertson, Christian Conservative delegates, and their supporters rallied for "pro-family" views; essentially, these included expressions of antiabortion, antifeminism, anti–sex education, anti–liberal media, and anti–gay rights views.[6] Vice President Dan Quayle, one of the rally speakers, attacked "liberal elites," given their alleged scorn for "family values." Another participant, a Louisiana delegate, commented that the assembled participants' "values derive from the Scriptures and from Judeo-Christian values 2,000 years old," and not from "the changing events of the world" (Von Drehle, 1992). Robertson had clearly established himself as a major player in the Republican Party at this time, and during his convention speech of August 19, he drew a contrast between the "visions" of Bush and Clinton, such that "George Bush's vision for America . . . is one of faith in God, strong families, freedom, individual initiative and free enterprise," whereas Bill Clinton's vision "is a liberal welfare state that dominates every facet of our lives, burdens free enterprise, redistributes wealth, raises taxes and weakens the family." Robertson added that Clinton would "make sexual preferences a privileged minority under our civil rights laws" and was "running on a platform that calls for saving the spotted owl but never once mentions the name of God" (Toner, 1992).

Robertson's complaints echoed many of those of Buchanan, who, in his "culture war" convention speech, had attacked such Clinton-associated targets as abortion on demand, "discrimination against" religious schools, "special rights" for homosexuals, and the right of women to serve in combat. Both Robertson and Buchanan put forth a view of modern social life as an arena for the forces of good (i.e., their branch of the Republican Party) and near evil (i.e., liberalism and Clinton as the figurehead of the liberal Democratic Party) (Grant, 1996, pp. 61–65).

By August 20, the convention's final night, in which President George Bush and Vice President Quayle were to be nominated and give their acceptance speeches, the conservative tone was thus pretty well set. Gay men and lesbians continued to be the targets of scorn by Republican speakers, albeit in coded form, such as in the following excerpt from Quayle's acceptance speech:

> When family values are undermined, our country suffers. All too often, parents struggle to instill character in their sons and daughters, only to see their beliefs mocked by those who look down on America. Americans try to raise their children to understand right and wrong, only to be told that every so-called "lifestyle alternative" is morally equivalent. That is wrong. (Malkin, 1992c)

Election Results

It has been said by various political analysts and interpreters that although the convention's stern moral conservative tone may have helped to rally the base of culturally conservative Republicans, other more moderate ("swing" or independent) voters may have been turned off by its message. Finally, on election day, November 3, Clinton won 43% of the popular vote and 370 electoral votes; Bush won 38% of the popular vote and 168 electoral votes; Independent (and largely self-financed) candidate H. Ross Perot came in with 19% of the popular vote and no electoral votes. The weak economy was believed to be the primary reason for the election result, although Clinton's effective campaign tactics and Bush's less-than-effective campaign undoubtedly each played a role in the outcome. A CNN poll indicated that Clinton captured 71% of the gay and lesbian vote, compared with Bush's 17% and Perot's 12% of the same vote (Malkin, 1992a).

One could very well argue that the political events of 1992, along with the first year of Clinton's presidency, set the stage for both the later elections in 1994 and 1996 and the subsequent polarized political climate. The Religious Right has continued to retain a moral hegemony over much of the Republican Party; this can be seen in a variety of instances, including the continued calls for school prayer, tax breaks for private schools, the antigay "defense of marriage" act, and harsh antiabortion legislation. The Right also played a role in the Republicans' dealings with Clinton, including its rejection of Clinton's desire to change the legal status of gays in the military (with the resulting "compromise" policy of "Don't ask, don't tell"); the rejection, for apparent ideological reasons, of various Clinton appointees; the forced resignation of Joycelyn Elders as surgeon general based on her lack of enthusiasm for "abstinence education"; and the unwillingness to spend money on such legislative programs as crime prevention, the 1993 urban stimulus package, and the health care plan. In many of these instances, both allies and critics saw Clinton as being altogether too willing to give in on such "wedge" issues as abortion and gays in the military. In 1994, the Republicans regained control of Congress, and the newer leaders, such as Newt Gingrich, Tom Delay, Dick Armey, Trent Lott, and Don Nickles were significantly further to the right than previous Republican congressional leaders.

Developments in Later Years

In more recent years, we have seen the following events, all of which have added to the cultural and political polarization of the gay rights movement and the Right.

Within the United States, there have been various state and local initiatives prohibiting government from including homosexuals as a protected class under civil rights laws. Even in states, such as Idaho and Maine, in which such ballot measures failed, they often did so by very close margins. On the federal level, Congress narrowly rejected a bill in 1996 that would have prohibited workplace discrimination on the basis of sexual orientation.

In 1998, Matthew Shepard, a 21-year-old undergraduate at the University of Wyoming, was brutally assaulted and killed by two men, who were both later convicted of second degree murder. Across the country, rallies and vigils were held for Shepard, although in Wyoming, Rev. Fred Phelps from Topeka, Kansas, and his followers held a "God hates fags" rally near Shepard's funeral. Shepard's death gave impetus to an expansion of the federal definition of "hate crimes" to include sexual orientation. Shepard's mother, Judy Shepard, became involved in the campaign against antigay hate crimes (Matthew Shepard Foundation, 2004). One other consequence of a growing awareness of both antigay hate crimes and a disproportionately high rate of violence affecting gay teens was the foundation in the late 1990s of the Harvey Milk School, an alternative school offering various social services for at-risk, openly gay adolescents in New York City. Such a school is also tied to an organization, the Gay, Lesbian, and Straight Education Network, which advocates for lesbian, gay, bisexual, and transgender students.

In 1996, with fairly little debate, Congress passed and President Clinton signed into law the Defense of Marriage Act, a Republican-sponsored measure aimed at preventing gay marriage. The law specified that no state would be required to recognize the validity of a gay marriage performed in any other state. Several states either then passed, or had already passed, their own version of the same law. The act defined marriage, under federal law, as the "legal union of one man and one woman." Critics of this law called it institutionalized bigotry and homophobia, and the constitutionality of the law was also immediately challenged in the courts. Later, in 2003, during the administration of President George W. Bush, conservatives began discussing the possibility of a constitutional amendment to prevent same-sex marriage, and Bush himself came out in favor of this proposed amendment. This was in response to two court rulings: first, a Supreme Court decision in June 2003 banning sodomy statutes (and thus a legal basis for criminalizing homosexuality) and second, a decision in November 2003 by the Massachusetts Supreme Court allowing gay marriage to take place in the Commonwealth of Massachusetts. Although conservatives, such as Bush, decried these decisions as the result of "activist" judges, they were also accused of trying to create a diversionary wedge issue as a presidential election year ensued. Their efforts to initiate such an amendment failed in a Senate vote in 2004. Nevertheless, some observers were expecting that various state antigay marriage amendments would be likely to impel significant numbers of Christian conservative voters to go to the polls in November. In fact, the election resulted in 11 more states passing such amendments. It has also been reported that Bush won 79% of the 26.5 million evangelical votes and 52% of the 31 million Catholic votes (Cooperman & Edsall, 2004).

Facing discrimination, gays have continued to press for equality and recognition, whether as individuals or through such social actions as mass mobilizations for gay rights. One such event was a protest march involving some 300,000 gay rights protesters in Washington, D.C., in 1993. Gays have also sought equality in the area of marriage. The notion of gay marriage took on a new momentum when the Netherlands became the first country to allow gay marriage, followed by other countries. In addition to developments in Massachusetts, there were also positive changes in the status of gays in states such as California, Vermont, and New Jersey, all of which began offering a variety of rights to gay men and lesbians.

Within various Christian religious organizations, a variety of responses to the ordination of gay clergy has occurred. For example, in 1994, the Presbyterian Church (U.S.A.) General Assembly barred clergy from blessing same-sex unions. Later, though, in 2001, the General Assembly voted to allow the local governing bodies the option of ordaining gays. In 1994, the House of Bishops of the Episcopal Church began to open itself up to the possibility of same-sex unions. Other denominations, such as the Evangelical Lutheran Church, engaged in dialogue on the issue. And in 1995, Reverend Jeanne Audrey Powers, a leading member of the United Methodist Church, came out as gay, the highest ranking official in her denomination ever to do so. Later, again within the Episcopal Church, an openly gay minister, Gene Robinson, was consecrated a bishop of the Diocese of New Hampshire, making him the first openly gay Episcopal bishop and the highest ranking gay clergyman in the United States. His ordination as bishop led conservative Anglican factions that believe that homosexuality is a sin to announce a state of "impaired communion" with the United States. In the meantime, the Catholic Church, under the leadership of Pope John Paul II and the ultraconservative Cardinal Joseph Ratzinger, prefect of the Vatican's Congregation for the Doctrine of the Faith (now Pope Benedict XVI), took various steps to marginalize gay Catholics as well as to oppose gay marriage, in spite of a legitimation crisis within the Church over child sex abuse by clergy.

Most recently, Vice President Dick Cheney and his wife, conservative activist and author Lynne Cheney, have broken ranks with President George W. Bush and the moral conservatives and have declared that the gay marriage issue (and by implication, the notion of gay rights) ought not to be a federal matter, stating that "freedom means freedom for everyone to enter into any kind of relationship they want" (Janofsky, 2004). The Cheneys' status as parents of an openly gay daughter, Mary Cheney, was spotlighted several times in the campaign, such as in the media furor that followed her gay identity being mentioned by John Kerry, the Democratic presidential candidate.

❖ A THEORETICAL UNDERSTANDING OF CLAIMS-MAKING

An entity such as the Religious Right represents claims-making par excellence. Of course, a full sociohistorical analysis of the religious conservative movement in the United States, as well as of its relationship to the topics of sexuality and homosexuality, would necessarily begin with the earliest days of America's colonial history and would thus be way beyond the scope of this much more temporally focused examination. Nonetheless, as we have seen, the Religious Right as a social movement was a claims-maker in 1992, making strong use of the political process, and of the Republican Party within this process, so as to put forth its moral message, with which it attempted to bring about legislative and cultural change, and it continues to be a claims-maker to this day. As an entity, the Religious Right consists of a variety of affiliated groups and organizations led by key officials and drawing on a number of specific resources—money, media exposure, symbolic organizational resources, access to the Republican hierarchy, and a grassroots following of mobilized true believers, among other things.

One aspect to focus on here is what Spector and Kitsuse (1977) call the "mechanism" for pressing claims, namely the channels through which the claims are pressed, the strategies for illustrating the group's argument, and the use of mass media. Obviously, a major party convention is a large-scale mass media event, and the activities occurring within this event get magnified, particularly by newspapers and by television. The strategies entailed in the presentation of claims within this event context are based on the moral absolutism of the claims—hence the repeated arguments about right and wrong. They are also based on a more pragmatic consideration: specifically, trying to help convince the electorate that the Republicans are a party of moral principle but that the Democrats are not and thus to turn out voters who will be likely to vote Republican.

However, Spector and Kitsuse (1973) note that "one important contingency in the processing of complaints is identifying the party to whom the complaint should be addressed" (p. 151). When we examine the role of the Religious Right in the national elections of the 1990s and beyond, we see that there are two distinct audiences: the Republican

Party, in which groups such as the Christian Coalition, the Traditional Values Coalition, the Family Research Council, and their respective allies see themselves as having an ownership share, and the general electorate, who, thus far, had remained less than fully convinced by the conservative moral message. However, as in other cases of "intraparty protest movements," the claims-makers here may not necessarily have expected to win their position in any sudden or absolute sense but rather in smaller, more incremental steps.

In contrast, although gay activists may have been participants in dialogue with both political parties in 1992—whether from a coopera- tive or from a confrontational stance—there is no analogy of its rela- tionship to the Democratic Party to the hegemony of the Religious Right over the Republican Party.

In addition, this case illustrates a relationship between opposing sets of claims-makers. Spector and Kitsuse (1973) point out that the actions of particular claims-makers "may provoke a reaction from other groups that prefer the existing arrangements or would stand to lose something if they were changed" and, further, that the conflicts between opposing groups "may escalate the visibility of the whole debate and facilitate the creation of public awareness of the imputed condition" (p. 151). Indeed, the focus here has been on the specific rela- tionship between Christian Conservative activists affiliated with the Republican Party and gay political activists, largely affiliated with the left end of the political spectrum or with the Democratic Party, and on this relationship at a specific moment in time.

Indeed, one can look at the gay community as itself a claims- maker, one engaged in the act of making a different type of moral claim; that is, one based on a recognition of a fundamental right to fair- ness, equality, and inclusion. Like the Religious Right organizations, gay rights organizations have shown a willingness to use political mech- anisms to press claims, with varying degrees of success.

As a result of the claims-making process, gay activists and Christian conservatives enter into one another's claims; each side becomes, in a sense, a construct, or element of the issued claim. Such mutual demonization processes help to construct a sense of social reality in which gays and Christian conservatives are alternatively presented as "threats" to some cherished value, as intolerant of their opponents, as narrow and extremist zealots for their cause. Gays accuse preachers and other Christian conservatives of gay bashing and condoning murder; conservatives accuse gays of bringing forth Sodom and Gomorrah. These polarized images each side holds of the other only get confirmed in angry moments of street confrontation, in which the two sides occasionally meet. This raises the issue of meaning and its production, an issue of particular importance to social constructionist analysis. As Berger and Luckmann (1967), in a major treatise on social constructionism, suggest, shared meaning is a product of the "typifications" of ordinary language, a language used by us to socialize one another and to *objectify* reality. Within such a process, our subjective biases—that is, our very sense of reality—come to seem objective. What Berger and Luckmann call *objectivation* takes our individual experiences and transforms them into something common and shared (i.e., a sense of "we" or "ours"), with this collective consciousness then transmitted over generations (and perhaps to be lost, eventually, in light of new arrangements). Objectivation also takes place on two different levels: an everyday life level, in which actors express their subjective experience by encoding them in typifications (e.g., saying such things as "I'm sick," "I'm in love," "I'm a conservative," "I'm studying business"), and a second-order *explanatory* level. This latter context, which Berger and Luckmann term *legitimation,* is abstracted from the activities and typifications through which an entire institutional order (i.e., a society as a whole) is both explained and justified by various parties. Hence the institutional order can further be seen in terms of second-order "symbolic universes," which Berger and Luckmann term *sheltering canopies* that integrate and give meaning to both individual biographies and the institutional order. From here, we can examine the "conceptual machineries of universe maintenance"; that is, the mythologies, theologies, philosophies, and sciences, and the social organization of such machineries. Hence we can see the gay-right dialogue as one of an attempted self-legitimation by each side and delegitimation of the other side. That is, there can be a variety of ways in which one might interpret one's own experiences, be these experiences of bodily pleasures or spiritual imaginings. The language used by each side—including and especially the language filtered through the media—reflects the meanings held by them about the social reality of the pressed claims. As we consider, further, the sorts of claims put forth in this case, we can see that these are based on ideas that are properly seen as cultural, institutional, and intersubjective. That is, they are shared by groups of relatively like-minded individuals who are bound by shared cultural values and institutional ties. As we continue to examine the conflict between sexual liberty and moral traditionalism, we continue to see examples of the truism that the personal (i.e., one's faith or one's sexual orientation) is political. In a world of nonstop global media, the personal-political is also fodder for an extensive viewing audience.

❖ DISCUSSION QUESTIONS

1. What is meant by claims-making? How do both the Religious Right and the gay community represent the act of claims-making? What are their main goals?

2. To what extent should the political process be used to promote a "moral agenda"? Whose morals should be promoted?

3. Is it possible for a person to be both actively gay and religiously devout? Explain.

4. What examples have you seen of how the media depicts both religious social activists and gay men and lesbians? Is there a difference in the depiction of gays generally versus those depicted as gay "activists"?

5. What do you think are the consequences for politics of the movement for gay rights?

❖ HOMEWORK ASSIGNMENTS

1. Using the Web sites listed in this chapter, identify and describe how a particular issue, such as gay marriage or hate crime legislation, is characterized by both pro-gay and religious-conservative groups and organizations. How is the particular issue framed by each side?

2. Using the Internet as well as library and archival sources, do a content analysis of the media's depiction of the actions of either a gay rights or a religious conservative group within a particular campaign (i.e., a particular presidential election, the campaign for and against hate crime legislation, etc.). Compare and contrast how the depictions work for both mainstream and nonmainstream media sources.

3. Interview any two or three gay individuals, as well as two or three persons of faith, to inquire into their views of gay rights and other social issues.

❖ NOTES

1. See Tuchman (1978) for an insightful discussion of the construction of news frames. Tuchman, a leading sociologist of mass media, derives much of her thinking from the work of Goffman (1959, 1986).

2. For simplicity, the term *gays* in this chapter refers to both gay men and lesbian women.

3. Adele Stan (1995), in "Power Preying" reports that "He [Buchanan] draws key staffers and a significant following from the [Christian] Coalition's ranks, and he conceivably could take his faithful with him if the Republican Party fails to toe his ideological line." Some additional evidence and suggestions are presented in other news reports and commentaries. For example, Michael Lind, in an August 19, 1992 op-ed article in the *New York Times*, wrote on Buchanan and the "Buchanan-Robertson brigades," calling Buchanan the "undisputed leader of the masses of the American right." It is noteworthy that both Buchanan and Robertson would each go on to a later run for the presidency but that, whereas Robertson would run as a socially conservative Republican, Buchanan would run first as a Republican and later (in 2000) as a right-wing populist, the leader of, as he put it, the "peasants with pitchforks" faction.

4. Ann Powers (1993), who sees sexual identity categorical boundaries becoming ever blurred, offers an analysis of the "queer politics" of such groups as ACT UP and Queer Nation, saluting what she describes as such groups' "revitalized street protest, mixing righteous rage with postmodern style and media savvy." According to Powers, such "queer groups offered politics that felt completely of the moment."

However, in a critique of the radical, constructionist politics of queer theory, gay author (and former *New Republic* editor) Andrew Sullivan writes (1993):

The trouble with gay radicalism, in short, is the problem with subversive politics as a whole. It tends to subvert itself. . . . the radical politics of homosexuality, like the conservative politics of homosexuality, is caught in a political trap. The more it purifies its own belief about sexuality, the less able it is to engage the broader world as a whole. The more it acts upon its convictions, the less able it is to engage in politics at all. For the "queer" fundamentalists, like the religious fundamentalists, this is no problem. Politics for both groups is essentially an exercise in theater and rhetoric, in which dialogue with one's opponent is an admission of defeat. It is no accident that ACT UP was founded by a playwright, since its politics was essentially theatrical: a fantastic display of rhetorical pique and visual brilliance. It became a national media hit, but eventually its lines became familiar and the audience's attention wavered. New shows have taken its place and will continue to do so—but they will always be constrained by their essential nature, which is performance, not persuasion. (p. 32)

5. The appropriation of the term "queer" by young gay activists is discussed by Duggan (1992), who sees "queer" as part of a critique of "the liberal and nationalist strategies in gay politics" and as part of a "constructionist turn in lesbian and gay theories and practices." Duggan adds that "The notion of a 'queer community' . . . is often used to construct a collectivity defined solely by the gender of its members' sexual partners," one "unified only by a shared dissent from the dominant organization of sex and gender" (p. 20). Duggan goes on to refer to "queer theory," locating this in the work of Foucault, particularly his *History of Sexuality,* and in the elaboration of the theory by gay constructionists, noting that "Queer theories do their ghetto-busting work by placing the production and circulation of sexualities at the core of Western cultures, defining the emergence of the homosexual/heterosexual dyad as an issue that *no* cultural theory can afford to ignore" (p. 23). However, she notes the gap between academic queer theory, which she sees as "breaking into the mainstream," and a "queer politics" that "occupies the critical margins" as "the language and logic of liberalism still occupy the progressive edge of the possible in mainstream U.S. politics" (p. 27).

6. See Tanya Melich (1996) for insightful background on the workings of Operation Rescue (p. 235).

❖ REFERENCES

AIDS activists clash with police. (1992, August 18). *Washington Post,* p. A19.

Berger, P., & Luckmann, T. (1967). *The social construction of reality: A treatise in the sociology of knowledge.* Garden City, NY: Doubleday.

Berke, R. (1992, August 17). Unhumbled, Buchanan backs Bush. *New York Times,* p. 8.

Cooperman, A., & Edsall, T. (2004, November 8). Evangelicals say they led charge for the GOP. *Washington Post,* p. A1.

Duggan, L. (1992, January–March). Making it perfectly queer. *Socialist Review,* 22(1), 11–32.

Gallagher, J., & Bull, C. (1996). *Perfect enemies: The religious right, the gay movement, and the politics of the 1990s.* New York: Crown.

Goffman, E. (1959). *The presentation of self in everyday life.* Garden City, NY: Doubleday Anchor Books.

Goffman, E. (1986). *Frame analysis.* Boston, MA: Northeastern University Press.

Grant, G. (1996). *Buchanan: Caught in the crossfire.* Nashville, TN: Thomas Nelson.

Harris, J., & Jenkins, K. (1992, August 20). Va. delegates welcome Falwell back. *Washington Post*, p. A37.

Janofsky, M. (2004, September 26). Social conservatives criticize Cheney on same-sex marriage. *New York Times*, p. A25.

Jordan, M. (1992, August 21). Voters decry GOP "gay bashing." *Washington Post*, p. A27.

Kitsuse, J., & Spector, M. (1973). Toward a sociology of social problems: Social conditions, value-judgments, and social problems. *Social Problems, 20*, 407–419.

Kolbert, E. (1992, August 19). Networks focus on shift to the right. *New York Times*, p. A14.

Lind, M. (1992, August 19). Buchanan, conservatism's ugly face. *New York Times*, p. A21.

Malkin, M. (1992a, November 5–11). A Clinton victory. *Bay Windows*, p. 1.

Malkin, M. (1992b, August 20). GOP convention engages in unprecedented bashing. *Bay Windows*, p. 1.

Malkin, M. (1992c, August 27). The party's over. *Bay Windows*, p. 3.

Marcus, E. (1992). *Making history: The struggle for gay and lesbian equal rights, 1945–1990.* New York: Harper Collins.

Matthew Shepard Foundation. (2004). Our story. Retrieved April 25, 2005, from http://www.matthewshepard.org/story.html

Melich, T. (1996). *The Republican war against women: An insider's report from behind the lines.* New York: Bantam Books.

Parenti, M. (1986). *Inventing reality: The politics of mass media.* New York: St. Martin's Press.

Powers, A. (1993, November/December). Queer in the streets, straight in the sheets: Notes on passing. *Utne Reader,* (60), pp. 74–80.

Rosenbaum, D. (1992, August 15). The 1992 campaign: Parties' core differences in platforms. *New York Times*, p. 26.

Schulman, S. (1994). *My American history: Lesbian and gay life during the Reagan/ Bush years.* New York: Routledge.

Spector, M., & Kitsuse, J. (1973). Social problems: A reformulation. *Social Problems, 21*, 145–159.

Spector, M., & Kitsuse, J. (1977). *Constructing social problems.* New York: Aldine.

Stan, A. (1995, November/December). Power preying. *Mother Jones, 20*(6), 34–46.

Sullivan, A. (1993, May 10). The politics of homosexuality. *New Republic, 208*(19), 24–33.

Toner, R. (1992, August 20). Republicans send Bush into the campaign under a banner stressing "family values." *New York Times*, p. A1.

Tuchman, G. (1978). *Making news: A study in the construction of reality.* New York: Oxford University Press.

Von Drehle, D. (1992, August 18). A celebration by religious right as platform panel sees the light. *Washington Post*, p. A17.

❖ ADDITIONAL RESOURCES

Boswell, J. (1981). *Christianity, social tolerance, and homosexuality: Gay people in Western Europe from the beginning of the Christian era to the fourteenth century.* Chicago: University of Chicago Press.

D'Emilio, J. (1998). *Sexual politics, sexual communities.* Chicago: University of Chicago Press.

Duberman, M. (1994). *Stonewall.* New York: Plume Books.

Harding, S. (2001). *The book of Jerry Falwell: Fundamentalist language and politics.* Princeton, NJ: Princeton University Press.

Hunter, J. (1992). *Culture wars: The struggle to define America.* New York: Basic Books.

Marsden, G. (1991). *Understanding fundamentalism and evangelicism.* Grand Rapids, MI: Eerdsmans.

Rauch, J. (2004). *Gay marriage: Why it is good for gays, good for straights, and good for America.* New York: Times Books.

Rimmerman, C., Wald, K., & Wilcox, C. (Eds.). (2000). *The politics of gay rights.* Chicago: University of Chicago Press.

Rosenstiel, T. (1993). *Strange bedfellows: How television and the presidential candidates changed American politics, 1992.* New York: Hyperion.

Wills, G. (1990). *Under God: Religion and American politics.* New York: Simon and Schuster.

Wuthnow, R. (1989). *The struggle for America's soul: Evangelicals, liberals, and secularism.* Grand Rapids, MI: Eerdsmans.

❖ WEB SITES

AIDS Coalition to Unleash Power. (n.d.). ACT UP/New York [Home page]. Retrieved April 25, 2005, from http://www.actupny.org/

American Center for Law and Justice. (2005). [Home page]. Retrieved April 26, 2005, from http://www.aclj.org

American Family Association. (2005). AFA Online [Home page]. Retrieved April 26, 2005, from http://www.afa.net

Christian Coalition of America. (2005). Christian Coalition of America: America's leading grassroots organization defending our Godly heritage [Home page]. Retrieved April 26, 2005, from http://www.cc.org

Eagle Forum. (n.d.). EagleForum.org: Leading the pro-family movement since 1972 [Home page]. Retrieved April 26, 2005, from http://eagleforum.org

Family Research Council. (2005). Family Research Council: Defending family, faith, and freedom [Home page]. Retrieved April 26, 2005, from http://www.frc.org

The Fight the Right Network. (n.d.). [Home page]. Retrieved April 25, 2005, from http://www.critpath.org/ftrn/ftrn.html

Focus on the Family. (2005). Family.org: A Web site of Focus on the Family [Home page]. Retrieved April 26, 2005, from http://www.family.org

Gay and Lesbian Alliance Against Defamation. (2004). GLAAD: Fair, accurate and inclusive representation [Home page]. Retrieved April 25, 2005, from http://www.glaad.org

Gay, Lesbian, and Straight Education Network. (2004). [Home page]. Retrieved April 25, 2005, from http://www.glsen.org/cgi-bin/iowa/home.html

Human Rights Campaign. (2005). Human Rights Campaign: Working for lesbian, gay, bisexual and transgender equal rights [Home page]. Retrieved April 25, 2005, from http://www.hrc.org

Marriage Equality, Inc. (2002). Marriage equality: Because marriage matters [Home page]. Retrieved April 25, 2005, from http://www.marriageequality.org

National Gay and Lesbian Task Force. (2004). [Home page]. Retrieved April 25, 2005, from http://www.thetaskforce.org

People for the American Way. (n.d.). People for the American Way: Taking action to defend democracy [Home page]. Retrieved April 25, 2005, from http://www.pfaw.org

Promise Keepers. (2005). Promise Keepers: Men of integrity [Home page]. Retrieved April 26, 2005, from http://www.promisekeepers.org

Fifteen-year-old Sakia Gunn, who was stabbed to death in downtown Newark, New Jersey, in 2003.

9

Small Murders

Rethinking News Coverage of Hate Crimes Against GLBT People

Kim Pearson

❖   ❖   ❖

When 15-year-old Sakia Gunn was stabbed to death on a downtown Newark, New Jersey, street corner in the early morning hours of May 11, 2003, allegedly by a man who was angry that she and her friends rebuffed his advances by declaring themselves to be lesbians, a colleague of mine remarked, "If the press doesn't cover this story the way they covered Matthew Shepard, I'm going to be so mad." The colleague, a white lesbian feminist, expressed concerns that Gunn's murder would be ignored because she was African American and poor.

Indeed, the beating and torture murder of Shepard, a 20-year-old Wyoming college student, attracted international press attention that

---

Author's Note: This essay is based in part on a paper delivered at the Fourth Biennial Conference on Feminisms and Rhetorics, October 25, 2003.

ultimately elicited widespread expressions of shock, sympathy, and calls for stiff penalties for hate crimes. As horrific as Shepard's murder was, it was not unique. Although reliable figures are not easy to obtain, the Federal Bureau of Investigation (FBI) reports that there were 10 bias murders based on sexual orientation in 2002 and 2003 alone (FBI, 2002, 2003). This figure is suspect, however. The 2003 report states that there were six people murdered because of their sexual orientation, and all of the victims were male. Although Sakia Gunn's murder was ruled a bias crime, it appears not to have been counted in the FBI's statistics.

Whatever the real figures are on antigay hate murders, it is clear that no other hate murder of a gay, lesbian, bisexual, or transgendered (GLBT) person has attracted the kind of press interest accorded to Shepard, so for some activists and press critics, Shepard's death has become a kind of yardstick for assessing the coverage of other murders of gay people.

This chapter examines how much attention the mainstream press paid to Gunn's murder, as well as the reasoning process behind the decisions journalists made about whether to cover her case and how. The conclusions drawn from this investigation of press coverage shows the need for journalists to reassess the process by which stories are judged and ultimately deemed publishable, particularly stories that lie along what news diversity expert Dori Maynard (2005) calls the "fault lines" of U.S. social structure: race, class, gender, generation, and geography. Because the foundation of American journalism is based on the libertarian philosophy that the press provides a free marketplace of ideas, journalistic efforts to provide truthful, fair, and comprehensive coverage to all communities may still be warped by the media's failure to recognize the subtle remnants of an oppressive epistemological[1] perspective. In other words, although journalists have made a conscious effort to rid the newsgathering process of race, class, and gender bias over the last 35 years, those biases may still be encoded in seemingly neutral journalistic practices.

This chapter is divided into four parts. First, there is a brief summary of the aftermath of Gunn's murder. Second, there is an analysis of how thoroughly her murder was covered in comparison to Shepard's, as well as the responses to requests to journalists for opinions about the coverage. In short, considerably more attention was paid to Shepard's story, but the explanations advanced by journalists for those disparities raise as many questions as they answer. In some instances, to paraphrase theologian Gayle Baldwin (2004b), the problem may reflect a failure of journalistic imagination.[2] Third, this case is placed in the context of the history and philosophy of mainstream journalistic practice. Fourth, the critical lens of African-American feminist thought is employed to suggest some ways of re-visioning murder coverage that might elicit fairer reporting that better fulfills the mission of providing the information vital to citizens in a democracy.

❖ SAKIA'S MURDER AND ITS AFTERMATH

On the night that Gunn died, witnesses say she had been waiting at a bus stop with four friends, all between the ages of 15 and 17. The girls had been partying at the Chelsea piers in Manhattan, a popular hangout for local area GLBT youth of color.

One of the girls, Valencia Bailey, told *Gay City News* reporter Mick Meenan (2003) about the confrontation that ended with Sakia's death. According to Meenan's article, two men in a white car pulled up to the corner where the girls were standing, The men tried to talk the girls into getting into the car, only to be rebuffed. An argument ensued. Richard McCullough, 29, got out of the car. He grabbed one of the girls by the neck. Shortly before, Chantell Woodridge, 17, another lesbian among the group returning from New York, had just said goodnight to her friends and was walking down Market Street, when she heard a ruckus behind her. She quickly returned to find her sister, Kahmya, being choked by McCullough. The following account of Sakia's murder is quoted directly from Meenan's (2003a) article.

> [Woodridge said,] "He had [Kahmya] by the neck. He told Sakia, 'Come here.' She said, 'No, you're not my father.' Me and Valencia was fighting him. He grabbed Sakia by the neck and put a knife there. She started fighting him and got away. She swung once at him. When she tried to swing again, he stabbed her." Sakia's killer jumped into the white vehicle and it sped away. Valencia raced to a car that had stopped for a red light.
>
> "'Please, mister, please,' I said as I was banging on his window. 'Can you please take us to the hospital?'"
>
> The young women were acutely aware that Sakia was bleeding profusely. The anonymous Good Samaritan took all five young women in his car to University Hospital, a short distance away. However, Sakia's massive blood loss spelled the impossible for the doctors who tried to keep her alive.

"She died in my arms in the emergency," said Valencia. "They rolled her into the back and tried to save her. But they couldn't."

One of the witnesses was able to supply police with a partial license plate number of the assailants' car, and police used that information to eventually identify her attacker as Richard McCullough, a 29-year-old father of two. On May 16, Newark Mayor Sharpe James held a press conference to announce that McCullough had turned himself in to police and had been charged with bias murder, intimidation, and weapons offenses (Smothers, 2003). McCullough's mother, Benita McCullough, offered her sympathies to Gunn's family but insisted that her son was not antigay, noting that he had been raised in part by a lesbian grandmother ("A Sakia Gunn Story," 2003). That same day, a coffin bearing Gunn's body, her favorite basketball, and a rainbow flag was placed in a cemetery next to Westside High School, where she had been a tenth grader and aspiring WNBA star.

Gunn's murder set off antiviolence vigils and rallies in Newark, and more than 2,500 people attended her funeral (Meenan, 2003). There were also vigils as far away as Duluth, Minnesota ("Northland briefs: Gay," 2003). News of the slaying spread throughout online outlets such as Indymedia.org. *Gay City News* covered the funeral thoroughly; the *Newark Star-Ledger* ran a smaller story.

Although news reports described the crowds that week as consisting mostly of young Latinas and African-American females, observers such as Rev. Kevin Taylor, pastor of Unity Fellowship Church–New Brunswick, noted the diversity of the mourners, including "thugged-out straight boys." Despite their differences in sexuality and gender identity, Taylor said they were united in their grief and fear of more murders. Some of the young people later told stories of being harassed and physically attacked in their schools, homes, and neighborhoods because of their actual or perceived sexuality. Some were convinced that the only way to protect themselves was to be prepared to fight and die as Sakia had, because school officials, police officers, and other authority figures were unable or unwilling to protect them. As one of the adult volunteers who tried to help comfort the young mourners, Taylor said, "They were two tears away from a riot."[3]

The outpouring of grief took city and school officials by surprise, according to city health commissioner Cathy Cuomo-Cacere ("It's a shame," 2003). Youthful friends and admirers formed an organization, Sakia Gunn Aggressive'z and Fem'z, to demand improved police protection, diversity training for school officials and police, antiviolence education, and the establishment of a gay and lesbian community center. They began wearing buttons and t-shirts with Gunn's picture, along with rainbow rings and other accessories. More significantly, they began speaking out about the problems they had experienced as GLBT youth of color, such as bullying; harassment from peers, teachers, police officers, and others; social isolation; and rejection by parents and clergy.

At Gunn's funeral, Mayor James promised support for the establishment of a drop-in counseling center. Rep. Donald Payne (D-NJ) promised to push for federal hate-crimes legislation. Fernard Williams,[4] the principal at Gunn's high school, however, refused requests that her friends be allowed to organize a memorial at the school, as had been done for other victims of violence. The rumor spread quickly (partly through a July 14 interview with Jamon Marsh on *Democracy Now!*) that Williams dismissed the request by saying that Gunn's death was a natural consequence of her lesbianism. School officials banned the wearing of Sakia Gunn clothes and accessories because, they said, it violated rules against wearing gang attire. Williams refused most calls from the press, but in an Associated Press story in the Lexis-Nexis database that was circulated on the first anniversary of Gunn's death, he denied having rejected the request for an in-school memorial. He added, "It was difficult for me to open up the school to the media because I didn't want to open up some of the wounds [the students] are trying to heal" (Meenan, 2004).

Nonetheless, by June 2003, an adult coalition of gay activists calling itself the Newark Pride Alliance had formed to support the youth group's demands. An outspoken, well-connected activist named Laquetta Nelson, the former president of New Jersey's Stonewall Democrats, emerged as the group's leader. Another key member of the leadership included Elder Reverend Jacquelyn Holland, pastor of Newark's Liberation in Truth Unity Fellowship Church, which has an active state-funded HIV/AIDs ministry, Loving in Truth. According to an interview published in the *Advocate*, Holland said, "We want to let them know it's OK to be who they are. [Gunn] didn't do anything wrong by being a lesbian" (DuLong, 2003).

In the following weeks, more rallies in Gunn's memory followed in Newark, as well as demonstrations in Boston ("Boston pays tribute," 2003) and New York, and memorials in many of the gay pride parades that took place in June. Former Vermont governor and Democratic presidential candidate Howard Dean said Gunn's murder was another reason for the need for federal hate-crimes legislation, and he called upon the mayor of Newark to aggressively address the concerns of city activists (Schindler, 2003). Coincidentally, the organizer of the Boston rally was writer-activist Jacquie Bishop, who had spent part of her youth in the Newark area, frequenting many of the same hangouts that Gunn would visit some 20 years later. Bishop sent an e-mail about Gunn's murder on May 13, 2003, that said, in part:

> I know this girl. No, I never met her, but I know what it's like to ride home and feel your lover's kisses dry like paint. I know what it's like to count the change in my pocket wishing I didn't have that last drink so I could have taken a cab home from the station.
>
> I know what is like to be young and gay and scared, and full of bravado, wondering, always wondering if someone will try to hurt me. More than 20 years later, I know what it is like to see my sisters, my daughters, walk the same streets I did, trying to find their way home.
>
> I raise this glass to Sakia Gunn.

By that September, the Pride Alliance had joined forces with prominent writer and activist Amiri Baraka, the father of Shani Baraka, a Newark schoolteacher who was murdered along with her girlfriend, Rayshon Holmes, on August 12, 2003. Amiri Baraka, along with his allies and protégés, has been a political factor in Newark since the 1967 riots, when the militant artist led a grassroots organization that helped elect Newark's first African-American mayor. Activists first mentored by Amiri Baraka still play important roles in local politics and policy. His son, Ras Baraka, is a city councilman and deputy mayor.

Shani Baraka and Rayshon Holmes were shot to death at the home of Shani Baraka's sister, Wanda Wilson. According to the Baraka family, Wilson's ex-husband, James Coleman, 35, had beaten Wilson and had threatened to kill her on several occasions. Wilson had made a dozen 911 calls about Coleman, had taken out a restraining order, and had pressed charges against him. Police were seeking to arrest Coleman on domestic violence charges at the time of the murders. Coleman has since been indicted for the murders and is awaiting trial.

Shani Baraka had been a basketball coach and mentor for Gunn; she was one of the small cadre of adults on hand to comfort the legions of youthful mourners at her funeral. She and Holmes had been popular members of the African-American gay community in Newark.

The Pride Alliance's effort was also endorsed by the New Jersey branch of the NAACP and Cory Booker, whose challenge to James' mayoral reelection had garnered national press in 2002. Booker is a city councilman who runs a nonprofit organization in Newark, Newark Now, which sponsors a variety of community improvement programs, including housing rehabilitation, civic education, and youth leadership programs.

At the same time, a student at Michigan State University in East Lansing Michigan, La Joya Johnson, started an online petition drive to protest the refusal of the principal of Gunn's high school to allow a moment of silence in her honor. She ultimately garnered more than 3,000 signatures ("MSU student receives," 2004). Meanwhile, the Newark Pride Alliance established relationships with national gay rights organizations that have not been known for their outreach to people of color, such as the Gay, Lesbian, and Straight Education Network, the Gay and Lesbian Alliance Against Defamation (GLAAD), and Parents and Friends of Lesbians and Gays (PFLAG). In fact, they established a chapter of PFLAG in Newark, led by Amina Baraka, the mother of Shani Baraka, and LaTona Gunn, the mother of Sakia Gunn.

The combined result of their advocacy was that on the first anniversary of Gunn's murder, a moment of silence was held for her and all Newark students murdered during the previous school year. In addition, facilitators with the Gay, Lesbian, and Straight Education Network conducted workshops with Newark schools officials and staff.

On the legal front, McCullough was formally indicted in November 2003. He chose to waive his right to appear in court at his arraignment, and his attorney entered an innocent plea on his behalf ("Suspect skips hearing," 2003). McCullough's trial was scheduled to begin in November 2004, but his lawyer delayed its start with a failed challenge to the constitutionality of the hate-crimes statute that formed the basis of the bias crimes charges. He is facing a sentence of 118 years if convicted of the original charges. On April 21, McCullough was sentenced to 20 years in prison after pleading guilty to charges of aggravated manslaughter, aggravated assault, and bias intimidation in Essex County Superior Court. In exchange for the plea, the prosecution dropped murder charges ("Man admits killing," 2005).

❖   COVERING MURDER: PHILOSOPHICAL
        AND HISTORICAL CONTEXTS

Journalists who are called on to cover a murder have to make a variety
of ethical judgments that are rarely discussed but widely understood.
In principle, everyone's life has infinite value, but in reality, not everyone's death makes equal claim on the space allotted for news. Death,
like all other human affairs, is subject to tests of newsworthiness, tests
that are taught by professors and mentors and lived by journalists
as if they arose from nature itself, not from potentially biased human
design.

Reporters who cover the police beat have an informal classification system for determining how much coverage a murder is likely to
get. The conventional wisdom is that the murder of a wealthy white
person is "big." The murder of a poor person of color is considered a
"little" murder, especially if the killer was also a poor person of color.
Dave Krajicek (2003), a veteran reporter and former Columbia University journalism professor, provides examples of this hierarchy:

> Journalist Russell Baker described a pecking order of "good" and
> "little" murders during his years covering crime in Baltimore.
> Murders of prominent citizens, children and attractive women were
> good. Murders of down-and-outers or those who dabbled in the
> vices were little. Baker wrote, "Murders of black people were not
> 'little murders.' They weren't murders at all."

Edna Buchanan found the same attitude three decades later in
Miami. She wrote,

> Often assistant city editors, short on space and patience, would
> insist that I select and report only the "major murder" of the day.
> I knew what they meant, but I fought the premise. How can you
> choose? Every murder is major to the victim . . . A bright young
> reporter I talked to recently casually referred to what he called
> dirt-bag murders: the cases and the victims not worth reporting.
> There is no dirt-bag murder. The story is always there waiting to
> be found if you just dig deep enough. (Krajicek, 2003)

In 2002, retired *New York Times* reporter and columnist Tom Wicker
(personal communication, April 3, 2002) made similar comments in

response to my inquiry about the *Times'* coverage of another homicide story I was examining—the 1991 deaths of 25 workers at a chicken processing plant in Hamlet, North Carolina. Despite the fact that the case set important legal precedents and led to an overhaul of worker safety practices in North Carolina and elsewhere, my students and I found national news coverage to be fairly limited. The specifics of the Hamlet story are not germane to this chapter, but Wicker's observation about the role of race and class in news coverage is:

> I do believe, on general principle, that if coverage of the story was scanty, it may well have been affected by class bias, as you suggest. Most of the workers were blacks, as I recall; if they had all been white college kids, or just mostly, coverage might well have been more extensive—in the *Times* as in any other paper.

Reporters will tell you that this tier system for allocating news coverage is not necessarily a matter of race or class bias; it is a matter of reader or audience interest. For editors, "audience" may be sliced even more finely to refer to those readers or viewers most attractive to advertisers. Also, editors and producers are "gatekeepers" and tend to want to publish or air news reports that interest them or the types of people they associate with (i.e., upper middle class white people). When a murder gets played up in a news outlet, it is a sign that someone has decided that this story has meaning for that news outlet's core audience.

These are things that must be understood when considering the press coverage of the victims of hate crimes based on gender or sexual orientation. It came about, in part, due to the push to diversify professional newsrooms and news coverage in the wake of the urban rebellions of the 1960s. Then-president Lyndon Baines Johnson commissioned a panel of experts to analyze America's racial divide and propose solutions. The resulting Kerner Commission Report concluded that the press had helped to create the racial divide, noting that "The press has been basking in a white world, looking out of it, if at all, with a white man's eyes and a white perspective" (Favre, 1999). Despite more than three decades of effort, there is still disagreement about the best way to achieve equitable and comprehensive coverage of race and gender in the news, and the diversification of the newsroom has proven to be elusive. According to the American Society of Newspaper Editors' (2004) most recent survey, in 2003, 12.94% of the employees at

U.S. newspapers were people of color, but 31% of the U.S. population was nonwhite.

The conversation about what constitutes equitable and comprehensive coverage of GLBT people is much newer. In a widely read survey published in 2000, "Lesbians and Gays in the Newsroom: Ten Years Later," most of the 363 GLBT journalists said that although it is now easier to be "out" as a journalist than it once was, news coverage of GLBT stories and issues is often inadequate. Ninety-two percent of respondents said that they were open about their sexuality or gender identity at work. However, only 46% said that local coverage of violence against GLBT people was "good to excellent," and the percentage of respondents who thought the coverage of the lives of lesbians was good to excellent was a dismal 12% (Aarons & Murphy, 2000).

❖ MEDIA COVERAGE OF THE GUNN MURDER

Between July 2003 and June 2004, I posted a monthly count on my Web log ("blog"), Professor Kim's News Notes (http://professorkim .blogspot.com), comparing the number of stories about Gunn's murder to the number of stories about the 1998 Matthew Shepard murder. The count was based on queries to the Lexis-Nexis database, a service that archives newspaper and broadcast stories from around the world.

According to writer Andrew Sullivan (Bozell, 2004), Lexis-Nexis logged a total of 3,007 stories in the first month after Shepard's murder. I did not count the total number of stories from all sources on Shepard because Lexis-Nexis can only return 1,000 hits at a time, and the total number of stories on Shepard exceeded that amount from the beginning.[5] However, instead of comparing the total number of stories about Shepard and Gunn, I compared only the total number of stories about Shepard in major newspapers to the total number of stories about Gunn from all sources.

Lexis-Nexis lists 53 publications in its category of major newspapers, ranging from the *Boston Herald* to the *South China Morning Post*. A full list is appended.

In the first month following Gunn's murder, eight stories about her appeared in the database. To compare, in the first month following Shepard's murder, 449 stories about him appeared in major newspapers. The disparity remained striking throughout the year (see Table 9.1).

Table 9.1   Shepard-Gunn Story Count

Months After Event	Matthew Shepard	Sakia Gunn
Month event occurred	448	8
1	507	11
2	512	11
3	549	15
4	568	18
5	657	19
6	659	21
7	683	21
8	692	22
9	694	22
10	699	28
11	735	28

The staggering difference in the number of stories was used as a basis for conversations with reporters, journalism scholars, and activists about the considerations governing journalists' decisions about the appropriate level of press attention for stories such as Gunn's.

E-mail messages were sent to a reporter for the *Star-Ledger* who wrote many of that paper's initial stories, but he never responded. I also posted queries to the journalism history (Jhistory) listserv, which has more than 400 subscribers, many of whom are current and former journalists, and the National Association of Black Journalists (NABJ) listserv. NABJ has more than 3000 members.

This was the text of my June 16, 2003, query to Barry Carter of the *Newark Star-Ledger:*

I am a professor of journalism and professional writing at The College of New Jersey who is interested in issues related to diversity in news coverage. I am writing to you as a reporter who seems to have been heavily involved in covering the murder of Sakia Gunn and the subsequent rallies and protests. I was wondering whether you thought the coverage of this story has been sufficiently adequate and comprehensive.

Let me tell you why I am asking. Although there has understandably been consistent coverage of these events in the *Star-Ledger*, coverage in other national and regional news organizations seems to have been rather thin. In fact, a Lexis-Nexis search I conducted today produced only eight hits.

By contrast, there had been more than 300 items logged in the Lexis-Nexis database in the month after the murder of Matthew Shepard in 1998. As you may know, some activists have been quick to assume that there would be less interest in Sakia Gunn's murder than in Matthew Shepard's because of the race, class, and gender differences between them.

Whatever the reason, I think there may be a story in the differing patterns of news coverage, and hope to gain a better understanding of it by contacting reporters who have worked on both stories, activists and others. I would appreciate any thoughts you have as the person who seems not only to be the lead reporter on this story for the *Star-Ledger*, but the person whose work is most frequently cited on Web sites that mention this story as well. Thanks in advance for your consideration of this request.

On June 17, I wrote a lengthy query to the Jhistory list that said, in part:

Some activists close to this story believe that it (and similar recent tragedies) should be accorded the kind of media attention given to the hate-motivated murder of Matthew Shepard a few years ago. My cursory research indicates that it has not, and I'm interested in knowing why. I am hoping that someone on this list who either covered or studied the coverage of the Matthew Shepard story can lend some insight.

I summarized the news reports on Sakia Gunn's murder and then added:

I can think of reasons for the disparity in coverage apart from the fact that Shepard was a well-to-do, white boy-next-door who happened to be gay, and Gunn was a working-class, black, cross-dressing girl. However, the reasons that emerge provoke more questions than answers. For example, Shepard was murdered in a particularly grisly and drawn-out way, dying five days after he was initially attacked. Gunn's death happened quickly, in the dead of night. Shepard was murdered four months after the lynching of James Byrd, Jr. in Jasper, Texas, shocked the nation into renewed attention to hate crimes. Does this mean that a killing has to be especially lurid to get attention?

Because of Gunn's preference for dressing like a boy, transgender activists count her among their number, and believe her defiance of gender norms was a factor in her death. Transgender activists particularly allege that violence against them is routinely ignored—especially when the victim is a person of color. Certainly, I have seen little national attention to the recent unsolved murders of such transgendered victims as Nizah Morris, Gwen Araujo, Fred Martinez and others. (For more examples, see the Web site of the GenderPac advocacy group: http://www.gpac.org/violence/. Click on some of the pictures at the top of the page to read stories of some of the victims.) As the Gunn murder story proceeds toward trial, is this a story angle that deserves exploration? I have other thoughts and questions, but I've gone on quite a bit now. I'd be interested in your collective wisdom and educated speculation.

On July 16, 2003, I sent this query to the NABJ list:

Earlier this week, I was interviewed on the syndicated news show *Democracy Now!* as part of a discussion of the aftermath of the murder of 15-year-old Sakia Gunn, who was stabbed to death this past Mother's Day morning in downtown Newark, New Jersey, allegedly because she and her friends told two men who made sexual advances toward them that they were gay. Despite the fact that the murder set off rallies and marches in Newark, Boston, New York and elsewhere, two months later, there have only been 11 stories in major news outlets, according to Lexis-Nexis. Two months after Matthew Shepard died, there were about 500 stories. Activists working on this issue say that it's harder to get media attention for gay, lesbian, bisexual, and transgendered victims of color.

Anyway, I've been writing about this in my Web log, Professor Kim's News Notes (http://professorkim.blogspot.com), and I'm curious to know what folks here think.

I was unsuccessful in my efforts to reach someone who had covered Matthew Shepard's murder, but I did get a few responses from the Jhistory list. One from Barbara Freeman (personal communication, June 17, 2003), an associate professor in the School of Journalism and Communication at Carleton University, said,

> I think there are several reasons for the relative lack of coverage, as our colleague has pointed out. But also, Shepard was "crucified," and that would certainly have a resonance in a Christian-centered country like the USA whose fundamentalists abhor homosexuality as sinful.

A private e-mail suggested that since Gunn could be considered a cross-dresser, it might be appropriate to compare the coverage of her murder to that of Brandon Teena, the female-to-male transsexual whose life and death were the focus of the feature film *Boys Don't Cry*.

I received only four responses from the NABJ list. The list moderator thanked me for raising the issue. Another reporter said "only 11 stories in densely-populated Newark? Hmmm. . . ." The exchanges with the other two journalists, former *Boston Globe* reporter Michelle Johnson and former Newark *Star-Ledger* reporter Todd Steven Burroughs, are provided in some detail later in this chapter.

Because the coverage of Shepard's murder was so extensive and the coverage of Gunn's murder was so scant by comparison, many of the conversations focused on why journalists would tend to be more interested in one story as opposed to the other. Some reporters were sure that differences in the race, class, and gender of the two victims played a role. Shepard was a well-to-do, white boy-next-door who happened to be gay, and Gunn was a working-class, African-American, cross-dressing girl.

However, the journalists and media critics I consulted said that it is not that simple. Some journalists point to the structure of the Newark media market. Todd Steven Burroughs (personal communication, August 31, 2004), a Newark native and former reporter for the Newark-based *Star-Ledger*, attributed the *quantity* of the mainstream news coverage to the lack of an alternative news outlet and the fact that the "economically depressed city is not its main audience (i.e., readers, subscribers, etc.)." Although an alternative news outlet might not have affected mainstream news coverage, it might have brought broader attention to the story. In addition, Burroughs said, "to New York City print [media], Newark is often just that armpit over THERE, in JERSEY."

Laramie, Wyoming, is not a major media market either, but that did not stop the onslaught of coverage following Shepard's murder. Although the structure of the Newark news market may be part of the issue, it does not seem to be the entire explanation.

Michelle Johnson (personal communication, July 18, 2003), a former reporter and columnist for the *Boston Globe* who is active in both the National Association of Black Journalists and the National Association of Lesbian and Gay Journalists, said, "I can't say that I've drawn any conclusions about race/coverage. Sometimes it doesn't appear to be a factor, as in the case of a 3-year-old black girl who was shot and killed here [in Boston] recently (received maximum coverage) versus the near silence about the case in NJ."

Johnson's response suggested another potential explanation for the disparity in news coverage. Former *Philadelphia Inquirer* reporter Jack Lule (2001), who is now a journalism professor at Lehigh University, wrote an interesting book, *Daily News, Eternal Stories*, which argues that journalists fall back on certain archetypal myths in framing their reporting. One of them is The Victim. According to Lule, stories that invoke the myth of The Victim serve an important cultural function: "They attempt to reconcile people to the vagaries of human existence, to cruel fate, to bizarre happenstance, to death itself" (p. 43). Lule also cites Jungian writer Joseph Henderson's observation that The Victim of myth is often cast in heroic terms: "Over and over again one hears a tale describing a hero's miraculous but humble birth," his proof of great strength, his battle with evil, "and his fall through betrayal or a *heroic* sacrifice that ends in his death" (pp. 43–44).

That could account for why the murder of a 3-year-old would get more attention in the mainstream press than that of a 15-year-old butch lesbian on a city street corner in the middle of the night. The 3-year-old might have been seen as the blameless victim of caprice, betrayed by a community that failed to protect her from violence. Sakia Gunn, however, might have been viewed less sympathetically because she was on the streets at a time when many adults would agree that a 15-year-old should be home in bed.

Coincidentally, Cathy Renna (2003), a media relations manager for GLAAD, made a similar point in a column for *Gay City News* about her experiences of working with reporters on the Shepard story over the years:

Whether I'm talking to a reporter or an auditorium of college students, one of the most common questions I'm asked is, "Why did Matt's murder get so much attention?" Truth is, there's no simple answer to that question. . . . I do know that there are some answers we don't explore enough. For example, we know the people with privilege and power in our community stood up when Matt was killed, prompting the media to take notice. People who identified with Matt leveraged their resources to pressure others into doing something. It is as simple and yet also more complex than that. However, my phone did not ring off the hook for other hate victims like Latina transgender teen Gwen Araujo or Sakia Gunn and J. R. Warren, both teens of African descent.

A spokesman for NLGJA said that the association had decided not to issue a statement about coverage of Gunn's murder. Marshall McPeek (personal communication, July 22, 2003), NLGJA vice president for broadcast, said that the association's rapid response task force came to the decision after it was unable to come up with compelling reasons why editors outside of the local region would find the story compelling. According to the NLGJA Web site, the rapid response task force is a "journalist-to-journalist" effort to identify and address inaccurate or biased news coverage related to gay, lesbian, bisexual, or transgendered people. The team thought Sakia Gunn's murder was a local story, and "It looks like the local coverage has been fine," McPeek said.

However, there are many other story angles that might interest editors in regions outside of New Jersey, including the following:

1. CNN aired a story about why GLBT youth hang out at the Chelsea piers. Editors in other locales might consider whether there are similar places in their regions that draw teens who say they have nowhere else to go. What happens there? How old are the kids? What do their parents think? Are they safe? What is the response of police and other officials? Are there advocates for them?

2. Are women targets of violence whenever they are assumed to be lesbians? In addition to the Gunn case, a woman in Washington, D.C. was allegedly gang-raped on September 28, 2003, after she stated that she was not interested in men.

3. Gunn's family and friends, along with advocates for gay youth, are trying to build a community center in her honor. They say

that if such a place had existed in Newark, she might not have felt the need to be on that corner in the middle of the night. Are there spaces in other communities in which GLBT youth, especially youth of color, feel comfortable? If not, what are the consequences? What is the feeling about how such concerns should be addressed?

4. Finally, young activists in Newark say that local school administrators have not attempted to create safe spaces for them at school. They not only complain that they are not protected from bullying by their peers but cite instances of callousness by administrators. Again, what is the situation in other locales? What is the response?

It is interesting that an Associated Press story citing the lack of press coverage of Sakia Gunn's murder subsequently appeared in news outlets in the United States and Europe a couple of weeks later. In the story, *Gay City News* reporter Mick Meenan offered this explanation for why neither Gunn's murder nor the mainstream press's lack of coverage failed to incite gay activists or the gay press to greater action: "I think there's racism in the LGBT community, and no doubt there's classism" (Strunsky, 2003).

Although attention to the story from the gay and alternative media might well be characterized as anemic, it was stronger than the response from the African-American or feminist media. Culture critic and scholar Mark Anthony Neal (2003) argues that the African-American press has downplayed Gunn's story because it is reluctant to condemn African-American men who attack African-American women and children. The reasons for this reluctance, Neal argued, are historical. Writing for Africana.com, Neal said:

Gay men are often "bashed" because of an affinity to women and lesbians are bashed because they *are* women. In many regards homophobia is rooted in misogyny—a hatred of women. Too often forms of sanitized and user-friendly sexism and misogyny circulate throughout the black community in the silence around black male violence against black women young and old. Had McCullough been a white man (or a police officer), is there any doubt that Gunn's death would have been a national controversy?

As legal scholar Devon Carbado describes this reality, black men are "up in arms when white men abuse black women because they want it known that black women's bodies will no longer be the terrain for white male physical or sexual aggression." But he adds that "When the abuser is a black male, the response is less politically strident" because the "assault on the black woman, even if ultimately criticized and condemned, is sometimes understood to represent an assertion of black male masculinity . . . a response to white male racism." This explains, in part, why some in the black community have sought to vigorously rehabilitate the images of black male celebrities like Mike Tyson, R. Kelly, and even the late Tupac Shakur, after they were accused of sexually abusing black women and girls. It also explains, in part, why stories like that of Gunn or Cherae Williams, who in September 1999 was brutally beaten by two NYC police officers after she accused them of failing to intervene in a domestic dispute with her black boyfriend, get pushed to the back pages of our newspapers and journals.

The African-American press may not have been paying much attention to Gunn, but like most of the mainstream press, it was paying considerable attention to the issue of gay marriage. If the BlackPressUSA Web site is any indication, moral and religious judgments about homosexuality override any other news value. BlackPressUSA is a news service sponsored by the National Newspaper Publishers Association, the trade association for African-American newspapers. It published a story in August 2003 about African-American churches' conflicting views of sexual orientation and another in February 2003 about HIV. The murders of Gunn and other African-American hate-crime victims were not mentioned until December 2003, and then only obliquely.

Here is how that oblique reference happened. In November, BlackPressUSA editor George Curry, one of the nation's most respected journalists, kicked up dust with his column "Mixed Feelings About Same-Sex Marriages." Curry's position on civil rights issues is usually fairly liberal—he supports affirmative action and hate-crime laws, for example. However, Curry said that his religious beliefs about homosexuality left him "torn between feeling that homosexuals should not be discriminated against because of their sexual orientation and believing that same-sex marriages should not be sanctioned by the government or the church" (Curry, 2003).

Curry went on to criticize those who equated the push for gay rights with the civil rights movement, asserting:

Sure there are some things that are common to both movements, but except in limited individual cases, gays and lesbians have never suffered anything approaching the oppression of African-Americans. They were not lynched because they were gay, they were not brought here in chains because of their sexual orientation, they were not deprived of the right to vote because they like people of the same gender, and no White girl in the United States has ever been killed for whistling at a White woman. (Curry, 2003)

The column prompted a rare public statement from ten African-American gay journalists ("Open letter to," 2003), some of whom had never revealed their sexual orientation before, according to industry blogger Richard Prince. The letter was published on the BlackPress USA site. Among other things, the journalists took Curry and the African-American press to task and indirectly referred to Gunn:

As for lynchings, we remind Mr. Curry, one of the most powerful Black journalists in America, of the scores of anti-gay murders that occur annually. This year, five Black and Latina transgender women were murdered in Washington, D.C. This summer, a 15-year-old Black woman from New Jersey was stabbed to death at a train station after identifying herself as a lesbian to a man who tried to pick her up. This gruesome list goes on, and it only includes those that the police actually classified as being motivated by the victim's sexual orientation. . . .

For too long lesbian and gay African Americans have sat on the sidelines, made invisible by our fear of our brothers and sisters who claim to know the mind and will of God. . . . We have been vilified, marginalized and . . . lynched.

Meanwhile, those, who believe our lives and our love to be "aberrant" and "ungodly" have used selected Scripture as their weapon of choice, poisoning the African-American community against its own sons and daughters, brothers and sisters—with catastrophic consequences for our community, its health, its cohesion, its progress.

No more. Like all African Americans, we demand our day in the sun. We will fight the bigotry against us from within our community and without.

Sakia Gunn was the "15-year-old Black woman from New Jersey" referred to in the letter.

It is, however, dangerous to make facile assumptions based on the kind of statistics I have cited. A similar analysis about the murder of Jesse Dirkhising, a 13-year-old Arkansas boy at the hands of two gay men, was conducted in 2002. According to police records, Dirkhising was bound, gagged, imprisoned, repeatedly raped, and smothered in what the defendants claimed was an episode of rough consensual sex. Conservative media activists, such as Brent Bozell (2004), president of the Media Research Center, say that the failure to accord Dirkhising's murder the kind of attention given to Shepard is indicative of a pro-gay press bias. As he put it:

> In this modern media age, ratings-obsessed news programs rush to report on lurid murders of children (can you say JonBenet Ramsey?). But in this case, it seems that the liberal media did not dare incur the wrath of the militant gay movement by reporting a grisly murder story that had as its villains two homosexuals. Had Dirkhising been openly gay and his attackers heterosexual, you can bet the mortgage that the crime would have led every network's evening newscast. (pp. 122-124)

However, the news media does not in fact rush to cover every lurid child murder. If you compare the coverage of Dirkhising's murder to those of other child sex-murder victims, such as Megan Kanka, Polly Klaas, Sherrice Iverson, and Danielle van Damm, there are large discrepancies in news coverage that correlated with a number of characteristics of the victims that had nothing to do with their implied or presumed sexual orientation or that of their killers (Pearson, 2002). These characteristics included race (white victims got more attention than nonwhite victims), the victims' economic class (wealthier victims got more attention than poorer victims), and whether a political movement emerged from the murder (such as Megan's Law, which requires that convicted sex offenders be part of a public registry upon release, or California's Good Samaritan law, which requires that witnesses to murders make some effort to help the victim, if only by alerting the police). Dirkhising fell at the lower end of a number of all of these scales.

Defenders of the news media's relative inattention to the Dirkhising case argued that Shepard's murder deserved more coverage because it was a hate crime. Conservative critics said that such a determination was further evidence of the problem with hate crimes because it makes some victims more important than others. Dirkhising's murder deserved more attention than it got because it was a tragic case of abuse and murder of a child at the hands of people who were supposed to be family friends (Dirkhising's mother allowed her son to spend weekends with the men and to work in their beauty salon). Dirkhising's poverty may be a better explanation for the failure to give more attention to this tragic story (LaJoya Johnson, personal communication, September 2, 2004).

In fact, what makes the limited coverage of the Gunn story even more striking is that its circumstances and aftermath are arguably more similar to Shepard's than a case such as Dirkhising's. Like Shepard, Gunn died as a result of an encounter with hostile strangers. Like Shepard, Gunn's story is being prosecuted as a hate crime. Like Shepard, Gunn's murder gave rise to a movement.

It may be that this kind of criticism by conservatives makes advocates for journalism diversity reticent about pressing too strongly. In developing their own vision of what it means to adhere to professional norms that require independence from factions, leaders and members of such groups as NABJ and the NLGJA walk a tightrope between perceived obligations to the marginalized communities they represent and charges from critics that they are not journalists but ideologues. Under attacks from critics such as William McGowan, author of "Coloring the News: How Crusading for Diversity has Corrupted American Journalism," the NABJ has taken pains to point out instances in which it has taken positions in the name of journalistic objectivity that have incited protests from NABJ members.

Professional journalists continue to debate, and LaJoya Johnson (personal communication, September 2, 2004), the young Michigan activist, suggests the disturbing possibility that although Gunn's story might indeed be underreported, there are additional hate-crime victims whose stories are not being reported at all. She offers this advice to reporters: "Just know that there are stories like Sakia's that happen everyday but no one hears about them because no one bothers to write about them. This is not something that happens every blue moon." To find these stories, Johnson said, reporters should "just look in the urban community. Get to know lgbt youth in the community. Go to the local hang out spots. Go to the local community centers or high schools."

❖ AN AFRICAN-AMERICAN FEMINIST PERSPECTIVE
    ON THE COVERAGE OF SAKIA GUNN'S MURDER

African-American feminist thought, as elucidated by Patricia Hill
Collins (1990), views the social location of African-American women as
a function of intersecting systems of race, class, and gender oppression.
These interlocking hierarchies have served not only to restrict opportunities for African-American women but to locate and define the positions of those who are either not African-American or not female
within the hierarchy. One goal of African-American feminist thought is
to give voice to experiences that would otherwise be silenced. As Hill
Collins explains:

> Black feminist thought consists of theories or specialized thought
> produced by African-American women intellectuals designed to
> express a Black woman's standpoint. The dimensions of this stand-
> point include the presence of characteristic core themes, the diver-
> sity of Black women's experiences in encountering these core
> themes, the varying expressions of Black women's Afrocentric
> feminist consciousness regarding the core themes and their expe-
> riences with them, and the interdependence of Black women's
> experiences, consciousness, and actions. This specialized thought
> should aim to infuse Black women's experiences and everyday
> thought with new meaning by rearticulating the interdependence
> of Black women's experiences and consciousness. Black feminist
> thought is *of* African-American women in that it taps the multi-
> ple relationships among Black women needed to produce a self-
> defined Black women's standpoint. Black feminist thought is for
> Black women in that it empowers Black women *for* political
> activism.

In her 2004 book *Black Sexual Politics*, Hill Collins argues that

> Like [most] African-American girls and women, regardless of
> sexual orientation, they were seen as approachable. Race was a
> factor, but not in a framework of interracial race relations; Sakia
> and her friends were African-American, as were her attackers. In
> a context where Black men are encouraged to express a hyper-
> heterosexuality as the badge of Black masculinity, women like
> Sakia and her friends can become important players in supporting

patriarchy. They challenged Black male authority, and they paid for the transgression of refusing to participate in scripts of Black promiscuity. But the immediate precipitating catalyst for the violence that took Sakia's life was her openness about her lesbianism. Here, homophobic violence was the prime factor. Her death illustrates how deeply entrenched homophobia can be among many African-American men and women, in this case, beliefs that resulted in an attack on a teenaged girl.

One expects racism in the press to shape the reports of this incident. In contrast to the 1998 murder of Matthew Shepard . . . no massive protests, nationwide vigils, and renewed calls for federal hate crimes legislation followed Sakia's death. (pp. 114–116)

My tentative conclusions about the role of race, class, gender, and sexuality in the coverage of Sakia Gunn's murder are more nuanced than those of Hill Collins, but the data on the coverage of Sakia Gunn's story is consistent with the expectation implied in Hill Collins' supposition. Indeed, the coverage of Gunn's murder has been slight, compared to that of Matthew Shepard. Where Hill Collins sees racism, there is evidence that racial bias is one of many factors that might have contributed to the scanty coverage.

However, some of the other factors that might have helped limit coverage are themselves a byproduct of race, class, and gender divisions. For example, Burroughs (personal communication, August 31, 2004) said that the newspapers in and around Newark are more interested in the more affluent suburbs than in the impoverished city. Indeed, many metropolitan newspapers have shifted resources from reporting on urban neighborhoods to providing news, entertainment, and lifestyle features designed to appeal to advertiser-attractive suburban readers.[6] I have had several informal conversations over the last 10 years with current and former reporters at major metropolitan newspapers who have lamented that the shift in coverage priorities, as well as heightened productivity pressures, have reduced their opportunities to cover their city's neighborhoods well. It is possible that such structural shifts made it difficult for reporters to grasp the full significance of Sakia Gunn's story.

My conscious application of an African-American feminist perspective to the practice of journalism is a departure from traditional journalism practice. In adopting this perspective, I acknowledge that my own journalistic practice is conditioned by my experiences as an African American woman from an urban, working-class background who has experienced and witnessed the kind of verbal and physical harassment described by witnesses to Gunn's murder.

Those who might argue that the adoption of such a perspective makes my approach to this issue less objective than a more traditional approach miss three important points. First, one of the goals of journalism diversity is to ensure that the worldviews of people with experiences such as Gunn's are better represented in news coverage. Second, looking at news stories through varied critical lenses can help reporters find fresh story angles that will both engage readers and enlighten them. Finally, the adoption of a particular critical perspective does not preclude the consideration of evidence and viewpoints that may not support that perspective.

Admittedly, the conclusions advanced here need further research and analysis; however, the goal of this chapter is to provide an opening for more systematic inquiry and conversation among journalists in the future.

The goal of diversity in news coverage should be to help journalists acquire the ability to see a story from multiple perspectives, including from the bottom and the margins. Reporters and editors can begin disseminating multiple persepectives by recognizing that no one group has a monopoly on the "truth." The "truths" of marginalized persons are as valid and deserving of media attention and space as the "truths" of their more mainstream counterparts. Addressing issues such as race, class, gender, and sexuality in the news requires most journalists to examine closely communities that are often quite different from their own. I only hope that journalists begin examining and depicting these communities in ways that are contextually accurate and multidimensional in scope.

❖ LEXIS-NEXIS' LIST OF MAJOR NEWSPAPERS

This list is accurate as of May 18, 2005. The newspapers are listed alphabetically.

Atlanta Journal-Constitution

Baltimore Sun

Boston Globe

Boston Herald

Buffalo News

Chicago Sun-Times

Christian Science Monitor

Columbus Dispatch

Daily News (New York)

Daily Telegraph

Daily Yomiuri

Denver Post

Dominion (Wellington, New Zealand)

Dominion Post (Wellington)

Evening Post (Wellington)

Financial Times (London)

Gazeta Mercantil Online

Guardian (London)

Hartford Courant

Herald (Glasglow)

Houston Chronicle

Independent

Irish Times

Jerusalem Post

Journal of Commerce

Los Angeles Times

Miami Herald

New Straits Times (Malaysia)

New York Times

New Zealand Herald

Newsday

Omaha World Herald

Pittsburgh Post-Gazette

Plain Dealer (Cleveland)

Press (Christ Church, New Zealand)

San Diego Union-Tribune

San Francisco Chronicle

Scotsman

Seattle Times

South China Morning Post

St. Louis Post-Dispatch

St. Petersburg Times

Star Tribune

Straits Times (Singapore)

Tampa Tribune

Times Picayune (New Orleans)

Toronto Star

USA Today

Washington Post

❖ DISCUSSION QUESTIONS

1. Is there hate crime legislation in your city or state? Are sexual
   orientation and gender identity included in the law? If there is a
   hate crimes law, how are hate crimes reported? Is there agreement about the crimes that should be included? One of the curious facets of the Sakia Gunn story is that despite the fact that her
   assailant was charged with bias murder, the FBI hate crimes
   report does not list any bias murders of lesbians in 2003. Ultimately, McCullough was convicted of a lesser charge. How is this
   reported in the hate crime statistics?

2. Pretend that in May 2003, you were an assignment editor for a major news outlet. Based on the initial facts of Sakia Gunn's murder, would you have covered it? Why or why not? How much attention would you have devoted to it? If you would not have covered it initially, is there a point when you might have picked the story up?

❖ HOMEWORK ASSIGNMENTS

1. Write a news or feature story that answers at least one of the following questions in detail: Where do GLBT youth go in your community? Is there a GLBT community center? Are its clients diverse in sexual orientation, gender identity, age, sex, race, and ethnicity? If not, why not? Is there antiviolence education in the public schools? Is there a local chapter of the Gay, Lesbian, and Straight Education Network?

❖ NOTES

1. Epistemology is the branch of philosophy concerned with how we determine what is true and important.

2. Baldwin is studying the disparate responses of religious communities to the murders of Shepard and Gunn. More information is available at http://www.und.edu/dept/philrel/Baldwin.htm and http://www.godandsexuality.org/products.asp?prod=29&cat=4&hierarchy=0%7C1.

3. Rev. Taylor made these comments at a Unity Fellowship Church–New Brunswick service on May 17, 2003.

4. Williams' first name has been variously reported as Ferdinand and Fernand. This spelling comes from a listing on the Newark Public Schools Web site, http://www.nps.k12.nj.us/schools.html.

5. Sullivan's total comes from Bozell (2004), p. 124.

6. For an example, see former *New York Times* Managing Editor Arthur Gelbs' memoir, *City Room* (2003).

❖ REFERENCES

Aarons, L., & Murphy, S. (Eds.). (2000). *Lesbians and gays in the newsroom, 10 years later.* Los Angeles: Annenberg School for Communications, University of Southern California.

American Society of Newspaper Editors. (2004, April 20). Newsroom employ-
    ment drops again, diversity gains [Press release]. Retrieved May 14, 2005,
    from http://www.asne.org/index.cfm?id=5145

Baldwin, G. (2004a). Gayle Baldwin. Retrieved May 14, 2005, from http://
    www.und.edu/dept/philrel/Baldwin.htm

Baldwin, G. (2004b). The resurrection of Matthew Shepard and Sakia Gunn's
    rainbow children: Issues of race and the religious imagination in response
    to hate crimes. Retrieved May 14, 2005, from the God & Sexuality: An
    Academic Conference on Religion and Issues of Sexuality and Gender,
    Bard College, Annandale on Hudson, NY Web site: http://www.godand
    sexuality.org/products.asp?prod=29&cat=4&hierarchy=0%7C1

Bishop, J. (2003, May 16). In memory of Sakia Gunn. Retrieved May 14, 2005,
    from the Keith Boykin.com Web site: http://www.keithboykin.com/
    arch/000741.html

Boston pays tribute to Sakia Gunn. (2003, June 27–July 3). Gay City News, 2(26).
    Retrieved May 14, 2005, from http://www.gaycitynews.com/gcn226/
    bostonpaystribute.html

Bozell, B. (2004). Weapons of mass distortion. New York: Crown Forum.

Curry, G. (2003, December 8). Mixed feelings about same-sex marriages.
    Retrieved May 18, 2005, from http://georgecurry.com/columns/index1
    .shtml?id=1071279229

DuLong, J. (2003, June 24). Young and in danger in New Jersey. Advocate, (892), 26.

Favre, G. (1999, June 4). We cannot rest now: The 1999 Hays-Press Enterprise
    Lecture. Retrieved May 14, 2005, from http://www.asne.org/ideas/99
    favre.htm

Federal Bureau of Investigation. (2002). Hate crime statistics. Retrieved May 14,
    2005, from http://www.fbi.gov/ucr/hatecrime2002.pdf

Federal Bureau of Investigation. (2003). Hate crime statistics. Retrieved May 14,
    2005, from http://www.fbi.gov/ucr/hatecrime2003.pdf

Northland briefs: Gay, lesbian vigil set for today. (2003, May 22). Retrieved May
    14, 2005, from the Duluth-News.com Web site: http://www.duluthsuperior
    .com/mld/duluthsuperior/news/5918492.htm

Gelbs, A. (2003). City room. New York: Berkley Books.

Hill Collins, P. (1990). Defining black feminist thought. Retrieved May 14, 2005,
    from http://www.hsph.harvard.edu/Organizations/healthnet/WoC/
    feminisms/collins2.html

Hill Collins, P. (2004). Black sexual politics: African Americans, gender and the new
    racism. New York: Routledge.

"It's a shame that you have to walk down the street not knowing what's going
    to happen to us": The Sakia Gunn murder. (2003, July 14). Retrieved May
    14, 2005, from http://www.democracynow.org/article.pl?sid=03/07/14/
    1454250

Krajicek, D. (2003). The crime beat. Retrieved May 14, 2005, from http://www
    .justicejournalism.org/crimeguide/chapter01/chapter01_pg06.html

Lule, J. (2001). *Daily news, eternal stories: The mythological role of journalism.* New York: Guilford Press.

Maynard, D. (2005). Fault lines. Retrieved May 14, 2005, from the Robert C. Maynard Institute for Journalism Education Web site: http://www .maynardije.org/programs/faultlines/

McGowan, W. (2001). *Coloring the news: How crusading for diversity has corrupted American journalism.* San Francisco: Encounter Books.

Meenan, M. (2003, May 16–22). Lesbian teen dies in hate stabbing. *Gay City News, 2*(20). Retrieved May 14, 2005, from http://www.gaycitynews.com/ gcn220/lesbianteendies.html

Meenan, M. (2004, May 13–19). Sakia Gunn memorialized: Family joins Newark activists in honoring young lesbian. *Gay City News, 3*(20). Retrieved May 14, 2005, from http://www.gaycitynews.com/gcn_320/sakiagunnmemo rialized.html

MSU student receives award for activism. (2004, December 2). Retrieved May 14, 2005, from the pridesource.com Web site: http://www.pridesource .com/article.shtml?article=10380&section=news

Neal, M. A. (2003, December 15). Critical noir: Remembering Sakia. Retrieved May 14, 2005, from http://www.africana.com/articles/daily/mu20040114 sakia.asp

Open letter to George Curry from gay black journalists. (2003, December 20). Retrieved May 14, 2005, from the Richard Prince's Journal-Isms Web site: http://www.maynardije.org/columns/dickprince/031219_prince/

Pearson, K. (2002, March). Liberal media bias? I must be missing something. Retrieved May 18, 2005, from http://kpearson.faculty.tcnj.edu/Articles/ Dirkhising.htm

Renna, C. (October 9–15, 2003). Learning from Laramie's legacy. Retrieved May 18, 2005, from http://www.gaycitynews.com/gcn_241/learningfromlaramies .html

The Sakia Gunn monthly story count. (2003, August 31). Retrieved May 14, 2005, from the Professor Kim's News Notes Web log: http://profes-sorkim.blogspot.com/2003_08_01_professorkim_archive.html

A Sakia Gunn story that I had missed. (2003, December 19). Retrieved May 14, 2005, from Professor Kim's News Notes at http://professorkim.blogspot .com/2003/12/sakia-gunn-story-that-i-had-missed.html

Schindler, P. (2003, June 6–12). Howard Dean steps up on Newark. *Gay City News, 2*(23). Retrieved May 14, 2005, from http://www.gaycitynews .com/gcn223/howarddean.html

Smothers, R. (2003, May 16). Man arrested in the killing of a teenager in Newark. *New York Times,* p. B4.

Smothers, R. (2004, May 12). Newark preaches tolerance of gays year after killing. *New York Times.* Retrieved May 14, 2005, from http://professorkim .blogspot.com/2004/05/new-york-times-new-york-region-newark .html

Strunsky, S. (2003, August 9). A young lesbian's stabbing death is far from resolved. Retrieved May 18, 2005, from the Associated Press state and local wire on the Lexis-Nexis Database.

Suspect skips hearing on Gunn slaying. (2003, December 11). Retrieved May 14, 2005, from the PlanetOut.com Web site: http://www.planetout.com/pno/news/article.html?2003/12/11/4

❖ ADDITIONAL RESOURCES

Criminal Justice Journalists. (2003). Covering crime and justice: A guide for journalists. Retrieved May 14, 2005, from http://www.justicejournalism.org/crimeguide/

GenderPac. (2005). Gender Public Advocacy Coalition [Home page]. Retrieved May 14, 2005, from http://www.genderpac.org. (In addition to educating readers about transgenderism, Genderpac publishes stories about victims of gender bias crimes.)

Newark Pride Alliance. (2004). [Home page]. Retrieved May 14, 2005, from http://www.geocities.com/newark_pride_alliance/ (A site for the advocacy group established in Sakia Gunn's memory.)

Sgt. Leonard Matlovich comes out of the closet on the cover of *Time* magazine in 1975.

SOURCE: *Time* Magazine © 1975 Time, Inc. Reprinted with permission.

10

Media Coverage
of the U.S. Ban on
Gays in the Military

Rhonda Gibson

❖   ❖   ❖

In its first 150 years, the United States military did not officially exclude or discharge gay men or lesbians because of their sexual orientation. Sodomy, however, was considered a crime as early as the Revolutionary War, and Lt. Gotthold Frederick Enslin earned the dubious distinction on March 11, 1778, of being the first known member of the U.S. military to be literally drummed out on charges of sodomy. Gen. George Washington himself issued the order that Enslin was "to be dismiss'd [sic] with Infamy" (Shilts, 1993, p. 12).

During World War I, the punishment for gay soldiers was first codified into American military law. Prior to this action, soldiers or sailors accused of sodomy were often discharged under the label of "conduct unbecoming." The Articles of War of 1916, which became effective in 1917, included assault with the intent to commit sodomy as a felony.

A revision of the Articles of War 3 years later named sodomy itself as a specific felony, the crime now being the sexual act itself, regardless of whether it was consensual or involved assault. In 1922, the first regulation of sexual thought and propensity was established: Beginning that year, enlisted personnel in the army who were charged with or suspected of homosexual acts were discharged under Section VIII, "inaptness or undesirable habits or traits of character."

During the 1940s, when the United States entered World War II, psychiatric screening became a part of the military induction process. During this time, professionals in the fields of psychiatry and psychology considered homosexuality to be an indicator of psychopathology, which made one unfit for military service. As a result, the military shifted from its earlier focus on homosexual acts, which were classified as a criminal offense, to a focus on eliminating homosexual people from its ranks. In 1942, revised Army mobilization regulations included for the first time language that defined both the homosexual and the "normal" individual and clarified procedures for rejecting homosexual draftees. Consequently, acknowledging a homosexual orientation would bar an individual from military service—a policy that was viewed at the time as enlightened, compared to simple criminalization of homosexual conduct.

In 1950, the newly created Department of Defense issued Army Regulation 600-443, which divided homosexuals into three classes. Class I homosexuals were defined as those engaging in activities involving force, fraud, intimidation, or the seduction of a minor. These individuals were required to face a general court-martial. Class II homosexuals were identified as those who either engaged in or attempted to engage in homosexual acts. Enlisted personnel in this class could accept a dishonorable discharge, and officers could submit a letter of resignation in lieu of general court-martial. Class III personnel were those who exhibited or admitted homosexual tendencies but who had not committed any provable offenses. They were given either a general or an honorable discharge. The regulation was liberalized in 1955 and 1958, allowing greater opportunity for Class II and III homosexuals to receive honorable or general discharges.

In spite of all of the regulations against sexual minorities, gay men and lesbians were actually allowed to serve in the military in times of extreme personnel shortages, such as during World War II and even during the 1990 Persian Gulf War and the recent conflicts in Iraq and Afghanistan. During times of personnel shortages, the military institutes a "stop/loss" policy, of which the aim is to slow the number of discharges from the armed forces, ensuring adequate manpower to fulfill whatever military missions a war requires. Gay discharges have dropped every time the country has entered a war, from World War II to the present, but the allowances are temporary, and as the war efforts end, antigay policies are again put into effect (Shilts, 1993).

During the anticommunist hysteria of the 1950s, national security was advanced as the central reason for keeping gays[1] out of military and government service. Gay men were considered at higher risk for blackmail, in spite of there being no evidence that this actually occurred. By the 1960s, after the McCarthy era passed, the most often articulated reason for barring gay men from the military was that the presence of those suffering from homosexuality, still classified as a mental disorder, would undermine the "good order, discipline and morale" (Shilts, 1993, p. 17) of the fighting forces.

Things began to change in the 1970s. The American Psychiatric Association removed homosexuality from its list of psychiatric disorders in 1973, and the American Psychological Association and the American Public Health Association passed similar resolutions in 1975. As the U. S. gay civil rights movement was gaining strength, and young people became more disillusioned with authority, the military's ban on homosexuals became a target for protest and court challenges. The most well known of the early challenges was mounted in 1975 by Sgt. Leonard Matlovich, a highly decorated 12-year veteran of the Air Force who hoped that because of his distinguished combat career, he would represent a perfect test case to fight the ban on gays in the military. He publicly announced his homosexuality and was promptly discharged. In December 1978, however, the U.S. Court of Appeals ruled that Matlovich's discharge had been illegal, and in 1980, a federal judge ordered the Air Force to reinstate Matlovich with back pay. Similar court cases were filed throughout the 1970s, and although they were largely unsuccessful, they highlighted the number of gay men and lesbians who were actually serving honorably in the military. In addition, they showed, in spite of clear regulations against homosexuals, how varied the response was among military leaders who were aware of gay men and lesbians serving in their units.

In spite of the changing psychological and societal views about homosexuality, as well as all the legal challenges to the military ban, the U.S. armed forces made no move to liberalize their policy. In fact, in 1982, the Department of Defense policy was revised to establish uniform procedures concerning homosexuality across the service branches. The policy stated unequivocally that homosexuality was incompatible with military service. Department of Defense Directives 1332.14 and 1332.20, issued in January 1982, dealt with the administrative discharge of gay and lesbian enlisted personnel and officers, with the following rationale:

> Homosexuality is incompatible with military service. The presence in the military environment of persons who engage in homosexual conduct or who, by their statements, demonstrate a propensity to engage in homosexual conduct, seriously impairs the accomplishment of the military mission. The presence of such members adversely affects the ability of the Military Services to maintain discipline, good order, and morale; to foster mutual trust and confidence among service members, to ensure integrity of the system of rank and command; to facilitate assignment and worldwide deployment of service members who frequently must live and work under close conditions affording minimal privacy; to recruit and retain members of the Military Services; to maintain the public acceptability of military service; and prevent breaches of security.

A Government Accounting Office report from the early 1990s stated that nearly 17,000 men and women were discharged in the 1980s under the category of homosexuality (Herek, 1993).

In 1992, the plight of gays in the military received unparalleled public attention due to the brutal murder of Seaman Allen Schindler, who was beaten to death by fellow sailors because he was gay. As a result, legislation to overturn the ban was introduced that year in the U.S. Congress. By then, a number of gay civil rights organizations demonstrated renewed interest in the fight for equitable treatment within the military ranks, and some colleges and universities banned military recruiters and Reserve Officer Training Corps (ROTC) programs from their campuses in protest of the policy. Although Congress did pass a law forcing the military to accept homosexuals, those who opposed the ban were heartened by the arrival of Arkansas Gov. Bill Clinton into the 1992 presidential race. Clinton made a campaign promise to end the military's ban against gay men and lesbians, and the first major news story in the period between his election and inauguration was his announcement that he planned to follow through on his campaign promise and issue an executive order rescinding the ban on sexual minorities in the military. Immediately, the Joint Chiefs of Staff, led by Chairman Gen. Colin Powell, came out strongly against lifting the ban, and Sen. Sam Nunn, a Democrat from Georgia and chairman of the Senate Armed Services Committee, announced on television that he would prevent the president from acting on his pledge. Conservative members of Congress, both Democrats and Republicans, also publicly opposed Clinton's proposal and threatened to put a more explicit ban into law. On January 30, 1993, Clinton reached a tentative compromise with congressional leaders. It delayed the issuing of a presidential order until July 1993 to give Congress time to hold hearings on the issue and allow the orderly implementation of the new proposal, called "Don't Ask, Don't Tell, Don't Pursue." The new policy was officially announced on July 9, 1993, by Clinton, who had carefully negotiated to secure the approval of the Joint Chiefs of Staff. "Don't Ask" differed from the previous military ban in three major aspects: service members and recruits could no longer be asked if they were gay, sexual orientation alone would not be grounds for discharge "absent of conduct," and no investigation could be initiated solely to determine the sexual orientation of a service member. However, a serviceman or -woman who acknowledged his or her homosexuality would still not be allowed to serve.

Congress went a step farther. In response to the strong opposition of the Senate and House Armed Services Committee to changing the ban, Congress approved legislation that prohibited open lesbians and gays from serving in the military. A key difference between the Clinton compromise and the tougher congressional law was that the Clinton proposal would have been issued with a Defense Department Directive, which could have been changed in the future by an executive order. However, because Congress actually passed legislation banning openly gay men and women from serving in the military, for the policy to be altered in the future, Congress will have to hold hearings on specific legislation and take a formal vote. The congressional language enabled the specifics of the Clinton plan to take effect while codifying into law a broad statement of policy that bars gays from military service. Some gay and lesbian activists considered this more of a setback than any move forward.

Civilian courts have issued contradictory opinions about the constitutionality of the "Don't Ask" policy, and some have ordered the reinstatement of openly gay military personnel who were involuntarily discharged. Higher courts, however, have upheld the policy. According to the Servicemembers Legal Defense Network, which monitors implementation of the policy, discharges based on charges of homosexuality have actually increased since the Clinton compromise was reached. The network also claims that harassment of gays and lesbians has intensified at some bases, in spite of the policy's expansion to include "Don't Harass" as a provision. They cite the 1999 murder of PFC Barry Winchell as a dramatic example. Winchell was beaten by Pvt. Calvin Glover and other members of Winchell's unit at Fort Campbell, Kentucky. Glover beat Winchell to death with a baseball bat while he slept, a crime that, prosecutors argued, was prompted by Winchell's perceived homosexuality. Glover was sentenced to life in prison, but a report by the Army Inspector General exonerated all officers of blame in Winchell's murder and identified no climate of homophobia at the base in Kentucky.

Although the issue was not a prominent one in the 2004 presidential campaign, many retired high-level military personnel have recently denounced the ban. Three retired officers, Generals Virgil Richard and Keith Kerr and Admiral Alan Steinman, came out publicly in the *New York Times* in late 2003 and criticized the "Don't Ask, Don't Tell, Don't Pursue" policy as ineffective. Richard summed up the officers' reason for going public with their sexual orientation and their beliefs: "There are gays and lesbians who want to serve honorably and with integrity, but have been forced to compromise. It is a manner of honor and integrity" (Files, 2003). Currently both opponents and proponents of the military ban on homosexuals are waiting to see what effect the Supreme Court's June 2003 decision in *Lawrence v. Texas*, overturning state sodomy laws, will have on both the military's sodomy statute and the "Don't Ask, Don't Tell" policy. As of this writing, a number of high-level military officials have come out of the closet, and many straight ones are calling for an end to the ban, but thus far there has been no action. An end to the ban does not seem likely under the current administration.

❖ THE MEDIA AND THE MILITARY

Until World War II, gay men and lesbians were basically unmentionable in American newspapers and magazines (Alwood, 1996). The few references that occurred were in small neighborhood or tabloid newspapers and mocked gays or characterized them as a menace to society. News coverage increased in the 1940s, when military psychiatrists began a campaign to weed gays out of the armed forces and stories about the military's efforts appeared in major newspapers and magazines such as the *New York Times* and *Saturday Evening Post.*

Newsweek magazine drew public attention to the military's efforts in a story titled "Homosexuals in Uniform," published in the June 9, 1947, issue. The story focused on the military's intensified antihomosexual campaign and reported that, although Army regulations strictly forbade the drafting of sexual minorities, between 3,000 and 4,000 individuals had been discharged during World War II for being homosexual, and some others had been released as neuropsychiatric cases. The story explained that psychiatrists in induction-station interviews attempted to determine who was homosexual by effeminate looks or behavior and by repeating certain words from the homosexual vocabulary and watching for signs of recognition. The article noted that a good many of the soldiers identified as homosexual begged to be cured, but doctors usually doubted their sincerity and recommended discharge. Going against prevailing psychiatric thought, the story reported that at least half of the confirmed homosexuals were well adjusted to their condition and neither needed nor would respond to treatment.

The *Newsweek* piece also focused on the phenomenon of the "blue discharge." Early in the war, suspected homosexuals were sent up for court-martial, but in 1943 and 1944, the Army decided to separate most of them quietly with a "blue" discharge (neither honorable nor dishonorable) unless some other breach of military law had been committed. On July 1, 1947, however, a new policy went into effect. Instead of leaving the service with the vague and protective "blue" discharge, those homosexuals who had not been guilty of a definite offense would receive an undesirable discharge. Those found guilty of homosexual violence or of impairing the morals of minors would receive a dishonorable discharge.

During World War II, the press was especially receptive to publicizing the military's antigay campaign because of the government's strict wartime constraints on what the media could report. The public was starved for information, so newspaper editors would print what they could, even if the topic was as controversial as gays in the armed forces. Increased media visibility for sexual minorities was, in this case, not necessarily a positive thing: The terms *pervert* and *deviant* were often used as synonyms for *homosexual*, and almost every description of gay men during this time was in the context of how they were unfit for military service. Lesbians remained virtually invisible in the news media.

One lasting result of the news coverage of the military's antigay efforts during World War II was the establishment of psychiatrists and psychologists, invariably heterosexual, as "experts" on the topic of homosexuality (Alwood, 1996). Clinical psychiatry was beginning to establish itself as a respected science, and those in the field considered homosexuality to be a potentially treatable mental disorder. Thus psychiatrists were added to journalists' "golden Rolodexes" of expert sources on homosexuality, joining law enforcement officials, who could speak to the "dark," criminal side of homosexuality, and members of the clergy, who were called on to provide information about the assumed immorality of homosexuals. Actual gay men and lesbians were almost never interviewed or included in these early news stories.

Occasional news reports about efforts in the armed forces and the State Department to weed out undesirable homosexuals continued into the 1950s with Sen. Joseph McCarthy's hunt for dangerous subversives, a group that included communists and homosexuals, terms that sometimes seemed to be interchangeable during the senator's hearings.

No Longer Silent: Sgt. Leonard Matlovich and Col. Margarethe Cammermeyer

Press coverage of gays in the military dramatically increased in 1975, when Air Force Technical Sergeant Leonard Matlovich acknowledged his homosexuality to his superiors, a move that, he said, was made deliberately to provoke a discharge to challenge the military's ban against sexual minorities. The 32-year-old highly decorated veteran of three Vietnam tours seemed to gay activist Frank Kameny to be the perfect candidate to challenge the military's ban on homosexuals (Aiken, 1975). Kameny enlisted American Civil Liberties Union (ACLU) attorney David Addlestone to help mount a legal battle, building their challenge to Matlovich's likely dismissal around an exception rule included in the Air Force's policy on homosexuality, which stated that the Air Force could retain a homosexual service member under unusual circumstances. In addition to arguing that the exclusionary policy was unconstitutional, Matlovich's team planned to argue that his exemplary record itself constituted the unusual circumstance that should permit him to remain in the Air Force.

Media coverage was intense. *Time* magazine, on September 8, 1975, featured Matlovich on the cover for a story on the struggle for gay rights. The cover showed Matlovich in a blue Air Force uniform complete with military ribbons—the 12-year military veteran had been awarded a Bronze Star, Purple Heart, and an Air Force Commendation Medal for his exemplary service in Vietnam. The picture was accompanied by the words "I Am A Homosexual." This was the first time an openly gay man had appeared on the cover of *Time*.

After declaring his homosexuality, Matlovich was deemed unfit for further military service and recommended for a general discharge rather than the honorable discharge that his distinguished record would normally have demanded. Matlovich challenged the ruling, and in December 1978, the U.S. Court of Appeals ruled that his discharge had been illegal and sent the case back to a lower court to decide on the issue of reinstatement. Meanwhile, the Matlovich case continued to attract much media attention and kept the issue of gays in the military on the public radar. In 1978, NBC News broadcast "Sgt. Matlovitch vs. the Air Force," one of the first gay rights feature stories aired on national television.

In 1980, a federal judge ordered the Air Force to reinstate Matlovich with back pay. Within a few months, Matlovich announced a settlement with the military; he dropped the case in exchange for a $160,000 payment, much to the dismay of many gay activists, who wanted his case to go to the Supreme Court. Matlovich died on June 22, 1988, from complications of AIDS. With full military honors and a 21-gun salute, he was interred in the Congressional Cemetery in Washington, D.C. He intended his grave to serve as a memorial for all gay and lesbian veterans, and so rather than recording his name, the headstone reads simply "A Gay Vietnam Veteran." Also inscribed on the stone are the words "Never Again" and "Never Forget" beneath two triangles, and the inscription, which he wrote himself: "When I was in the military, they gave me a medal for killing two men and a discharge for loving one."

Another highly decorated soldier, Col. Margarethe Cammermeyer, also won her battle against the military's ban on lesbians and gay men. Born in Oslo, Norway, in 1942 during the Nazi occupation, Cammermeyer joined the Army Student Nurse Program during college in the United States and went on active duty after graduation in 1963.

She married a fellow soldier and served in Vietnam for 14 months, earning the Bronze Star for Meritorious Service. Cammermeyer divorced after 15 years and four sons, coming to the realization that she was a lesbian. In 1988, having earned the rank of colonel, she accepted the position of chief nurse of the Washington State National Guard. The following year, during an interview for high-level security clearance, she told military officials about her sexual orientation. She was discharged in June 1992 and immediately filed suit in Federal District Court in Seattle, challenging the ban on gays in the military and requesting reinstatement. A judge ruled the ban unconstitutional, and Cammermeyer was reinstated in the National Guard in June 1994 in her previous position as chief nurse. A made-for-TV movie based on her 1994 autobiography *Serving in Silence* starred Glenn Close and received three Emmy awards. In March 1997, after 31 years of service, Margarethe Cammermeyer retired with full military privileges.

The Outing of Pete Williams

Although there were occasional news stories in the 1980s about additional legal challenges to the military ban or about gay bashing in the armed forces, the main gay-related news story of the decade was the emerging AIDS epidemic. Gay civil rights proponents and public health officials were often critical of the limited funding for research and treatment coming from President Ronald Reagan's administration. One tactic these activists used to garner publicity and affect policy making was the "outing" of closeted homosexuals who were involved in some type of public antigay behavior, usually in politics (Gross, 2001). The most prominent "outer" was journalist Michael Signorile, best known for exposing the "secret" gay life of multimillionaire publisher Malcolm Forbes in *Outweek* in 1990. Signorile's defense of outing was simple: He thought it good journalism to expose hypocrisy among public officials. Signorile had long been receiving tips about Assistant Secretary of Defense Pete Williams, chief spokesman for the Pentagon, from people angry over the Department of Defense's policy of excluding lesbians and gay men from the military, and these tips increased with Williams' greater media visibility during the 1991 Persian Gulf War. In June 1991, Air Force harassment of Capt. Charles Greeley, who had marched in a Gay Pride parade the day before he was to be discharged, was the catalyst that led to Williams' outing. Members of the gay activist group Queer Nation put up posters in Washington with Williams' picture and a caption that read, "Absolutely Queer. Pete Williams, Pentagon Spokesman, Tap Dancer. Consummate Queer." In smaller print, the posters read, "Gay Bush appointee sits by while gay servicemen and women are burned." The *Advocate* made the outing official in a story by Signorile in August that linked the outing of Williams to the military's increasingly violent exclusion of gays from the military. Many major news outlets picked up the story, although some of them ran it without actually naming Williams. Within weeks of the *Advocate* story, the *New York Times* and the *Washington Post* ran editorials attacking the military's antigay policy, and *Time* published a lengthy account of the controversy surrounding the issue that was clearly sympathetic to the gay cause (Gross, 2001). Williams, who did not lose his job in spite of being outed, was quickly hired by NBC News after the Republicans lost the White House in 1992.

Bill Clinton's Fight to End the Ban on Gays in the Military

In the fall of 1991, Clinton was asked at a Harvard University forum about his views on the military's long-standing ban on gays and lesbians and if he would issue an executive order to rescind the ban if he won the race for the presidency. Clinton answered "yes" and explained: "I think people who are gay should be expected to work and should be given the opportunity to serve the country" (Rimmerman, 1996, p. xix). Although Clinton later admitted he had not given the issue much thought before the Harvard forum (Clinton, 2004), his statement launched 2 years of heavy media coverage of the issue of gays in the military.

News coverage intensified in May 1992, when gay sailor Keith Meinhold announced his homosexuality during an interview on *ABC World News Tonight*. Meinhold, who had joined the U.S. Navy at the age of 18 in 1980 and served with distinction for 12 years, hoped his case would shed light on the many gays and lesbians serving with honor in the armed forces and possibly lead to a reversal of the military's ban. Meinhold told ABC News on June 29, 1992, "I'm supposed to be out there fighting for American values, to retain those, and the Navy is just absolutely violating those, the civil rights of Americans." Although his sexual orientation was well known inside his unit and by his base commander prior to his announcement, discharge proceedings were begun after Meinhold's appearance in the news. On November 6, 1992, a federal judge ordered the U.S. Navy to reinstate Meinhold, an event that was heavily covered by print and television media.

News coverage peaked again in January 1993, when President-Elect Clinton announced his plan to lift the ban after a 6-month study period. Immediately, members of Congress and the Joint Chiefs of Staff expressed strong opposition to the president's proposal and took their case to the press. The issue dominated radio call-in programs and newspaper headlines for a week (Bawer, 1993), much to the dismay of the new Clinton administration: "I didn't want the issue to get any more publicity than it already had, not because I was trying to hide my position, but because I didn't want the public to think I was paying more attention to it than to the economy" (Clinton, 2004, p. 483). Also that month, three U.S. Marines in North Carolina were charged with assaulting a gay man who was dragged out of a bar and beaten. The Marines were reportedly protesting Clinton's plan to lift the ban.

Senate Armed Services Committee Chairman Sam Nunn held hearings on the matter during the spring of 1993. The hearings contained several dramatic moments, including Col. Fred Peck's outing of his son Scott. Peck, the U.S. Army spokesman in Somalia, testified that he supported the ban because of antigay sentiment among soldiers. He publicly stated his fear that if his son were in the military, his life would be in jeopardy from his own troops. Peck's testimony, along with that of many other military officials strongly opposed to lifting the ban, made for great television, as did the passionate responses from gay civil rights advocates who considered the military's response to be blatant discrimination. The issue was receiving almost daily news coverage during the first half of 1993 and focused media attention on other gay-related events, such as the third gay rights National March on Washington on April 15, 1993. Part of the march coverage focused on highly decorated Army Sgt. Joe Zuniga, who had been named Sixth Army Soldier of the Year. Zuniga acknowledged that he was gay during a fund-raiser for the National Gay and Lesbian Task Force on the evening before the march, stating that he wanted to give a human face to the issue. Reporters had been alerted to Zuniga's announcement and linked coverage of the march to the president's attempt to lift the military ban.

Clinton was not the only one distressed by the amount or type of news coverage on the gays in the military controversy during the first months of his term. Military leaders were especially bothered by servicemen and -women such as Zuniga who publicly announced their homosexuality to the press. There were attempts to crack down on anyone talking to journalists, and commanders went to great lengths to identify anonymous sources used in TV and print news reports (Shilts, 1993).

News coverage continued, however, with the next spike occurring the following month when Nunn proposed a "Don't Ask, Don't Tell" compromise under which the military services could not question members about their sexual orientation, but overt homosexual behavior or open statements of homosexuality would lead to discharge. The final news peak that year occurred in July, when Clinton agreed to the compromise policy. Television coverage of the aftermath of the compromise agreement continued as the battle moved to the federal courts, and the controversy generated, on average, at least one major network news story a week until the end of the year (Gonzenbach, King, & Jablonski, 1999; Steele, 1997).

❖ ANALYSIS OF MEDIA COVERAGE

There is much disagreement about the quality and tone of news coverage of Clinton's unsuccessful attempt to lift the ban on gays in the military and the eventual "Don't Ask, Don't Tell, Don't Pursue" compromise. Some critics charge that news reports were slanted against lifting the ban (Rimmerman, 1996; Shilts, 1993; Wilcox & Wolpert, 1996), but there is evidence that many reports were actually positive toward the president's actions, focusing more on his arguments about why sexual minorities should be allowed to serve in the military than on those who opposed gays in the armed forces (Gibson & Hester, 2003; Gonzenbach et al., 1999).

Oddly enough, it was the journalistic quest for balance and fairness that led to slanted media coverage, according to Professor Janet Steele (1997), who studied television news coverage of the issue. Steele analyzed the way in which television news organizations selected and used unofficial sources in covering the 1992–1993 controversy over gays in the military. She studied all of the 155 news stories about the topic on NBC, ABC, and CBS and determined that the broadcast media framed the issue as being a conflict between two opposing interest groups: the military and its supporters in Congress versus protesting gay servicemen and women backed by gay civil rights organizations. Steele likens this to "game story" coverage of one "team" versus another.

TV producers and correspondents sought commentary from advocates of what they considered to be the two sides of the dispute, which meant that they made almost no effort to obtain the views of social scientists or other more neutral experts who could have placed the controversy in a broader social or historical contest. The vast majority of the stories on gays and military service were focused on conflict-laden events such as a presidential meeting with military advisors, a court ruling, or hearings by the Senate Armed Services Committee. Only a few stories attempted to place the events into a more general social or historical context; these included reports on the integration of gays and lesbians into the NATO, Canadian, and Dutch militaries. One story, an NBC "America Close Up Report" on February 9, 1993, examined the issue of gays in the military in light of the history of racial segregation and integration in America's armed forces.

Although both proponents and opponents of sexual minorities in the military were included in news coverage, the types of sources selected to represent the two sides were not "equal," according to Steele. The unofficial sources who explained the military's point of view were usually active duty or retired officers and former public officials, in contrast to the political outsiders (gay and lesbian civil rights activists) who spoke for those gay men and lesbians in the armed forces who were challenging the military ban. Only rarely were more prestigious sources used for the progays in the military side, such as in a *CBS Evening News* report on February 13, 1993, that included a statement from Roman Catholic Cardinal Roger Mahoney of Los Angeles that he believed there might be a place for gays in the U.S. military. Military sources against lifting the ban included retired generals, such as Norman Schwarzkopf, who were already familiar and credible to television viewers. In a May 11, 1993, report on ABC's *World News Tonight,* Schwarzkopf was described in glowing terms: "The general commanded the kind of celebrity status that is rarely seen on Capitol Hill. Chairman Nunn wanted a photo. The committee wanted his opinion, and General Schwarzkopf was not shy about giving it." In another example, a November 11, 1992, NBC News story introduced retired Army Col. Harry Summers as a "well-known authority on military affairs," granting him a level of status and expertise that gay political organizers David Mixner and Robert Hattoy, also in the segment, could not match. Thus, although the journalistic convention of balance was achieved, it was in a way that may have legitimated the views of one side but marginalized those of the other. The selection of experts and the way in which they were paired worked to the advantage of those for the ban, according to Steele: The pairing of military sources with gay activists and advocates often bestowed insider status on the former and relegated the latter to the role of outsider.

Steele argues that if television news organizations had framed the controversy in a more thematic way, they might have turned to historians, sociologists, legal scholars, and other analysts who could have placed the issue in a broader social or historical context, raising questions about the assumptions underlying the arguments of what were characterized as the two sides of the dispute. Gay journalist Randy Shilts, whose 1993 book *Conduct Unbecoming* chronicles more than 200 years of military efforts to exclude homosexuals, agreed. He argued that coverage focused too much on conflict and fights and did not delve into deeper, broader issues, such as the social, cultural, or historical dimensions of the issue, the changing role of gays in the United States, conflicting religious attitudes, or the historical role of the military in integrating diverse groups into American society.

Other critics of press coverage of the gays in the military issue claim that the military and its allies were overly influential in setting the tone of press coverage, providing compelling visual images to dominate television news coverage. They believe that Nunn's ability to dominate the debate with his dramatic hearings put the president and opponents of the ban on the defensive from the very beginning (Rimmerman, 1996). Powerful visual images—such as Col. Peck's emotional testimony and a tour taken by Nunn and other congressional leaders of two Navy ships so they could get a full understanding of the close living quarters faced by those in the military—received much television and print news coverage (Bawer, 1993). Nunn pointed out for the accompanying C-SPAN camera the closeness of the bunks and asked soldiers, all of whom were against lifting the ban, how they felt about the possibility of gays in the military. A *CBS Evening News* report on May 10, 1993, showed footage from the claustrophobic tour and included numerous sound bites from Navy personnel who were distressed at the possibility of living with gay men in such cramped quarters.

In response, gay and lesbian activists hoped they too could mobilize the news media to show the faces of those who had served honorably in the media, such as Meinhold and Zuniga. The tactic had worked in the African-American Civil Rights movement—contrasting the faces of peaceful protesters with the often vicious actions of the police was a powerful tool. In the coverage of gays in the military, however, the Congressional hearings took center stage, overshadowing the images of gay and lesbian service members who wanted to continue their military careers.

Some members of gay civil rights organizations were critical of the language used in many of the television and print news reports. For example, an April 25, 1993, report on ABC's *World News Sunday* about the National March on Washington stated that polls showed most Americans did not like the "gay lifestyle," a term that groups such as GLAAD say is insulting because it fails to recognize diversity among sexual minorities. They point out that news personnel would not refer to any one "straight" lifestyle. Another term offensive to many gay rights supporters, *gay agenda*, was common in news stories, and not just in direct quotations and TV sound bites. Reporters and television correspondents often used this phrase to refer to any progay proposal, and again gay activists questioned the presence of any monolithic "gay agenda." Gay civil rights proponents were also critical of many antigay sound bites and quotes that they believed were slurs. The ABC report on the march on Washington that contained the phrase "gay lifestyle" also contained a sound bite from an unnamed antigay demonstrator: "You deserve no rights. I'll tell you how to stop AIDS, stop being a homosexual, that's how you stop AIDS." A previous ABC report on November 15, 1992, featured a sound bite from Admiral Thomas Moorer (ret.): "These people are involved in what I consider to be a filthy, disease-ridden practice." And a Virginia state senator, Warren Barry, was reported on all three networks as having referred to the gays in the military controversy as "fags in the foxhole." GLAAD and other gay rights organizations argue that such negative statements would not be included in news stories if they were aimed at women or racial minorities.

In spite of much criticism of news coverage of Clinton's attempt to lift the ban on gays in the military, there is some evidence that many of the news stories featured sources that were primarily favorable toward the president's stance, and not all of these sources were outsiders. In a June 10, 1993, report on ABC's *World News Tonight*, anchor Peter Jennings quoted former senator and conservative Barry Goldwater as being for lifting the ban on gays in the military. Goldwater's argument was "You don't need to be straight to fight and die for your country. You just need to shoot straight."

Likewise, in a content analysis of all stories about the issue presented by the early evening news programs on the three major television networks, the *New York Times*, and the television news show

Nightline from September 1, 1992, to February 28, 1993 (a total of 356 stories), Gonzenbach et al. (1999) found that more articles contained comments supporting Clinton's position than opposing it. As with Professor Steele's analysis, however, the Gonzenbach et al. study revealed that the media appeared to focus more on political sparring surrounding the ban than on the direct emotional or social ramifications of the issue for the public. The reports mostly dealt with the posturing and interplay among various governmental organizations. Most of the coverage focused on conflict between Clinton and members of Congress or between Clinton and the military. When issues such as morale of the troops or gay rights were discussed, they were framed in terms of the governmental camps that took sides on these issues.

There were also some stories critical of Clinton's actions, but not from those opposed to gays in the military. After Clinton's July 19, 1993, announcement of the "Don't Ask, Don't Tell, Don't Pursue" compromise, some gay civil rights proponents were critical of the president. In a report that night on *World News Tonight*, Thomas Stoddard of the antiban organization Campaign for Military Service stated: "The administration labels its new policy Don't Ask, Don't Tell, Don't Pursue. The policy is more aptly called 'Let's Pretend.' Let's pretend gay people simply don't exist, even though we know they do." In a July 20, 1993, report on the *CBS Evening News*, a group of gay men and lesbian protestors were shown chanting "Bill Clinton, go to hell."

Editorial Stands

Many major U.S. newspapers published in-house editorials about the gays in the military controversy during 1993. These were accompanied by syndicated and local opinion columns and numerous letters to the editor. Many of the in-house editorials were supportive of Clinton's attempts to lift the ban on gays in the military. The *Atlanta Journal and Constitution*, for example, on May 17, 1993, wrote:

> So what, then, is the problem with gays in the military? There is none, except for the attitude of those who would serve with them. Things get dicey, we are told, when the "homosexual lifestyle" is introduced into the barracks. That's an interesting concept, using sexual preference as the single determinant of how people live their lives. It's ludicrous. Does being heterosexual determine how you'll behave in every situation? (Head, 1993, p. A11)

A July 21, 1993, column in the *Chicago Sun-Times* by the syndicated writer Carl T. Rowan was very critical of the "Don't Ask, Don't Tell" compromise, saying that gay men and lesbians deserved better: "Instead of liberating homosexuals from bigotry, Mr. Clinton consigned them to a second-class status where they must live a silent lie and pretend to remain celibate, even when off duty and off their bases." The Manchester, New Hampshire *Union Leader* took a different stance in a house editorial on that same date:

> The military is no place for social experimentation. The whole point here, one that U.S. military experts affirm, is that while experience shows that many anti-social types can coexist in harmony in a military setting, the inclusion of active or self-avowed homosexuals has a detrimental effect on military morale and efficiency. ("Mixed signals: Homosexuals," 1993)

Syndicated columnist Cal Thomas made the same point in a piece that appeared in the New Orleans *Times-Picayune* on November 26, 1993:

> The military ought not [to] be a laboratory for social and political experimentation. Already there are reports of a decline in the quality of new recruits. Official approval of homosexuals in the ranks would further erode that quality as significant numbers of people who might otherwise join would not, based on moral principles they see the military as having surrendered.

Only one of the three television networks featured actual in-house commentary on the issue. In a January 31, 1993, commentary on the *CBS Evening News*, Bruce Morton spoke for lifting the ban on gays in the military, stating "Having rules of behavior and enforcing them makes sense; telling people 'You're not full citizens' doesn't. We are all Americans, with the right to love our country and, if need be, to fight for it."

The Current Situation

The issue continues to receive occasional news coverage, most often in relation to legal challenges to the "Don't Ask, Don't Tell" policy or when there is an incident of gay bashing on a military base. In

2004, during America's war against Iraq, when the military was faced with a shortage of combat personnel, some newspapers ran editorials against the policy of discharging openly gay men or lesbians. A July 3, 2004, editorial in the Eugene, Oregon *Register-Guard* argued that "Odds are good that exhausted troops who long to return to their loved ones would welcome back all of the 770 qualified soldiers who were kicked out of the services last year because of their sexual orientation" ("An unnecessary policy," 2004, p. A16). The *Atlanta Journal-Constitution*, in a June 25, 2004, editorial, was more blunt: "The U.S. military's Don't Ask, Don't Tell policy, which keeps gay and lesbian troops in a strange twilight, has never made much sense. Now that troop levels are stretched to the breaking point, it has become ludicrous" ("Anti-gay military," 2004, p. A18). The topic was eclipsed in 2004, however, by another gay rights issue: same-sex marriage. As the country argues over whether same-sex couples should be allowed to legally marry or if an amendment prohibiting same-sex marriage should be added to the U.S. Constitution, the debate over gays in the military has been put on the media's back burner, at least for the time being.

❖ DISCUSSION QUESTIONS

1. Instead of episodic coverage of the gays in the military issue, coverage that has been compared to sports coverage of a game story, how might the print and broadcast news media have chosen to cover the issue? What kinds of stories might this type of coverage have produced? What sources might have been used?

2. Should news stories about gays in the military contain antigay slurs from sources? Should reporters treat this topic differently than stories that deal with women or racial minorities?

3. Should GLBT news reporters be allowed (or expected) to cover issues such as gays in the military? Why or why not?

❖ HOMEWORK ASSIGNMENTS

1. The 2003 U.S. invasion and subsequent rebuilding of Iraq has stretched the U.S. military to its limits in terms of personnel. Many of those who oppose the military's ban on homosexuals

have said that this situation just confirmed the ban's negative effects: At a time when all branches of the military desperately needed personnel, hundreds of individuals who openly stated their homosexuality were being discharged. Examine newspaper coverage of this debate from 2003. What sources were used on each side of the issue? Do the sourcing patterns match those identified in Steele's study of 1993, which showed anti–gays in the military sources to be more prominent and respected than pro–gays in the military sources, who were less well known and respected?

2. Interview members of the ROTC program at your university. Do they read or watch news coverage of the gays in the military issue? What do they think of such coverage? Is coverage fair to the military? Would they feel comfortable speaking to a newspaper reporter about the issue?

❖ NOTE

1. For simplicity, the term *gays* in this chapter refers to both gay men and lesbian women. The term *homosexual* is also used inclusively, primarily in a historical sense.

❖ REFERENCES

Aiken, D. L. (1975, July 2). A perfect test case. *The Advocate*. Retrieved July 2004 from http://www.advocate.com/html/stories/852/852_archives_167.asp

Alwood, E. (1996). *Straight news: Gays, lesbians, and the news media.* New York: Columbia University Press.

Anti-gay military asks for trouble. (2004, June 25). *Atlanta Journal-Constitution*, p. A18.

Bawer, B. (1993). *A place at the table: The gay individual in American society.* New York: Poseidon Press.

Clinton, B. (2004). *My life.* New York: Knopf.

Files, J. (2003, December 10). Gay ex-officers say "don't ask" doesn't work. *New York Times*, p. A18.

Gibson, R., & Hester, J. B. (2003, March). *Gays in the military: A second-level agenda-setting analysis of TV news coverage.* Paper presented to the Radio and Television Journalism Division of the Association for Education in Journalism and Mass Communication, Kansas City, Missouri.

Gonzenbach, W. J., King, C., & Jablonski, P. (1999). Homosexuals and the military: An analysis of the spiral of silence. *Howard Journal of Communications, 10,* 281–296.

Gross, L. (2001). *Up from invisibility: Lesbians, gay men, and the media in America.* New York: Columbia University Press.

Head, J. (1993, May 17). Military, not gays, is problem. *Atlanta Journal and Constitution,* p. A11.

Herek, G. M. (1993). Sexual orientation and military service: A social science perspective. *American Psychologist, 48*(5), 538–549.

Homosexuals in uniform. (1947, June 9). *Newsweek,* p. 54.

Mixed signals: Homosexuals as heroes. Why the rush? (1993, July 21). *Union Leader.* Retrieved May 20, 2005, from the Lexis-Nexis database.

Rimmerman, C. A. (1996). *Gay rights, military wrongs: Political perspectives on lesbians and gays in the military.* New York: Garland.

Rowan, C. T. (1993, July 21). Nunn undermines Clinton initiatives. *Chicago Sun-Times,* p. A31.

Shilts, R. (1993). *Conduct unbecoming: Gays and lesbians in the U.S. military.* New York: St. Martin's Press.

Steele, J. (1997). Don't ask, don't tell, don't explain: Unofficial sources and television coverage of the dispute over gays in the military. *Political Communication, 14,* 83–96.

Thomas, C. (1993, November 26). The moral flame. *Times-Picayune,* p. B7.

An unnecessary policy. (2004, July 3). *Register-Guard,* A16.

Wilcox, C., & Wolpert, R. M. (1996). President Clinton, public opinion, and gays in the military. In C. A. Rimmerman (Ed.), *Gay rights, military wrongs: Political perspectives on lesbians and gays in the military* (pp. 127–145). New York: Garland.

❖ ADDITIONAL RESOURCES

Katenstein, M. F. (1996). The spectacle of life and death: Feminist and lesbian/gay politics in the military. In C. A. Rimmerman (Ed.), *Gay rights, military wrongs: Political perspectives on lesbians and gays in the military* (pp. 229–247). New York: Garland.

Robert Crown Law Library, Stanford Law School. (2005). Don't ask, don't tell, don't pursue. Retrieved May 9, 2005, from http://dont.stanford.edu/

Servicemembers Legal Defense Network. (2004). Don't ask, don't tell: Lesbian & gay military resources. Retrieved May 9, 2005, from http://www.sldn.org

University of California Santa Barbara Center for the Study of Sexual Minorities in the Military. (2005). Retrieved May 9, 2005, from http://www.gaymilitary.ucsb.edu

After 23 years and four children together, Jehan Agrama and Dwora Fried got married in San Francisco on March 8, 2004.

SOURCE: © Jehan Arama.

11

Same-Sex Marriage in Cultural and Historical Context

A Guide for Beginning Journalists

Sine Anahita

❖ ❖ ❖

With increased media coverage about same-sex marriage in the United States, it is understandable that young journalists and future journalists might think that the issue is a new one. However, discussion about same-sex marriage is not really *that* new, as historical evidence documents the existence of same-sex marriage and other forms of same-sex partnership throughout Western history. For example, historians note that clergy performed church-sanctioned same-sex commitment ceremonies in pre-modern Europe (Boswell, 1994). Contemporary debates about same-sex marriage are really political debates about gender and sexuality and who should be allowed social and legal sanction for their relationships (Schwartz & Rutter,

1998). This chapter will put same-sex marriage in the United States into cultural and historical context. Although the issue of same-sex marriage is hardly new, it is true that the noise level of this contentious debate seems to have jumped recently.

❖ THE ISSUE OF SAME-SEX MARRIAGE

No matter what anyone says about marriage, the truth of the matter is this: The institution of marriage has been constantly changing (Graff, 1999). If you look only at Western history, ignoring all other cultures, the way marriage has been defined, who has been allowed to marry, and the reasons for marriage itself have been in constant flux. Today it is fashionable to say that traditional marriage has always been between one man and one woman, and even that marriage represents the foundation of Western civilization. These claims are patently wrong. The truth is that the latest debate about who should be allowed to marry legally, the question in this case being about same-sex couples, represents a continuation of discussions about marriage that began thousands of years ago.

It is true that in the last decade, the shouting match over marriage seems to have gotten louder. Since the 1990s, thousands of same-sex couples have pressed for the legal right to marry in the United States and in other nations, and opponents to the expansion of legal marriage rights to include same-sex partners have been equally vocal. Currently, the only state in the United States that allows same-sex couples to marry legally is Massachusetts (Gay & Lesbian Advocates & Defenders, 2004), and this right can still be overturned by a constitutional amendment. Indeed, Massachusetts voters will vote on a constitutional amendment in 2006. Vermont allows a parallel institution for same-sex couples—the civil union—and Connecticut will begin allowing civil unions in the fall of 2005. Civil unions offer state-level, marriagelike benefits to same-sex couples. There are also several pending sets of court decisions that may legalize same-sex marriage within the next few months in other states. In particular, California, New York, and Washington are states to watch. In these states, the pending lawsuits are similar to the one that legalized same-sex marriage in Massachusetts. Thus it is likely that a court decision striking down a state law forbidding same-sex marriage in any of these three states will also result in a guarantee of marriage rights for lesbian and gay couples. Meanwhile, as of May 2005, voters in 18 states have passed measures to ban same-sex marriages in their state through constitutional amendments (Peterson, 2005). In short, same-sex marriage is a political "hot button" issue, and impending court decisions and activism on all sides of the issue guarantee that it will be a hot one for years to come. This chapter will provide future journalists with an understanding of the cultural context surrounding the issue of same-sex marriage.

One question you may ask is this: Why would lesbian or gay people want to get married? The answer is that they want to marry for the same reasons straight couples want to marry (Graff, 1999). They want to solemnize their love and commitment in a public ceremony shared with friends and family. They want to feel they are a normative part of a couple-oriented society. They marry to establish kinship, family, and community (Stiers, 1999). Some want to raise children within a legally sanctioned and committed family unit. Aside from these reasons to marry, there are pragmatic and logistical reasons. For example, federal law awards 1,138 rights and protections to married couples that it denies to nonmarried individuals (Gay and Lesbian Advocates and Defenders, 2004). In most states, real estate property, bank accounts, household furnishings, even pets automatically pass from one spouse to the other upon the death of one member of a couple in the absence of a will. Life insurance, health insurance, property insurance—all of these benefits are unquestioningly granted to legally married spouses. Children born to one spouse are assumed to belong to the other spouse as well, without the nonbirthing parent having to file paperwork, such as adoption papers, to be considered a legitimate parent. The list of practical marriage benefits goes on and on, but as of this writing, same-sex couples are denied accessibility to any of these benefits except in Massachusetts—and then only state benefits of marriage apply, and none that are federally based. Thus in addition to the ideals of love, commitment, family, and community, lesbians and gay men also want to marry for the pragmatic and mundane reasons straight folks marry (Stiers, 1999).

Suppose a legislator has just proposed a new law banning same-sex marriage or that a lesbian or gay couple has just returned from Canada or Denmark, where same-sex marriages are legally performed, and is now demanding that your state recognize the marriage as legal? In what context should such a story be placed? One important thing to think about is how to avoid taking a polarized journalistic approach that sets up an overly simplified dichotomy or that analyzes the issue only in terms of the conflict involved (Colbert, 2003; O'Donnell, 2004). In other words, develop ways to frame the issue of same-sex marriages in new and unique ways. Same-sex marriages do not necessarily need to be juxtaposed with heterosexual unions. Although it is true that some particular elements of same-sex marriage may be different from those found in heterosexual unions, there are many more similarities than differences. Marriage is marriage, after all. With that being said, report about the issue using sources that represent a myriad of positions and avoid printing or broadcasting only positive or negative responses. Seek a strategic balance by citing sources who are authentic authorities on alternative sides of the issue but who are asked the same types of questions about the same issue (O'Donnell, 2004). Journalists who avoid framing the issue of same-sex marriage as a simplified dichotomy will help avoid solidifying the negative and problematic stereotypes that have plagued lesbian and gay communities for decades. Professional journalists can play a vital role in helping to further the cause of equality for lesbians and gay men through their writing (Jensen, 1996).

Same-Sex Marriage in Historical Context

Same-sex relationships that included the setting up of a common household in the manner of marriage have been documented throughout history. In fact, the institutionalization of same-sex unions through special ceremonies attended by friends, family members, and governmental and religious functionaries has been documented in multiple cultures, both Western and non-Western. Historians of marriage and family have explored documents that demonstrate the prevalence of institutionalized same-sex unions in ancient Greece, old Rome, early modern Japan, dynastic China, some pre-Columbian American Indian nations, 20th-century African groups, indigenous cultures in what is now Russia, and many other regions of the world (Boswell, 1994). From reading the accounts of the widespread institutionalization of same-sex relationships, it becomes apparent that our contemporary discussion about same-sex marriage is really not all that new. What *is* new is the claim that marriage has *always* been defined as an exclusive union between a man and a woman. In this regard, opponents of same-sex marriage are not only wrong but are also rewriting history by their denial of a rich store of verifiable historical evidence.

This chapter is not about ancient marriage customs, however. Instead, it is about setting a context for the contemporary discussion about same-sex marriage for journalism students. This story will thus begin in the not-too-distant past, in the 1770s. During this era, an upper-class Irish female couple eloped and established a household in rural Wales that thrived for over 50 years, lasting until one of the partners died (Grumbach, 1989). What might surprise observers today is that the local newspaper in the women's region described them as romantic partners, with no hint of perversity. That is because from the period of the Renaissance until the late 19th century, both men and women enjoyed participation in a normative social institution that has nearly vanished today, that of romantic friendship (D'Emilio & Freedman, 1988). Romantic friends established intense same-sex relationships that included the exchange of passionate love letters, hugging and kissing, even sharing a bed, and at least some degree of physical intimacy. However, only men and upper-class women were usually financially able to establish households with their romantic friend. Perhaps the most important point to be made about romantic friendships in terms of today's debates about same-sex marriage is the fact that romantic friendships were considered completely normal, even desirable in many ways. Far from being seen as weird or perverted, same-sex passionate relationships in which the partners were able to establish a common household were held to be an ideal (Faderman, 1981).

In the United States, the historical record of the 1800s is particularly rich in description of same-sex unions. Among educated women in the upper classes in the progressive northeast United States, monogamous, marriagelike unions were commonplace and known as "Boston marriages" (Faderman, 1981). Whether most such relationships included sexual intimacy is unknown, although surviving letters and diaries often hint at some degree of sexual activity. However, during the early to mid-1800s, when Boston marriages were popular, the concept of sexual passion was usually divorced from the concept of courtship and marriage. Sexual passion was not usually seen as important, or as problematic, in marriage (D'Emilio & Freedman, 1988). Thus, unlike in contemporary relationships, participants in a Boston marriage may or may not have considered genital activity to be an important element in their relationship.

In the 1800s, many women and some men took the social role of the other sex, "passing" so effectively that they were able to obtain legal marriage licenses and marry their beloved (D'Emilio & Freedman, 1988). A handful of historical cases that have come to light became "cases" only when the social deception became publicly known and discussed in local newspapers on the death of the passing partner. There is no doubt that there were many more same-sex marriages that were not similarly discovered by society, and it is probable that the other partner not only knew the "true" sex of his or her beloved but was actively complicit in the social deception.

Towards the latter part of the 19th and early 20th centuries, a new intellectual current became established that developed new ideas about individuals' interior landscapes and about sexuality in general. Known as *sexology*, the new field theorized that the quest for sexual satisfaction was a primary drive analogous to hunger or thirst. As common as this thinking is today, it was novel at the time, and suddenly the thought that romantic friends might be having sex with each other made romantic friendships suspect in the minds of many who were increasingly uneasy with the social changes being wrought. Sexologists proposed a new theory to explain the persistence of same-sex desire—"congenital inversion"—which posited that some individuals were born homosexual as a result of natural causes beyond their control and that if not carefully controlled by society, "congenital inverts" would seek to recruit others into their deviant and sick lifestyle. Paradoxically, congenital inversion theory worked both to free and to constrain those with same-sex desires. On the one hand, congenital inversion theory freed women and men to play out a homosexual identity by reasoning that although they were sick individuals, it was biologically inevitable for them to engage in homosexual behavior. On the other hand, congenital inversion theory constrained people who desired to maintain a relationship with someone of their own sex. By the early 20th century, behaviors and relationships that would have enjoyed the status of normalcy in earlier decades and centuries were now linked with sexuality, and were described as sick, weird, and even pathetic (Faderman, 1981).

In the 20th century, for the first time in history, it became acceptable for women of nearly all social classes and ethnicities to hold paying jobs outside of their homes. This shift in women's economic status had profound effects on the formation of households that were autonomous from families of origin (Faderman, 1992). Along with the shift toward increasing autonomy and economic independence for individuals came another profound demographic shift: the rural-to-urban migration. All over the United States in the early to mid-20th century, young people flocked to the swelling urban centers to take jobs. World War I and World War II also drew young people with same-sex desires away from their home communities and into cities (D'Emilio, 1983). These shifts greatly expanded the number of same-sex partnerships by making it economically feasible for partners to establish a household and to enter into marriagelike relationships free from the traditional constraints of their families and rural communities. Urban areas became home to thousands of same-sex couples, and many lesbian and gay subcultures flourished in cities' marginalized neighborhoods (D'Emilio, 1983). In the 1920s, for example, African-American lesbians discovered a remarkable degree of tolerance of their couple relationships in New York's Harlem. Faderman (1992) documents many same-sex African-American couples who married each other in elaborate wedding ceremonies. In many cases, the couple obtained a legal marriage license by having one member of the couple use a masculine first name or by having a gay man act as a surrogate "groom" for the application process. Local newspapers in the early part of the 20th century documented many working-class female couples who were legally married (D'Emilio, 1983). Also, throughout the early to mid-20th century, British newspapers ran articles of curiosity about the discovery of passing women that included a stable marriage-like relationship and, often, the joint raising of children (Oram & Turnbull, 2001).

By the 1950s, major cities were home to thriving, though secretive, gay and lesbian subcultures that included couples who organized their households and relationships in marriagelike ways. By the mid-1960s, activism in the gay and lesbian urban communities resulted in a remarkable change of tone in major urban newspapers' coverage about these communities (Faderman, 1992). The *New York Times* and the *San Francisco Chronicle* were instrumental in shifting the tone of news reporting away from derogatory terms toward more neutral and objective reporting of events pertaining to gay men and lesbians. In 1969, a growing sense of militance exploded in a 2-day riot in Greenwich Village (D'Emilio, 1983). However, newspapers failed to report on its significance at the time (Faderman, 1992), although the Stonewall Revolt, as it is commonly referred to today, is hailed as a decisive moment in the history of the struggle for lesbian, gay, bisexual, and transgender liberation.

In the years just after the Stonewall Revolt, gay men and lesbians engaged in militant tactics that contrasted sharply with previous decades of accommodation to the heterosexual status quo. Ironically, some of these tactics involved agitating to open one of the most conservative and conventional institutions of the state—civil marriage—to lesbian and gay couples (Chambers, 2000). For example, in the early 1970s, two African-American lesbians in Milwaukee staged a vociferous campaign for a marriage license, and although they ultimately were denied the right to marry legally, they nonetheless wed in a large Eastern Orthodox Catholic church wedding ceremony that garnered widespread media attention (Faderman, 1992). Nationally, same-sex couples were staging weddings in such large numbers that *The Advocate,* a gay magazine, noted it amounted to a marriage boom (Chambers, 2000). In the early 1970s, with activists' hopes riding high after the Stonewall Revolt, a handful of couples filed lawsuits challenging their states' refusal to issue them a legal license to marry. One gay couple brought their suit in Minnesota in 1970–1971. Hailed as one of the first same-sex couples to publicly attempt to obtain legal civil marriage in the modern era, the couple was not only featured in the gay and lesbian press but also in the widely popular *Look* magazine as part of a feature on the American family (Chambers, 2000).

Although none of the lesbian and gay couples in the 1970s were ultimately successful in challenging their states' laws regarding their right to a civil marriage, their attempts at obtaining legitimacy for their relationships heralded the multiple shifts family and marriage laws would take in the near future. Their activism also had unanticipated results. Many high-profile national organizations and well-known activists questioned the validity of a strategy to expand marriage to same-sex couples, arguing that marriage was an archaic and exploitative institution (Chambers, 2000; Graff, 1999). Many refused to support marriage initiatives, reasoning that other issues were much more urgent, such as working to decriminalize gay sex acts, eliminating police harassment, and overturning the laws sanctioning employment discrimination. High-profile national organizations, including the ACLU, initially refused to help litigation efforts. They justified their decision on what turned out to be legitimate fears that the 1970s' political climate would result in court defeats that would produce legal precedents that would hobble the movement for decades to come (Chambers, 2000).

The AIDS epidemic in the 1980s, coupled with the political retrenchment necessary for gay men and lesbians to survive the Reagan-Bush era, allowed conventionalism to sweep over gay and lesbian communities (Faderman, 1992). The new conventionalism resulted in a surge in the number of same-sex wedding ceremonies. Many liberal Protestant churches opened their doors to same-sex commitment ceremonies (Chambers, 2000), gay and lesbian couples married in droves. In fact, at the 1987 March on Washington, more than a thousand couples got married in a mass wedding ceremony held at the National Cathedral (Chambers, 2000). Most national gay and lesbian organizations actively sought to discourage the quest for legal marriage, continuing to justify their decisions on the importance of preventing paralyzing court precedents. Others reasoned that working to expand marriage rights would squander movement and organizational resources and would end up only supporting what many criticized as an inherently conservative, patriarchal, and exploitative institution (Chambers, 2000).

Contemporary Context for Same-Sex Marriage

In the 1990s, many legal strategies were devised and popularized by activist attorneys to protect same-sex relationships in the absence of legal civil marriage, such as wills, durable powers of attorney, relationship contracts, and the like (Ettelbrick, 1991). The concept of domestic partnership, which allows same-sex and nonmarried heterosexual couples limited marriagelike benefits, such as being able to purchase health insurance for a domestic partner, began to take root as universities, private employers, and a few municipalities worked to expand employment rights for their gay and lesbian workers. Many in the gay and lesbian community thirsted to be considered legitimate families, however (Andrews, 1995), believing the right to marry their partner to be an individual right (Chasin, 2000) and a matter of simple justice (Graff, 1999). Thus, in spite of the reticence and official discouragement expressed by national lesbian and gay organizations and the ACLU, individual couples in several states located attorneys willing to represent them in lawsuits seeking the legal right to civil marriage (Chambers, 2000). In 1990, a lawsuit filed against the state of Hawaii reshaped the national discussion about same-sex marriage. Known as *Baehr v. Levin*, the lawsuit involved three couples who were denied marriage licenses in Hawaii. The lawsuit's arguments claimed that denying the plaintiffs marriage licenses amounted to discrimination based on their sex (Fassin, 2001). Although the national ACLU and the Lambda Legal Defense and Education Fund both refused to assist the couples involved in the case, they continued their quest, working with two activist attorneys. The suit took more than 5 years to come to a conclusive end, but finally in 1996 the Hawaii State Supreme Court ruled that denying a marriage license to gay and lesbian couples amounted to illegal discrimination based on sex (Schwartz & Rutter, 1998).

Repercussions from the *Baehr v. Levin* decision reverberated throughout the country. Gay and lesbian couples across the nation relished the legal victory; conservative organizations were galvanized into action. As a result, state legislatures, including Hawaii's, passed statutes banning same-sex marriage. Lambda and the ACLU grudgingly shifted their public stance on the marriage issue and began to create a national marriage strategy (Chambers, 2000). Even though the Hawaii decision, and similar lawsuits filed in Alaska and other states, ultimately resulted in legislation banning same-sex marriage, the *Baehr* suit brought national and international attention to the issue of same-sex marriage (Graff, 1999). Consequently, by the mid-1990s, the issue of marriage overshadowed nearly all other issues related to gay and lesbian Americans (Chambers, 2000).

In Vermont, a case similar to the one filed in Hawaii and other states had a markedly different outcome. Relying on an old Vermont law that had been upheld by state courts as providing protection against all manner of discrimination, three Vermont couples, along with a bevy of national and local activist organizations, filed suit when the couples were denied marriage licenses (Chambers, 2000). In 1999, the Vermont Supreme Court unanimously decided that prohibiting same-sex couples from marrying was unconstitutional. However, in an acknowledgment of the furor that would soon erupt over the ruling, the court declared that although the state must extend all of the benefits of civil marriage to same-sex couples, it might do so in an alternative manner. Early in 2000, the state signed into law a statute outlining civil unions, a form of domestic partnership open only to same-sex couples, which provides all of the state benefits of marriage.

However, by the late 1990s, a conservative backlash pervaded state and federal politics, and the same-sex marriage issue was successfully exploited as a political issue (Schwartz & Rutter, 1998). Not only were restrictive laws passed in more than half of the states, but the Defense of Marriage Act (DoMA) passed Congress in 1996 and was signed into law by President Bill Clinton. DoMA has two provisions: First, it decrees that states are under no obligation to recognize a same-sex marriage performed in another state. Second, it stipulates that federal regulations relating to married people shall be construed as applicable only to heterosexual marriage (Chambers, 2000). Although many legal theorists believe that DoMA will ultimately be found unconstitutional, the bill garnered a lot of political and popular support in the mid-1990s. DoMA was seen as a politically expedient tool that worked to deflect political criticism from the Democratic Party, many of whose politicians publicly supported it (Schwartz & Rutter, 1998). Currently, there are only a handful of lawsuits pending that challenge DoMA. This is because DoMA and the legal history of the United States make the states responsible for defining who is eligible to marry, and thus most activism both for and against same-sex marriage has been waged at the state level.

There are three basic forms of state-based legislation: amendment to the state constitution, marriage statutes, and nonbinding resolutions (Peterson, 2004). Marriage statutes are generally of three types: They may prohibit same-sex marriage altogether, bolster already existing anti–same-sex marriage laws, or ban marriagelike benefits from applying to same-sex couples. The third form of legislation against same-sex marriage is nonbinding resolutions. These resolutions typically urge Congress to pass a federal constitutional amendment prohibiting same-sex marriage. Twenty states have introduced nonbinding resolutions; two states have passed such resolutions, and legislation is pending in other states.

In the latter part of 2004, three states emerged as especially significant in the debate over same-sex marriage: Massachusetts, California, and Oregon. The events that have played out in these states are having a ripple effect across the nation. We can expect activists on all sides of the marriage issue to attempt to deal with the fallout from decisions in these three states for the next several years.

In May 2004, Massachusetts became the first state to recognize same-sex marriage when its Supreme Judicial Court legalized the practice (Peterson, 2004). However, both the current governor, Mitt Romney, and the state's attorney general, Thomas Reilly, are hostile to the court's ruling and have allied with radical right organizations to prevent its full implementation. They are using a 1913 Massachusetts law that prohibits out-of-state couples from being married in the state if their marriage would not be legal in their home state as a strategy to prevent same-sex marriage from spreading beyond their state borders (Peterson, 2004). Although eight couples have filed a lawsuit to prevent the state's enforcement of the law, as of this writing, the outcomes of both the court ruling and the actions being taken by the governor and attorney general are not yet clear. What *is* clear, however, is that more than 6,000 same-sex couples legally married in Massachusetts in the new law's first year. The Massachusetts court ruling also has had significant ripple effects in other states, as conservatives recognize that their state laws banning same-sex marriage may be similarly vulnerable in their own courts (Silverman, 2004b). Because legal theorists believe that state constitutional amendments are a more impervious barrier to same-sex marriage rights, there has been a virtual stampede as state legislators and citizens' initiatives hurriedly placed proposed state constitutional amendments before voters in 2004. In Missouri, voters were in such a hurry to pass a state constitutional amendment banning same-sex marriage that they held a special election in August in spite of Republican worries that not having the issue on the November ballot would keep conservative voters home from the polls (Corrigan, 2004). The constitutional amendment passed by a wide margin, although opponents of the amendment outspent proponents by nearly 20 to 1 (Silverman, 2004b).

In 2004, California also was a significant player in the debate about same-sex marriage. Early in the year, a renegade San Francisco mayor, Gavin Newsom, ordered the city clerk to issue legal marriage licenses to same-sex couples. More than 4000 same-sex couples obtained licenses and married before a court injunction ordered a cessation. Then, in August 2004, the California Supreme Court nullified the 4,037 same-sex marriages that had been performed, ruling that only the court itself had the power to interpret marriage rights and that the mayor had usurped its power by granting the right to marry to same-sex couples. Although legal theorists believe that the court's decision is only a procedural ruling that will have no significant long-term effect on the right of same-sex couples eventually to marry (Silverman, 2004a), the disappointment and dismay felt by the gay and lesbian couples whose marriages had been declared void were palpable as photos of grieving couples splashed across major newspapers across the nation. As of mid-2005, California's legislature is poised to vote on a bill to extend marriage rights to same-sex couples (Peterson, 2005).

Because state statutes in Oregon do not define marriage as being exclusively for other-sex couples, in March 2004 the chief counsel for the Oregon Legislature declared it would be unconstitutional for Multnomah County commissioners to withhold legal marriage licenses from same-sex couples (Moorehouse, 2004). Within hours of the decision's announcement, approximately 3000 gay and lesbian couples obtained legal marriage licenses and married (McDonnell, 2004). But their euphoria was short-lived, as a circuit court decision just a month later, in April, ordered the county commissioners to cease issuing marriage licenses to same-sex couples (Peterson, 2004). Although a lower court ruling stated the marriages already performed were valid, and a state Court of Appeals upheld that decision, the ruling has been stayed until the Oregon Supreme Court issues a ruling in the matter. The state Supreme Court scheduled a hearing for November 17, 2004. However, conservatives in Oregon placed a proposed constitutional amendment banning same-sex marriage on the ballot for November 2, and it passed with just a 15% margin (Silverman, 2004b; McDonnell, 2004). The proposed constitutional amendment was a citizen's initiative, thereby effectively bypassing the legislature (Peterson, 2004). In mid-2005, Oregon's Supreme Court nullified the marriages that had been performed (Peterson, 2005).

Currently, 39 of the 50 states have laws that are modeled after the federal DoMA, which allows them to refuse to recognize same-sex marriages that are legally performed in another state. Four of these states had laws barring same-sex marriage that predated DoMA (Peterson, 2004). Five states adopted legislation in 2004 that prohibits same-sex marriage, prohibits marriagelike benefits for same-sex couples, or tightens previous laws against same-sex marriage. These states are New Hampshire, Ohio, Oklahoma, Utah, and Virginia. Eleven states debated such laws in 2004 but failed to pass them. Four states (Hawaii, Arkansas, Nevada, and Nebraska) had already amended their state constitutions in recent years to ban same-sex marriage. During the 2004 election season, 11 states passed state constitutional amendments banning same-sex marriage (Silverman, 2004b; Peterson, 2004). These states are Arkansas, Georgia, Kentucky, Michigan, Mississippi, Montana, North Dakota, Ohio, Oklahoma, Oregon, and Utah (McDonnell, 2004). Kansas voters passed a constitutional amendment after the November 2004 election (Peterson, 2005).

It would be a mistake, however, to assume that all proposed constitutional amendments and other initiatives opposed to same-sex marriage are successful. For example, numerous state legislatures have attempted to pass constitutional amendments, resolutions calling for a federal marriage amendment, or state statutes banning same-sex marriage but have either failed to muster enough political support or have not yet passed them. As of this writing, these states are Alabama, Arizona, Colorado, Delaware, Idaho, Iowa, Kansas, Maine, Minnesota,

North Carolina, Rhode Island, South Carolina, Vermont, Washington, and Wisconsin (Peterson, 2004). Even though Hawaii did pass a constitutional amendment against same-sex marriage, at the same time, it passed a law that allows for the registration of domestic partnerships that carries limited, state-level, marriagelike benefits. Seven states have passed laws instituting similar registry systems for same-sex domestic partnerships (Peterson, 2005). In addition, even though constitutional amendments and other legislation may be pending, there continue to be important and successful court challenges to the initiatives. As of this writing, for example, there are more than 20 lawsuits in 11 states that challenge state bans on same-sex marriage, and state courts are going to be called on to rule about the constitutionality of denying their lesbian and gay citizens equal rights to marry (Peterson, 2004).

Public Opinion About Same-Sex Marriage

At this point, journalism students might well wonder what the public really thinks about the issue of same-sex marriage. After all, you may be writing about this issue in the very near future. As the debate continues, you may want to know what ordinary folks think. Do common citizens really care if the nice lesbian couple next door is legally married? Does it matter to most parents if their beloved gay son is unable to marry his partner? Do most lesbian and gay couples want the right to marry? Just how important is the issue of same-sex marriage to most people? What do ordinary folks really think?

As you might guess, the results of polls about same-sex marriage rights vary according to the wording of the questions on the poll (Silverman, 2004b). If, for example, a poll asks respondents if they believe there should be basic rights for gay and lesbian partners, including the right to marry legally, the majority of those polled say yes, they support same-sex marriage. However, ask people a similar question in a different way—for example, whether only heterosexuals should be allowed to marry—and the majority also answer yes. Pollsters, of course, have understood for decades that they can manipulate the outcome of public opinion polls by tweaking the wording of questions, so this should come as no surprise. The wording of the first question uses an emotionally laden term, *basic rights*, that enjoys widespread popular support. Few Americans find it publicly acceptable to admit to a pollster that they are against anyone having "basic rights."

The Gallup Poll Organization has asked about people's opinions on same-sex civil unions for nearly a decade, with somewhat surprising results. Beginning in 1996, the organization asked whether people supported or opposed allowing homosexual couples the right to form civil unions that carried some limited marriagelike benefits. Despite the use of the emotionally laden term *homosexual*, the latest polls reveal that nearly half of Americans support civil unions and marriagelike benefits for same-sex couples (49%). This is a much higher figure than a decade ago, when fewer than one third of those surveyed were in support (28%), and illustrates the increasing social acceptance of the concept. It is interesting that age seems to have a marked effect on people's acceptance of same-sex unions. For example, a Gallup Poll conducted in 2003 discovered that more than two thirds (67%) of those who are between the ages of 18 and 29 say that allowing same-sex unions will either have no harmful effects on society or might even improve it. The age differences discovered in this particular survey might prove to be especially important as the older people who are more opposed to same-sex marriage are superseded by these younger people who are less opposed.

Among gay and lesbian people, 9 out of 10 prefer to live in a couple relationship (Schwartz & Rutter, 1998). Also, in spite of the decades-long debate within the gay and lesbian community about the desirability of pursuing marriage as a national movement strategy, the vast majority of gay men and lesbians would obtain a legal marriage if they were allowed to do so (Schwartz & Rutter, 1998). Even among those in the lesbian and gay community who personally choose not to marry, or who believe that marriage should not be an important political strategy for the movement, most also believe the state should not be allowed to prohibit same-sex marriage (Schwartz & Rutter, 1998).

The *Boston Globe* conducted a unique survey among same-sex couples in May 2004 when it sent reporters out to 11 cities where the first marriage licenses were being issued to same-sex couples in Massachusetts. Of the 752 couples interviewed, fully two thirds were women (Greenberger, 2004), illustrating that in Massachusetts, at least, lesbians were much more likely to marry in the early days of legal same-sex marriage than gay men were. Some other interesting demographic information that arose from the *Globe* survey was that the median age of the couples interviewed was 43 and that half of the couples had been partners for a decade or more. In addition, a third of the couples stated that they were raising children together. The longevity of the relationships, the shared raising of children, as well as the age of the couples who were marrying, tell a story of commitment, maturity, and responsibility that contrasts sharply with the negative stereotypes portrayed by those opposed to same-sex marriage.

An important issue for journalism students to consider is the role that advertising plays in shaping coverage of contentious issues in media that depend on advertising dollars. There have been significant changes in the ways that advertising has viewed gay men and lesbians, as marketers have taken note of the possibilities inherent in marketing to a consumer group that has more disposable income than the majority of Americans (Atkinson, 2003). In the past several years, advertisers have been featuring lesbian and gay themes. Several trend-setting newspapers, most notably the *New York Times,* now feature not only gay- and lesbian-themed advertising but also routinely publish same-sex wedding announcements (Society of Professional Journalists, 2002).

Many undergraduate students are unclear on the facts about same-sex marriage. Some falsely assume that same-sex marriage is legal in both Vermont and Hawaii, and there is little understanding about the difference between Vermont's civil union statute and the real, tangible benefits accorded to legal marriage in other states. Some do not understand the scary implications of the power of states to prohibit who may marry and share in the tangible benefits of marriage. Indeed, few students have ever contemplated the nature of marriage, or its history, or the fact that our current concept of marriage is peculiarly located within our own cultural milieu.

It is completely understandable that undergraduate students, including journalism students, may be generally quite puzzled about same-sex marriage. After all, it seems that court decisions and legislation are constantly destabilizing state marriage laws, making same-sex marriage legal in one state for a few days only to have another state court make it illegal or reversing the lower court's decision. The fact that all states with ballot initiatives banning same-sex marriage in the 2004 elections passed them seems to demonstrate a virtual mandate against any legal recognition of same-sex unions. Still, 60% of those surveyed in exit polls reported that they support civil unions for same-sex couples (Breslow & Malesky, 2004). The issue of same-sex marriage seems be in a constant state of flux. This general state of unrest, this constant shifting of the parameters about same-sex marriage, makes this era very exciting, but it also makes the job of journalists harder, as the current state of same-sex marriage will have to be researched nearly every time a story about the issue is written. Because marriage rights are defined by the states and because there is as yet no federal Constitutional amendment defining marriage, we will continue to see debates about the issue being played out state by state for the next few years (Schwartz & Rutter, 1998). However, no one can deny that social acceptance for gay and lesbian people has steadily increased throughout the last century. Even President George W. Bush, who was on record as being hostile to gay and lesbian political interests throughout his first term, gave his guarded support for same-sex civil unions and civil rights for gay men and lesbians in the waning days of the 2004 election (Breslow & Malesky, 2004). Just as it took a U.S. Supreme Court decision in the 1960s to nullify state laws prohibiting interracial marriage, it may take a similar Supreme Court decision to overturn state laws prohibiting same-sex marriage. Journalists have a unique role to play in the discussions about same-sex marriage and can play an important, liberating role (Jensen, 1996) through the choices they make in terms of style, tone, and even whom they choose to interview.

❖ DISCUSSION QUESTIONS

1. Does your local newspaper routinely publish wedding announcements of same-sex couples? If so, what do you notice about the tone of the announcements? Are there usually pictures of the couple? What might the publishing of such announcements mean for the couples involved, their friends and families, and your community? If your paper does not publish such announcements, what reasons does it give for not doing so?

2. Choose a story about same-sex marriage that has appeared in a local or regional newspaper, and analyze it using some of the ideas in this chapter. What connections does the author of the story make to the historical and cultural context of same-sex marriage? What tone does the article take? How would you rewrite the article, and why would you make those changes?

3. Suppose that you have been assigned to write a story about same-sex marriage in your state. What is the legal status of same-sex marriage in your state? How does it contrast with neighboring states? With Vermont, Massachusetts, and Oregon? What legislation or court cases are pending, and how might they affect the issue of same-sex marriage in your state?

❖ HOMEWORK ASSIGNMENTS

1. Interview a same-sex couple and an other-sex couple, both of whom plan to marry, and then write a story about your talks with them. Why do they want to marry? What similarities are there between the two couples' reasons for marrying? What kinds of wedding ceremonies do each plan to have? How can you write about the experiences of these two couples so that you avoid polarizing stereotypes?

2. What quirky and interesting angle might you take for a story about same-sex marriage? How can you write about the issue in a novel and unpredictable way? Some suggestions: interview a county clerk who issues marriage licenses, a veterinarian who has lesbian or gay clients, or a car salesperson. What kinds of everyday experiences have they had that illuminate the issue of same-sex marriage?

❖ REFERENCES

Andrews, K. (1995). Ancient affections: Gays, lesbians, and family status. In K. Arnup (Ed.), *Lesbian parenting: Living with pride and prejudice* (pp. 358–377). Charlottetown, P.E.I.: Gynergy Books.

Atkinson, C. (2003). Marketers warm up to gay audience. *Advertising Age, 74*(31), 4–5.

Boswell, J. (1994). *Same-sex unions in premodern Europe.* New York: Villard Books.

Breslow, P., & Malesky, R. (Producers). (2004, November 6). Gay marriage and civil unions. *Weekend Edition* [Radio broadcast]. Washington, DC: National Public Radio.

Chambers, D. L. (2000). Couples: Marriage, civil union, and domestic partnership. In J. D'Emilio, W. B. Turner, & U. Vaid (Eds.), *Creating change: Sexuality, public policy, and civil rights* (pp. 281–304). New York: St. Martin's Press.

Chasin, A. (2000). *Selling out: The gay and lesbian movement goes to market.* New York: Palgrave.

Colbert, J. (2003). Women, gender, and the media: A look at representation, coverage, and workplace issues. In F. Cropp, C. M. Frisby, & D. Mills (Eds.), *Journalism across cultures* (pp. 23–38). Ames: Iowa State University Press.

Corrigan, D. (2004). Gay marriage vote makes August ballot. *St. Louis Journalism Review, 34*(268), 23.

D'Emilio, J. (1983). *Sexual politics, sexual communities: The making of a homosexual minority in the United States, 1940-1970.* Chicago: University of Chicago Press.

D'Emilio, J., & Freedman, E. B. (1988). *Intimate matters: A history of sexuality in America.* New York: Harper & Row.

Ettelbrick, P. L. (1991). Legal protections for lesbians. In B. Sang, J. Warshow, & A. J. Smith (Eds.), *Lesbians at midlife: The creative transition* (pp. 258–264). San Francisco: Spinsters Book.

Faderman, L. (1981). *Surpassing the love of men: Romantic friendship and love between women from the Renaissance to the present.* New York: William Morrow.

Faderman, L. (1992). *Odd girls and twilight lovers: A history of lesbian life in twentieth-century America.* New York: Penguin.

Fassin, E. (2001). Same sex, different politics: "Gay marriage" debates in France and the United States. *Public Culture, 13*(2), 215–232.

Gay and Lesbian Advocates and Defenders. (2004). Marriage equality. Retrieved August 20, 2004, from http://www.glad.org/marriage/

Graff, E. J. (1999). *What is marriage for? The strange social history of our most intimate institution.* Boston: Beacon Press.

Greenberger, S. (2004, May 18). Survey finds women in majority. Retrieved August 20, 2004, from the *Boston Globe* Web site: http://www.boston.com/news/local/articles/2004/05/18/survey_finds_women_in_majority/

Grumbach, D. (1989). *The ladies.* New York: Random House.

Jensen, R. (1996). The politics and ethics of lesbian and gay "wedding" announcements in newspapers. *Howard Journal of Communications, 7*(1), 13–28.

McDonnell, E. (Executive Producer). (2004, November 3). Eleven states vote to ban same-sex marriage. *Morning Edition* [Radio broadcast]. Washington, DC: National Public Radio.

Moorehouse, C. (2004, March 17). Same-sex marriage gets real at Portland campus. Retrieved August 20, 2004, from the CNN.com Web site: http://www.cnn.com/2004/ALLPOLITICS/03/12/pcc/

O'Donnell, M. (2004). Going to the chapel: Same sex marriage and competing narratives of intimate citizenship. *Pacific Journalism Review, 10*(1), 9–28.

Oram, A., & Turnbull, A. (2001). *The lesbian history sourcebook: Love and sex between women in Britain from 1780 to 1970.* New York: Routledge.

Peterson, K. (2004, November 3). 50-state rundown on gay marriage laws. Retrieved May 9, 2005, from the Stateline.org Web site: http://www.stateline.org/live/ViewPage.action?siteNodeId=136&languageId=1&contentId=15576

Peterson, K. (2005, May 13). Same-sex unions—A constitutional race. Retrieved May 17, 2005, from the Stateline.org Web site: http://www.stateline.org/live/ViewPage.action?siteNodeId=137&languageId=1&contentId=20695

Schwartz, P., & Rutter, V. (1998). *The gender of sexuality.* Thousand Oaks, CA: Pine Forge Press.

Silverman, A. (Senior Producer). (2004a, August 13). Legal thinking behind gay marriage annulments. *All Things Considered* [Radio broadcast]. Washington, DC: National Public Radio.

Silverman, A. (Senior Producer). (2004b, August 4). Statehouse legislators work to ban gay marriage. *All Things Considered* [Radio broadcast]. Washington, DC: National Public Radio.

Society of Professional Journalists. (2002). NY Times announces gay unions in Sunday Section. *Quill, 90*(8), 39.

Stiers, G. (1999). *From this day forward: Commitment, marriage, and family in lesbian and gay relationships.* New York: St. Martin's Press.

❖ ADDITIONAL RESOURCES

Arnup, K. (1995). Living in the margins: Lesbian families and the law. In K. Arnup (Ed.), *Lesbian parenting: Living with pride and prejudice* (pp. 378–398). Charlottestown, PEI: Gynergy Books.

Axel-Lute, P. (2005). Same-sex marriage: A selective bibliography of the legal literature. Retrieved May 9, 2005, from http://law-library.rutgers .edu/SSM.html (Published by the Rutgers Law Library, this site contains citations of court cases and legislative activity in the United States [provided state by state] and other nations. An invaluable resource for researching the history of particular law cases in individual states. This site also contains an exhaustive list of books, Web sites, and scholarly articles on all sides of the debate.)

Equal marriage for same-sex couples. (2005). Equal marriage for same-sex couples: Queer gay marriage equality. Retrieved May 9, 2005, from http:// www.samesexmarriage.ca/ (This is a good site for information about Canada's same-sex marriage debate. Canadian activists have been pressuring provinces for the right to marry, and so far, they have had more success than activists in the United States. At least seven Canadian provinces allow same-sex partners to marry legally. Also interesting is the fact that many gay and lesbian Americans travel to Canada to become married even though their marriage will not be legally recognized in the United States.)

Gay and Lesbian Advocates and Defenders. (n.d.). GLAD: Equal justice under law. Retrieved May 9, 2005, from http://www.glad.org/marriage/ (This site is updated regularly and is a particularly rich source for those looking for tips about getting married. It includes thorough discussions about the benefits and liabilities of same-sex marriage for individual couples.)

Investigative Reporters and Editors, Inc. (IRE). (2004). [Home page]. Retrieved May 9, 2005, from http://www.IRE.org (Check out this site for help in getting beyond the predictable approaches to journalism. There are some cutting-edge articles that avoid the problems of oversimplification and polarization.)

National Public Radio. (2005). NPR: National Public Radio: News, arts, world, US. Retrieved May 9, 2005, from http://www.npr.org (NPR has run several features on same-sex marriage and is one of the best sources for updated information. Go to their search engine and type in "same sex marriage" to find a list of the latest shows and interviews.)

Stateline.org. (2005). Stateline.org: Politics & policy news, state by state. Retrieved May 9, 2005, from http://www.stateline.org (Despite its exclusionary title, this site is a good one to consult for a brief framework of current legal and court activity, state by state. The site appears to be updated regularly and was even updated the day after the momentous 2004 election. Use the search engine to search for applicable articles.)

12

Proving the Case

Psychology, Subjectivity, and Representations
of Lesbian and Gay Parents in the Media

Damien W. Riggs

❖　❖　❖

Representations of lesbian and gay parents within the media typically fall into two categories—the first, and seemingly most
entrenched, stereotype is that of the lesbian or gay (or bisexual or transgendered) parent as pathological (i.e., suffering from a disease). The
second category, and one that purports to be "prolesbian" or "progay,"
suggests that lesbians and gay men are "the same" as their heterosexual

Author's Note: I would first like to acknowledge the sovereignty of the Kaurna
people, the First Nations people on whose land I live in Adelaide, South
Australia. In doing so, I recognize the considerable privilege that I experience
as a white person, at the expense of indigenous people and regardless of my
identification as a gay man. I would like to thank Victoria Clarke for her inspir-
ing work on this topic area, and, as always, thanks to Greg for support and
proofreading and to our foster child, Gary, for making this all worthwhile.

counterparts. These depictions suggest that notions of pathology among GLBT parents represent outdated ways of thinking and further suggest that GLBT parents are "no different" than their heterosexual counterparts, aside from their "sexual object preference." The unfortunate consequence of this seemingly benign account is that the politics of sexuality as framed under *heteropatriarchy* and *heteronormativity* (i.e., the cultural system in Western societies that privileges heterosexual men over all others) are rendered invisible, and thus the normative status of heterosexuality is left unchallenged. This has the effect of denying the ongoing oppression that many lesbians and gay men face, because it relies on a model of same-sex attraction that denies difference and that therefore both denies the radical challenges that lesbians and gay men may present to the traditional ordering of gender and sexuality under heteropatriarchy and ignores the privilege that accrues to heterosexually identifying individuals under heteronormativity.

Such "pro" accounts of lesbians and gay men have experienced considerable prominence within recent media debates over lesbian and gay parenting and adoption in the United States. In particular, these accounts have emphasized the "sameness" discourse[1] outlined here to "prove" that lesbians and gay men can be fit parents (Clarke, 2002b). This is most often achieved through recourse to notions of "scientific fact"—advocates for and supporters of lesbian and gay parenting cite psychological research that claims to demonstrate that children raised in lesbian and gay headed households are (a) not at an increased risk of abuse (either within or outside of the home), (b) do not display an increased tendency to identify as lesbian or gay themselves, and (c) are no more prone to experiencing mental health problems as a result of being raised by lesbian or gay parents than are those children raised by heterosexual parents (e.g., American Psychological Association, 1995; Tasker & Golombok, 1997). Although such "evidence" is used to counter claims of pathology and to satisfy the burden of proof that seems to rest with lesbian and gay parents, it does little to challenge the heteronormative frameworks (i.e., those frameworks that suggest that heterosexuality is the "normal way to be") that shape debates over lesbian and gay parenting (Riggs, 2004b). Indeed, it may be suggested that by engaging in such debates *on the terms set by the heterosexual majority,* GLBT parents run the risk of reifying science (i.e., treating it as if it reflected some sort of "real truth") as the appropriate arbiter of truth claims and thus continuing to privilege the agendas set for parenting under heteropatriarchy (Clarke, 2000).

With this in mind, this chapter seeks to explore some of the ways in which psychological discourses are employed within the media to warrant particular truth claims in support of lesbian and gay parents. The chapter starts off by exploring the model of subjectivity (i.e., the way we understand ourselves and the identities we claim) that is evident in media accounts of lesbian and gay parents and how this is connected to psychological accounts of subjectivity. In the course of this exploration, I suggest that a focus on subjectivity may allow for an analysis of the media that examines how particular, intelligible subject positions are made possible for lesbian and gay parents through the use of "pro" accounts" (see also Clarke & Kitzinger, 2004). From here the chapter explores in detail two aspects of media representations of lesbian and gay parents. First, it looks at constructions of the (normative) family and how they are played out within debates over lesbian and gay parents. This entails paying attention to how these debates set up a series of exclusionary binaries that work to render lesbian and gay parents complicit with the hegemony (i.e., dominance[2]) of heterosexuality.

The second aspect of media representations of lesbian and gay parents explored within this chapter is one that focuses on how the notion of "expert evidence" is used to legitimate lesbian and gay parenting. In particular, such notions rely upon claims of "objectivity" to rhetorically justify the truth claims of pro accounts. In looking at how science is deployed within media accounts of lesbian and gay parenting, I suggest that we need to focus on how power is constituted through the use of scientific rhetoric and how this relates to the history of scientific research being used against lesbians and gay men (and indeed, how it continues to be used to these ends).

Having outlined how discourses of science are used within media debates over lesbian and gay parents, this chapter then examines in closer detail some of the limitations of this approach. In particular, it explores more thoroughly the power dynamics that underpin the fight for recognition of lesbian and gay parents and how these dynamics may well be reinforced by using science to "prove the case." This section also elaborates on the points made earlier in relation to complicity and agenda setting and what this means in regard to using the media to garner support for lesbian and gay parents.

The chapter then concludes by exploring what Lisa Blackman and Valerie Walkerdine (2001) have termed a "critical psychology of the media"—how critical approaches within the discipline of psychology may be used to better understand the media, and vice versa. Such an approach would recognize the ever-increasing connections between media representation and modes of being within Western societies and the implications of this for better understanding lesbian and gay parenting. In this way, a critical psychology of the media may prioritize political activism and encourage a focus on the political choices that often underpin lesbian and gay parenting (Pollkoff, 1987), something that is most often missing from accounts that currently circulate within the media. From this perspective, I suggest that readings of media representations need to move beyond simply recounting who is influencing whom and how viewers are resisting or being made complicit with hegemonic media representations and concentrate instead on the potential for developing radical understandings of lesbian and gay parenting through a sustained focus on the ideologies that underpin current accounts (Kitzinger, 1998).

❖ PSYCHOLOGY, MEDIA, AND SUBJECTIVITY

Long-standing debates within media studies have paid continued focus to the role of how people respond to or resist media messages. Eric Louw (2001) suggests that these debates may be epitomized by the contrasting foci that media studies have traditionally taken, that being a focus on either the production of media or the reception of media. He suggests that there has been a marked increase of research into media reception, to the detriment of research on media production. Similarly, Jenny Kitzinger (1998), in her work on representations of AIDS in the media, proposes that there is a need for a more complex account of media representation and that this must be accompanied by a move away from a sole focus on either production or reception.

Following on from these points, I suggest here that one way of achieving this may be to engage in a social constructionist approach to media studies (see, for example, Eldridge, 1993), whereby the focus is one that examines the mutuality of production and reception, so that the two may be understood as demonstrating how intelligible subject positions are made available through and with the media. Such an approach would thus refuse to separate the media (as an institution) from "consumers" of media and instead would consider subjectivity as a practice constituted in tandem with the media. Thus relatively recent developments in media technology (e.g., the widespread use of the Internet within Western societies) may be seen as both making possible new forms of subjectivity and being developed precisely through the desire for new ways of relating and being (e.g., see chapters 1, 6, 10, and 19 in Hawthorne & Klein, 1999). We may extend this metaphor of coconstitution to better understand how the media and psychology are thoroughly entwined with one another and what this means for the understanding of subjectivity that appears to dominate media debates over lesbian and gay parenting.

Psychology as a discipline continues to play an ever-increasing role in the production of media knowledge (Clarke & Kitzinger, 2004; Epstein & Steinberg, 1997; Gamson, 2001). Whether through the use of press releases to announce position statements on particular social issues (e.g., the American Psychological Association's [1995] recent statement on same-sex marriage) or when psychologists appear as "experts" on daytime talk TV (or indeed have their own programs, such as Dr. Phil McGraw, TV's "Dr. Phil"), psychology continually takes center stage in media representations of the world around us. The converse of this is likewise true: Psychologists are increasingly using the media to promote their services, to attract potential students to the study of psychology, and to counter claims made against the discipline by other disciplines and groups of people. In this way, the use of the media is of growing concern to psychologists and has engendered much discussion over how psychologists should be involved within it (e.g., Schwartz, 1999).

These interactions between psychology, media, and subjectivity have resulted in the need for researchers to focus on what particular types of subjectivity are produced as a result of these relations. In their work on critical psychology and media studies, Lisa Blackman and Valerie Walkerdine (2001) outline some of the key issues that arise from these interactions, with particular attention being paid to how much of the research in this area continues to privilege a model of subjectivity that would appear to undermine the potential for radical challenge that the "new medias" may herald. In particular, Blackman and Walkerdine focus on the neoliberal model[3] of the rational autonomous individual as it informs psychological discourse. They suggest that many of the ways in which psychology is taken up within the media only serve to perpetuate the hegemony of traditional psychological knowledge and thus encourage people to take on board an understanding of themselves as individual agents capable of change through practices such as "self-control" and "self-empowerment." Blackman and Walkerdine examine these practices for the ways in which they encourage forms of "self-government"—what Foucault (1991) has termed "technologies of subjectification." This may seem like an unnecessarily complex term, but it does serve to capture the very real effects that are produced through a reliance on psychological models of subjectivity within the media.

To elaborate: Such models reinforce the notion that people exist as isolated beings, divorced from cultural context or historical location. As a result, this understanding of subjectivity is predominantly apolitical— it fails to examine how political practices shape subjectivities through the promotion of particular normative ideals (traditionally, these are those of white, heterosexual, middle-class males). As a result, exclusionary practices (such as those perpetuated in the media in regard to lesbian and gay parents) are seen as the result of individual fault and hence require individual correction rather than redressing of social disadvantage and inequity (see Kitzinger & Perkins, 1993, for a more detailed account of how such individualized accounts work to locate blame within same-sex–attracted individuals). Bringing this back to Foucault's term, "technologies of subjectification," we may thus understand how psychology as a "technology" works to encourage forms of self-governmentality[4] that require people to subject themselves to dominant norms—to locate themselves within particular notions of "control," "causation," and "accountability" (see Riggs, 2005).

What does this all mean in regard to understanding media representations of lesbian and gay parents? As the next two sections will demonstrate, a focus on the coconstitution of subjectivity with psychology and the media may allow for a better understanding of how specific pro accounts of lesbian and gay parents may be seen to evidence technologies of subjectification that require lesbian and gay parents to locate themselves within particular psychological discourses of accountability. The point of this focus, then, is to examine how complicity with the media and psychology may do little to assert radical forms of lesbian and gay subjectivities and instead may only serve to more firmly entrench dominant stereotypes of lesbians and gay men.

The Normalization of Lesbian and Gay Parents

In her work on lesbian and gay parenting, Victoria Clarke (2002a) outlines a number of rhetorical strategies that she suggests are used to "normalize" lesbian and gay parenting practices. She suggests that these practices of normalization result in several key implications for lesbian and gay parenting, three of which will be the focus of this section: (a) the recentering of heteronormative assumptions about families and parenting, (b) how normalization constructs the categories of good and bad lesbians and gay men, and (c) the depoliticization of lesbian and gay parenting.

Practices of normalization draw on the previously outlined discourse of sameness, which

> highlight[s] the similarities between lesbian and gay and heterosexual families. This construction (often) "normalizes" lesbian and gay families—denying or downplaying "gayness" or difference and emphasizing the ways in which lesbian and gay parenting is "no different" from the heterosexual norm. (Clarke, 2002a, p. 99)

As Clarke suggests, such normalization effectively assumes the heterosexual nuclear family as the model for lesbian and gay parenting. This model takes as central a number of ideological assumptions about what constitutes a "good (heterosexual) family." Some of these are exemplified in media reports over lesbian and gay adoption in the United States, as *The Advocate* notes: "We think the court is wrong in thinking that the Constitution lets the government assume that sexual orientation has anything to do with good parenting" ("Florida maintains ban," 2004).

Here advocates of lesbian and gay adoption rights draw on the notion that sexual orientation is completely unrelated to parenting. As will be discussed further on in the chapter, this ideological assumption normalizes lesbian and gay parents by denying their sexuality and thus denying their experiences of difference and the oppression that they face as a result of their minority status. Lesbian and gay parents are thus encouraged to enact a form of desexualized subjectivity that is therefore considered unthreatening to the heterosexual moral majority. Similarly, it has been reported that "Good parenting is not influenced by sexual orientation. Rather, it is influenced most profoundly by a parent's ability to create a loving and nurturing home—an ability that does not depend on whether a parent is gay or straight" (American Civil Liberties Union, 1999).

This discourse on a "loving and nurturing home" is identified by Clarke and Kitzinger (2004, p. 206) as one that "sugar coats" lesbian- and gay-headed families and that thus fails to recognize the systemic problems underlying dominant constructions of "the family" as well as the "institutional, ideological and material validation and support which is bestowed on heterosexual families," a set of privileges that ignores how, for many lesbians and gay men, "family is about rejection, disappointment and pain." This recentering of a heteronormative understanding of the family is evident in media reports that suggest that

> State agencies and courts now apply a "best interest of the child" standard to decide [custody or visitation rights for lesbian and gay parents]. Under this approach, a person's sexual orientation cannot be the basis for ending or limiting parent-child relationships unless it is demonstrated that it causes harm to a child. (American Civil Liberties Union, 1999)

This rhetoric of "the best interests of the child" is thus used to warrant a particular reading of what constitutes appropriate parent-child relations. Recent research focusing on such rhetoric has demonstrated how it relies on an understanding of the family that privileges the heterosexual nuclear family and thus implicitly positions lesbian and gay parents (in particular, adoptive and foster parents) as being outside the category of "family" (Raymond, 1992; Riggs, 2004e, in press). These three examples of media accounts of lesbian and gay parents demonstrate some of the ideological assumptions that inform practices of normalization. They show how pro accounts that seek to "prove" the normality of lesbian and gay parents effectively deny lesbians and gay men's experiences of oppression by promoting an understanding of families and parenting that privileges the heteronorm.

One implication of this is that lesbian and gay parents who take up this normalizing discourse are encouraged to promote their own parenting abilities, and indeed their identification as parents, as representing a form of "healthy lesbian or gay subjectivity." As a result, this perpetuates the binary of "good" or "bad" lesbians and gay men that effectively positions lesbians and gay men who choose not to parent as "bad citizens" or as failing to conform to the heteronormative expectations that are promoted through discourses of normalization (Pollkoff, 1987). This works to reinforce a pathological model of *some* lesbians and gay men, whereby choosing *not* to parent demonstrates a form of lack or deviance.

The extension of this logic, which is evident in the media extracts shown here, is that in being "just like" heterosexual parents, lesbian and gay parents are positioned "as no longer pos[ing] a threat to heteronormativity" (Bernstein, 2001, p. 434). Thus in minimizing the role that sexual orientation plays in *anyone's* subjectivity, pro accounts of lesbian and gay parenting effectively minimize the political challenges that lesbians and gay men have long presented to heteropatriarchy. Moreover, such minimizing ignores the privilege that heterosexual parents experience as a result of their sexuality and that is enshrined in the law. One of the implications of this is that claiming normality for lesbian and gay parents works to depoliticize lesbian and gay subjectivities and thus dismisses one of the many motivations that may lead lesbians and gay men to choose parenting as a viable option. In other words, this depoliticization further marginalizes the standpoints of those lesbians and gay men who see parenting as a political act—normalization makes it seem as though such parents wish to be "just like" heterosexual parents, which may not necessarily be the case. Indeed, as Nancy Pollkoff (1987) suggests in the following quote, lesbian parents may be unwilling to talk about their role as a parent, as it may lead to accusations about complicity with patriarchal definitions of womanhood and mothering:

> It is rare to hear a lesbian say she wants a child because she wants to put her politics into practice, and childbearing is one way to do that. I am not sure I have ever heard a lesbian say she wanted a child because she wanted to make a public statement that there was another model for childrearing, and that it was better than the traditional model. (p. 50)

Following up the previous examination of practices of normalization, we may suggest that the voicing of the politics of lesbian and gay parenting is not heard precisely because "being political" is not considered a "normal thing" for parents to do (Riggs, 2004a), or that parenting itself is not something that may be considered an appropriately political act. This therefore demonstrates how normalization effectively excludes many lesbian and gay parents from representation within the media by making all forms of parenting conform to the heterosexual model for parenting.

"Expert Evidence" and the Hegemony of Science

Perhaps the most central aspect of media representations of lesbian and gay parents is the reliance on "scientific proof" to justify the legitimacy of lesbian and gay parenting. Some of the many examples of this include

> Psychologist Charlotte Patterson's report that "not a single study has found children of gay or lesbian parents to be disadvantaged in any significant respect relative to children of heterosexual parents" (http://www.thetaskforce.org/downloads/TalkingPointson Parenting.pdf).

> Judith Stacey's report that significant, reliable social scientific evidence indicates that lesbian and gay parents are as fit, effective, and successful as heterosexual parents (http://www.lethimstay .com/wrong_socscience_expert.html).

> The American Psychological Association's (1995) statement that because many beliefs about lesbian and gay parents and their children are open to empirical test, psychological research can evaluate their accuracy (http://www.apa.org/pi/parent.html).

> Scientific findings (reported on, among other places, the Family Pride Coalition's Web site) debunk the myth that gay men cannot be nurturing parents (http://www.familypride.org/issues/myths .htm).

Together, these few examples show some of the many rhetorical strategies that are used to warrant psychological knowledge (in particular) as representing an objective truth. One specific strategy mirrors the construction of the "good" or "bad" lesbian or gay man binary discussed in the previous section—that "significant, reliable social scientific evidence" is a powerful tool for debunking myths. Celia Kitzinger (1990) has termed this the "rhetoric of pseudoscience"—disproving your opponents' claims to truth by demonstrating their "bad science" (see also Riggs, 2004c). One example of this is provided in Judith Stacey's claim that

> Paul Cameron is the primary disreputable and discredited figure in this [anti–lesbian and gay parenting] literature. He was expelled from the APA and censored by the ASA for unethical scholarly practices, such as selective, misleading representations of research and making claims that could not be substantiated. ("Why it's wrong," 2004)

Here Stacey uses the authority of "good" social scientific research to disprove the claims of a "disreputable and discredited figure." In so doing, although she provides a means of supporting lesbian and gay parents in their fight for parenting rights, she also perpetuates the notion that scientific knowledge is the appropriate arbiter of what counts as "good parenting." This is reinforced in the statement of the American Psychological Association (Patterson, 1995), which suggests that "many beliefs about lesbian and gay parents and their children are open to empirical test." This is intended to demonstrate the importance of using psychological research to "evaluate [the] accuracy" of such beliefs, but it also demonstrates the risks that lesbian and gay parents and their supporters run when using science to determine what will count as "truth" (Clarke, 2000; Riggs, 2004a, 2004c)—that by definition, psychological knowledge represents the most accurate truth about parenting practices.

We only need to look back 30-odd years to see a vastly different story. It is as recent as this that same-sex attraction was classified as a pathology in the American Psychiatric Association's *Diagnostic and Statistical Manual of Mental Disorders* (*DSM-II*). This demonstrates the point that scientific knowledge is highly contextual and historical—it does not reflect *a priori* truths (i.e., it is not unquestionably true and does not exist as such outside of its cultural location), but rather is a marker of the current political and social status quo (Alwood, 1996; Kutchins & Kirk, 1997). In relation to lesbian and gay parenting, this suggests that using science to "prove the case" works to (a) reify and (b) recenter scientific knowledge, which has historically (and may well again in the future) been used to oppress lesbians and gay men (among others). Thus, as Joshua Gamson (2001) suggests, that which is considered "normal" is often a synonym for "power" (p. 76).

In this regard, then, the power that is evoked through the use of scientific discourse in media representations of lesbian and gay parents may be used against them. For example, Bill Maier, a clinical psychologist and vice president of the (right-wing, antigay) Focus on the Family Institute, is reported as saying that

Every responsible psychologist in the APA should be ashamed; the organization is obviously more concerned with appeasing its powerful gay lobby than it is with retaining any semblance of moral and ethical duty (Toalston, 2004).

This extract demonstrates one of the ways in which the power of scientific discourse can be used against lesbians and gay men, by constructing morality and ethics as being naturally oriented toward the values of the heterosexual majority. Even if lesbian and gay rights activists counter this with "proof" of the normality of lesbians and gay men, this does little to destabilize the hegemony of scientific knowledge and its ability to define what counts as moral and ethical. Indeed, Maier draws attention to a very important point—that although organizations such as the APA may seek to use psychological knowledge to refute antigay claims, they do so without challenging the underlying ideological assumptions about morality and ethics that are enshrined in the law (Bernstein, 2001). As a result, the APA (and those who use psychological knowledge in pro accounts more generally) is left open to accusations of bias and willful ignorance of the law that supports the institutions of heterosexual marriage and parenting.

Finally, and again in relation to constructions of "good" lesbians and gay men, the use of scientific discourse works to establish a power dynamic within which certain lesbians and gay men are held up as being "good citizens"—as accepting the definitions that science applies to them. By default, then, those lesbians and gay men who challenge the hegemony of science are positioned as being either pathological or delusional—as unable to comprehend the "benefits" of deploying scientific knowledge (Kitzinger & Perkins, 1993). This works to reassert the individualized model of subjectivity that is traditionally assumed within psychology and thus locates blame within particular lesbians or gay men rather than challenging the status quo. As a result, lesbian and gay parents are encouraged to buy into a form of subjectivity that accepts scientific arguments as legitimate and that thus encourages lesbians and gay men to open their lives to scientific scrutiny, measurement, and objectification. Psychological knowledge may thus be seen to promote forms of self-governance among lesbian and gay parents.

In summary, this section has shown some of the ways in which the use of scientific discourse can be used against lesbian and gay parents and, likewise, how discourses of science have been used previously to construct same-sex attraction as pathological. Science was discussed as a contextual, contingent, meaning-making practice rather than as one that has privileged access to "the truth." As a result, I suggest, lesbian and gay parents may well do themselves a disservice by relying on science to prove their "normality."

❖ LIMITATIONS OF THE "SAMENESS" DISCOURSE: COMPLICITY AND CO-OPTION

In this final section, we look at the limitations of the sameness discourse that appear evident in pro accounts of lesbian and gay parents. This entails a focus on the politics of lesbian and gay parenting and an examination of how the debates on parenting are framed within the media.

Drawing on George Orwell's novel *1984*, John Eldridge (1993) suggests that what appear as debates over social issues such as lesbian and gay parenting may more accurately be described as "one-sided debates" wherein the "opposing parties" are actually arguing very similar points and are both relying on a similar set of presumptions about the social and political spheres. This is particularly evident in debates over lesbian and gay parenting, as both those for and those against lesbian and gay parents accept relatively unproblematically the notions of "family" and "science" that inhere to the debates. Thus, for example, in the previous section, we saw Stacey claim that antigay researchers have questionable ethics, just as Maier suggests that the support for lesbian and gay issues given by the APA represents a crisis in its "ethical and moral duty." Both "sides" of the debate take as natural the role of science in determining rights to parent. Similarly, a normative construction of the family is evoked by both parties in the debate—those who support lesbian and gay parents seek to demonstrate that their families are built on love and that sexual orientation bears no consideration, just as those against lesbian and gay parenting "believe it best to move [foster] children into permanent homes with [heterosexually] married parents" (Kreisher, 2002).

Understood in this way, "debates" over lesbian and gay parenting may instead be understood as a power struggle over who has the right to access hegemonic representations of "the family" and "science." None of the media representations presented here challenge either of these categories, nor did there appear to be any examination of "the family" or "science" in the much broader review of media representations undertaken as the basis for this chapter. Thus the pro accounts represented here effectively concede ground to the heterosexual majority by engaging in debates over science and by employing scientific rhetoric to "prove the case." Such concessions may well work in the short term to generate "positive" representations of lesbian and gay parents in the media and, in some cases, may be an important aspect of legal challenges in regard to lesbian and gay adoption rights, but on the whole, they do little to challenge the networks of power within which they are located (Louw, 2001).

In addition, the particular forms of lesbian and gay subjectivity that are prioritized in these debates work to further marginalize lesbians and gay men who do not fit into the mold of "the family." In other words, the representations of lesbian and gay parents that appear in the media most often privilege white, middle-class lesbians and gay men—those people who can typically afford to fight the legal system for adoption rights or who have the time to push for representation within the media (Bernstein, 2001). As a result, these representations further marginalize those lesbians and gay men who do not fit within this category (for example, due to economic or cultural difference from the white, middle-class majority), in addition to those lesbians and gay men who choose not to parent. These points demonstrate how the fight for recognition within the media can lead to the further marginaliza- tion of groups of lesbian and gay men who already have little access to "positive" representation (Gamson, 2001).

This then leads us to a discussion of the politics of lesbian and gay parenting—something that has been present throughout this chapter. Polkoff (1987) suggests that lesbian and gay parents need to continu- ally question how the category "parent" itself may automatically ren- der lesbians and gay men complicit with heteropatriarchy. In other words, as a result of the terms "mother" and "father" typically being associated with hetero–mothering and fathering (Clarke, 2002b, Riggs, 2004d), lesbian and gay parents are always at risk of "passing by impli- cation"—of being assumed to be heterosexual simply because they are parents. For some lesbians and gay men this may be a useful tool for avoiding discrimination or harassment, but it also works to render invisible those lesbians and gay men who seek to politicize their par- enting role. Thus the sameness discourse itself is inherently a tool for silencing—by rendering lesbian and gay parents as "just like" hetero- sexual parents, the radical differences that lesbian and gay parenting may engender are routinely dismissed or ignored.

This then brings us back to the politics of science and, more specif- ically, the political climate within which debates over lesbian and gay parenting occur (Clarke, 2002b). If we are to understand these debates as happening within a climate that continues to privilege and normal- ize heteroparenting, then it is relatively simple to see how discourses of sameness work to co-opt lesbian and gay parents into this normative framework. Moreover, and in relation to psychology, this framework is one that merely adds lesbian and gay parents onto the existing model rather than developing alternate ways of relating to and understanding parenting (Clarke, 2002a). In this light, media representations of lesbian and gay parents that draw on pro accounts may themselves be seen as (a) implicated in the construction of "acceptable" forms of lesbian and gay subjectivity and thus (b) perhaps of little use to lesbian and gay parents who seek to destabilize the hegemony of heteropatriarchal understandings of families and parenting.

❖ CONCLUSIONS: CRITICAL
    PSYCHOLOGY AND THE MEDIA

It is useful to return to the points made about critical psychology in the introduction—that is, through the lens of a "critical psychology of the media," we may better understand how particular subjectivities are made intelligible through or with the media and the political implications of this for lesbian and gay parenting. Throughout this chapter, we have examined how scientific discourse is used to "prove" the normality of lesbian and gay parents through recourse to notions of "sameness." Yet, as Blackman and Walkerdine (2001) suggest:

> This approach, which calls for more positive images or stereotypes to replace those which are considered negative, still relies upon the very principle embedded within the psychological sciences—that we can "know" different populations through the uncovering of stable and enduring sets of traits that "make up" a person's character, personality and identity. (p. 8)

In contrast to this, a critical psychology of (and, indeed, in) the media may allow for a more thoroughgoing account of how the media, psychology, and subjectivities are coconstituted *as* particular political and social frameworks. In other words, we may ask questions such as, How do understandings of "the individual" in neoliberalism mesh with psychological accounts of subjectivity, and what are the implications of this for representations of lesbian and gay parents in the media? It is suggested here that in looking at these three aspects *together* it may be possible to elaborate an account of lesbian and gay parenting that may be resistive to co-option and complicity.

Such an approach would first need to examine the representation-subjectification nexus and (intimately related to this) question the limitations of available modes of being under heteropatriarchy. Thus, if we recall Nancy Pollkoff's (1987) statement that she does not hear lesbians say they choose to parent as a political choice, we may understand this lack of representation as being closely connected to the current range of intelligible subject positions available to lesbian (and gay) parents at the present time. This may also be related to the problems that arise when attempting to speak out as a lesbian or gay parent in a society that either devalues non-heterosexual parents, or in communities that are critical of those people who continue to choose parenting in the face of heteropatriarchal restrictions on women's and men's bodies. In order to counter this, one goal may be to continue to explicate why this is the case (both as a result of historical and cultural reasons) and how things may be done differently.

A critical psychological approach to media representation may seek to prioritize the political—to both look at and voice the views of lesbian and gay parents (for example) that have traditionally been marginalized or silenced and to continually encourage lesbians and gay men to examine their complicity in dominant understandings of families and parenting. An equally important aspect of such an approach would be to explore forms of relationality that privilege the experiences of lesbians and gay men. In his work on gay donor fathers, Paul van Reyk (2004) demonstrates a number of potential ways for relating to one another and thus for constructing families that need not rely upon a heterosexual model. Indeed, he suggests that "working in *radical* difference" may help lesbians and gay men to refuse a place within the hegemonic binaries of hetero- or homosexual and instead create communities that start from lesbians and gay men, rather than as a response to the terms set by heteropatriarchy.

In relation to the media, then, lesbian and gay parents may choose to engage in potentially more radical approaches to representation, rather than simply taking on board the tenets of "objectivity" and "truth." Challenging media representations requires more than simply diagnosing the oppressive aspects of media representation post hoc (as has been the work of this chapter). Instead, it is important to begin the work of developing alternate ways of understanding lesbian- and

gay-headed families. As lesbian feminists have long known (e.g., see chapters 6, 7, 13, and 14 in Pollack & Vaughn, 1987), this requires a willingness to refuse the power that comes from complicity with heteropatriarchy and to prioritize the knowledges held within lesbian and gay communities.

❖ DISCUSSION QUESTIONS

1. How are "pro" accounts, or positive representations of lesbian and gay parents, similar to accounts that seek to generate negative representations of lesbian and gay parents?

2. Describe an example of how you have felt compelled to "be controlled" or to "manage yourself" as a result of media representations.

3. List some of the normative assumptions about "the family" mentioned in this chapter and relate them to your own experiences of family—where do they differ and how are they the same?

❖ HOMEWORK ASSIGNMENTS

1. Compare the readings of lesbian parenting provided in Pollack and Vaughn (1987) with those available in Clunis and Green's (2003) text on lesbian parenting. Which account of families and parenting does each book prioritize? Whose agenda do you think the books are responding to?

2. Watch an episode of a TV talk show that features a "science expert" (e.g., most episodes of Dr. Phil). How is science used to justify particular explanations? How might these particular ways of looking at the world be oppressive to lesbians and gay men or to other marginalized groups?

3. Look at some examples of media reports on lesbian and gay parenting (e.g., those on the Web sites listed in the Additional Resources section) and list some of the labels they use to describe lesbian and gay parents. How do you think these labels challenge "negative" accounts of lesbian and gay parents?

❖ NOTES

1. A *discourse* may be defined as a set of meaning-making practices that frame how we understand particular cultural constructs—ways of looking at the world that lend such constructs a semblance of naturalness and thus make possible these particular ways of knowing and being.

2. The term *hegemony* refers to much more than simply "dominance." It may be understood as a practice for convincing oppressed groups to accept their disadvantage as normative by making hierarchies (i.e., in which heterosexuality seems "better" than homosexuality) seem as if they were naturally occurring.

3. *Neoliberalism* is a recent form of liberal governmentality that promotes an economic (as well as political and philosophical) mentality whereby actions are assessed for their profitability—a desire to conceive of human interaction as a set of balanceable transactions.

4. *Self-governmentality* is a form of political and social thinking that encourages people to enact self-control so that the policing of people becomes the work of the individual rather than the state.

❖ REFERENCES

Alwood, E. (1996). *Straight news: Gays, lesbians, and the news media.* New York: Columbia University Press.

American Civil Liberties Union. (1999). Overview of lesbian and gay parenting, adoption and foster care. Retrieved May 14, 2005, from the ACLU Utah Web site: http://www.acluutah.org/dcfsfacts.htm

Bernstein, M. (2001). Gender, queer family policies, and the limits of the law. In M. Bernstein & R. Reimann (Eds.), *Queer families, queer politics: Challenging culture and the state* (pp. 420–426). New York: Columbia University Press.

Blackman, L., & Walkerdine, V. (2001). *Mass hysteria: Critical psychology and media studies.* Hampshire, England: Palgrave Macmillan.

Clarke, V. (2000). "Stereotype, attack and stigmatize those who disagree": Employing scientific rhetoric in debates about lesbian and gay parenting. *Feminism & Psychology, 10,* 152–159.

Clarke, V. (2002a). Resistance and normalization in the construction of lesbian and gay families: A discursive analysis. In A. Coyle & C. Kitzinger (Eds.), *Lesbian and gay psychology: New perspectives* (pp. 98–116). Oxford, England: BPS Blackwell.

Clarke, V. (2002b). Sameness and difference in research on lesbian parenting. *Journal of Community and Applied Psychology, 12,* 210–222.

Clarke, V., & Kitzinger, C. (2004). Lesbian and gay parents on talk shows: Resistance or collusion in heterosexism? *Qualitative Research in Psychology, 1,* 195–217.

Clunis, D. M., & Green, G. D. (2003). *The lesbian parenting book: A guide to creating families and raising children.* Washington, DC: Seal Press.

Eldridge, J. (1993). News, truth and power. In J. Eldridge (Ed.), *Getting the message: News, truth and power* (pp. 3–33). London: Routledge.

Epstein, D., & Steinberg, D. L. (1997). Love's labours: Playing it straight on the Oprah Winfrey Show. In D. L. Steinberg, D. Epstein, & R. Johnson (Eds.), *Border patrols: Policing the boundaries of heterosexuality* (pp. 32–65). London: Cassell.

Florida maintains ban on adoptions by gays. (2004, January 29). Retrieved May 19, 2005, from *The Advocate* Web site: http://www.advocate.com/news_detail .asp?id=03902, http://www.advocate.com/new_news.asp?id=11137&sd= 01/29/04

Foucault, M. (1991). Governmentality. In G. Burchell (Ed.), *The Foucault effect: Studies in governmentality* (pp. 87-104). Chicago: University of Chicago.

Gamson, J. (2001). Talking freaks: Lesbian, gay, bisexual and transgender families on daytime talk TV. In M. Bernstein & R. Reimann (Eds.), *Queer families, queer politics: Challenging culture and the state* (pp. 68–86). New York: Columbia University Press.

Hawthorne, S., & Klein, R. (1999). *Cyberfeminism: Connectivity, critique, creativity.* North Melbourne, Victoria: Spinifex.

Kitzinger, C. (1990). The rhetoric of pseudoscience. In I. Parker & J. Shotter (Eds.), *Deconstructing social psychology.* London: Routledge.

Kitzinger, C., & Perkins, R. (1993). *Changing our minds: Lesbian feminism and psychology.* New York: New York University Press.

Kitzinger, J. (1998). Resisting the message: The extent and limits of media influence. In D. Miller, J. Kitzinger, K. Williams, & P. Beharell (Eds.), *The circuit of mass communication: Media strategies, representation and audience reception in the AIDS crisis* (pp. 199–212). London: Sage.

Kreisher, K. (2002, January). Children's voice article, January 2002: Gay adoption. Retrieved May 14, 2005, from the Child Welfare League of America Web site: http://www.cwla.org/articles/cv0201gayadopt.htm

Kutchins, H., & Kirk, S. A. (1997). *Making us crazy: The psychiatric bible and the creation of mental disorders.* New York: Free Press.

Louw, E. (2001). *The media and cultural production.* London: Sage.

Patterson, C. J. (1995). Lesbian and gay parenting. Retrieved May 14, 2005, from the American Psychological Association Web site: http://www.apa.org/pi/ parent.html

Pollack, S., & Vaughn, J. (Eds.). (1987). *Politics of the heart: A lesbian parenting anthology.* New York: Firebrand Books.

Pollkoff, N. D. (1987). Lesbians choosing children: The personal is political revised. In S. Pollack & J. Vaughn (Eds.), *Politics of the heart: A lesbian parenting anthology* (pp. 48–54). New York: Firebrand Books.

Raymond, D. (1992). "In the best interests of the child": Thoughts on homophobia and parenting. In W. J. Blumenfeld (Ed.), *Homophobia: How we all pay the price* (pp. 126–134). Boston: Beacon Press.

Riggs, D. W. (2004a). "Expert knowledge" and the fight for rights: Examining representations of lesbian and gay parents in the media. In *Conference Proceedings of the "Parenting Imperatives" National Parenting Conference.* Adelaide, Australia: Child and Youth Health.

Riggs, D. W. (2004b). On whose terms? Psychology and the legitimisation of lesbian and gay parents. *GLIP News, 3,* 3–6. Retrieved May 14, 2005, from http://www.psychology.org.au/units/interest_groups/gay_lesbian/glip_news_may04.pdf

Riggs, D. W. (2004c). The politics of scientific knowledge: Constructions of sexuality and ethics in the conversion therapy literature. *Lesbian & Gay Psychology Review, 5,* 6–14.

Riggs, D. W. (2004d). The psychologisation of foster care: Implications for lesbian and gay parents. *PsyPag Quarterly, 51,* 34–43.

Riggs, D. W. (2004e). Resisting heterosexism in foster carer training: Valuing queer approaches to adult learning and relationality. *Canadian Journal of Queer Studies in Education, 1.* Retrieved May 19, 2005, from http://jqstudies.oise.utoronto.ca/journal/viewarticle.php?id=3&layout=html

Riggs, D. W. (2005). Locating control: Psychology and the cultural production of "healthy subject positions." *Culture, Health & Sexuality, 7,* 87–100.

Riggs, D. W. (in press). Developmentalism and the rhetoric of "best interests of the child": Challenging heteronormative constructions of families and parenting in foster care. *Journal of GLBT Family Studies, 2*(1).

Schwartz, L. L. (1999). *Psychology and the media: A second look.* Washington, DC: American Psychological Association.

Tasker, F. L., & Golombok, S. (1997). *Growing up in a lesbian family: Effects on child development.* New York: Guilford Press.

Toalston, A. (2004, July 30). Psychologists' OK of same-sex unions called "gay agenda." Retrieved May 14, 2005, from the BP News Web site: http://www.bpnews.net/bpnews.asp?ID=18784

Van Reyk, P. (2004). Baby love: Gay donor father narratives of intimacy. In D. W. Riggs & G. A. Walker (Eds.), *Out in the Antipodes: Australian and New Zealand perspectives on gay and lesbian issues in psychology* (pp. 146–166). Bentley: Brightfire Press.

Why it's wrong: The social science case. A conversation with Professor Judith Stacey. (2004). Retrieved May 14, 2005, from the ACLU Let Him Stay Web site: http://www.lethimstay.com/wrong_socscience_expert.html

❖ ADDITIONAL RESOURCES

The Advocate. (2005). [Home page]. Retrieved May 19, 2005, from http://www.advocate.com (Online site of this award-winning gay and lesbian newspaper.)

Gamson, J. (1998). *Freaks talk back: Tabloid talk shows and sexual nonconformity.* Chicago: University of Chicago Press. (A very readable analysis of representations of LGBT people on talk shows.)

Gay and Lesbian Alliance Against Defamation. (2004). GLAAD: Fair, accurate and inclusive representation. Retrieved May 14, 2005, from http://www.glaad.org/

Gay Parent Magazine. (2005). [Home page]. Retrieved May 14, 2005, from http://www.gayparentmag.com/

Philadelphia Lesbian and Gay Task Force. (n.d.). Media monitoring form. Retrieved May 14, 2005, from http://www.op.net/plgtf/mediaform.htm (A form for reporting negative and positive representations of LGBT in the media.)

ProudParenting.com. (2005). [Home page]. Retrieved May 14, 2005, from http://www.proudparenting.com/ (Lesbian and gay parenting Web site.)

Terry, J. (1999). *An American obsession: Science, medicine and homosexuality in modern society.* Chicago: University of Chicago Press. (Documents how science has been used against lesbians and gay men and how this has appeared in the media.)

Comedienne and TV Talk show host Ellen DeGeneres at the GLAAD Media Awards.

SOURCE:© GLAAD, Los Angeles Chapter. Reprinted with permission.

13

From Zero to 24–7

Images of Sexual Minorities on Television

Rhonda Gibson

❖ ❖ ❖

A mericans watch an average of more than 4 hours of television a
day, or more than 2 months of TV a year, so you can understand
why media scholar George Gerbner (1998) called TV the universalizer:
the source of the most broadly shared images and messages in history.
As such, TV plays a large role in the socialization of young people and
the development of their belief systems. Those who study the effects
of television suggest that TV's representation of sexual minorities has
undoubtedly influenced the way Americans have come to understand
homosexuality and the way they respond, both socially and politically,
to sexual minorities and the issues relevant to them (Gross, 2001; Hart,
2000; Signorile, 1993; Tropiano, 2002). Positive representations of gay
men, lesbians, and bisexuals can help to decrease the stigma associated with homosexuality and the pervasive influence of heterosexism,
whereas negative images may reinforce existing homophobia (Mackie,
Hamilton, Susskind, & Rosselli, 1996). For years, sexual minorities

were virtually invisible on television, except as comic relief. The number and quality of GLBT characters gradually increased throughout the 1970s and 1980s, as society's attitudes toward homosexuality began to change. The real breakthrough event occurred in 1997 with the coming out of sitcom lead character Ellen Morgan, played by comedian Ellen DeGeneres. *Ellen* featured the first lesbian lead on a prime-time series, but it became more than that: It was a major media event. Since then, the number of GLBT main characters has exploded, shows with ensemble casts comprised of all gay or lesbian characters have premiered, and the first gay-themed cable channel has been launched. This chapter will examine changes in the portrayal of sexual minorities in television programming and will consider the implications of such portrayals on the viewing public.

❖ THE EARLIEST YEARS

Sexuality studies scholar Kylo-Patrick Hart (2000) suggests that the earliest representations of gay men on television—the 1960s and early 1970s—can be called the "ridicule" stage, with derogatory terms such as "homo," "fag," "fairy," and "pansy" encountered on talk shows and dramas. Likewise, jokes and derogatory comments about gay men were considered to be appropriate and entertaining content on variety and comedy shows during this "stage." Television producers avoided including anything in their content that appeared to condone homosexuality for fear of alienating viewers or advertisers (Alwood, 1996).

The generally taboo subject of homosexuality first appeared on television in locally produced talk shows in the mid-1950s. The shows, appealing to both the fears and curiosity of audience members, most often featured a group of so-called experts engaged in a panel discussion of the social "problem" of homosexuality. The topic was usually approached from a medical context, and panelists debated if and how gay men and lesbians presented a threat to American society, if homosexuality should be legal, what caused the disease, and what could cure it (Tropiano, 2002). Experts consisted of lawyers, physicians, psychologists, police, and clergymen—and they were invariably heterosexual. A favorite topic of conversation was the assumed danger posed to children by male homosexuals, who were considered by many to be sex-crazed perverts. Lesbians were usually ignored.

As early as 1954, the Los Angeles-based talk show *Confidential File* devoted entire episodes to homosexuality. On April 25, *CF* aired "Homosexuals and the Problem They Present," which used a format that became common in subsequent shows. It featured interviews with a psychiatrist and police officer, who characterized gay men as criminal and mentally ill, and included a look inside a gay bar. It also showed footage of a meeting of the Mattachine Society, a California-based homophile organization that advocated for legal equality, and included a conversation with the group's secretary, who characterized himself as a well-adjusted gay man and challenged many of the prevailing stereotypes. These early talk shows probably had both positive and negative effects on the public's attitude toward homosexuality (Tropiano, 2002). On one hand, they brought the previously off-limits subject out in the open, but the designation of homosexuality as a social problem and the common association of gay men with child molesters may have done more to strengthen rather than alleviate the public's fear of sexual minorities.

The first made-for-television documentary about homosexuality aired on September 11, 1961, on San Francisco public television station KQED-TV. *The Rejected* "offered the most comprehensive exploration of the subject to date" (Tropiano, 2002, p. 5), although it was exclusively about gay men. Also, although it equated homosexuality with other social ills, such as alcoholism, drug abuse, and prostitution, there were some positive references to sexual minorities. Psychiatrist Karl Bowman, for example, went against the official position of his profession and argued that homosexuality was not a mental illness. Members of the San Francisco chapter of the Mattachine Society proudly appeared, this time without concealing their names or faces. Viewer response to the program was generally favorable.

Network television followed with its first special report about homosexuality in 1967. *CBS Reports: The Homosexuals* aired on March 7 and was hosted by *60 Minutes'* Mike Wallace. Like earlier treatments, the show attempted to answer the major questions then associated with homosexuality: What causes it and whether it is harmful or curable. As usual, the show focused solely on gay men and presented heterosexual "experts," including psychiatrists, clergy, and law enforcement personnel. Sensational footage of a darkly lit gay bar and male prostitutes loitering on a street corner were thrown in, as well as interviews with a few gay men, some well adjusted and others full of shame and guilt. One of the most disturbed individuals shown was a

27-year-old man who sat in almost total darkness with his face hidden by a potted plant. The man characterized himself as sick, sexually and in other ways. Comments from Mike Wallace throughout the documentary added to this perception: He called gay men the most despised minority group in the United States and referred to the average gay man as promiscuous and not interested in or capable of maintaining a lasting relationship.

❖ ENTERTAINMENT TELEVISION

Historian Vito Russo (1987) has suggested that sexual minorities on television and in the movies prior to the 1990s can be separated into five archetypal figures: (a) the villain or pervert; (b) the tragic, often suicidal case; (c) the flamboyant comic relief; (d) the noble individual whose primary function is to teach a heterosexual about tolerance; and (e) more recently, the gay male best friend to a heterosexual woman. The earliest representations were usually one of the dual roles of victim and villain.

In the 1950s and 1960s, lesbians were perceived as less threatening than gay males, possibly because of the fear of gay men as child molesters. This may explain why the first treatment of sexual minorities on a prime-time drama dealt with lesbianism. On November 13, 1963, an NBC drama, *The Eleventh Hour*, focused on an unstable actress diagnosed with "lesbian tendencies." The show featured two psychiatrists who were on-call to help a patient through "the eleventh hour," the time when he or she was on the edge of a mental breakdown. In this particular episode, the actress, Hallie, was having difficulties with her on-stage performance and was at odds with the show's female director. The psychiatrist, Dr. Starke, learned from Hallie that she had experienced a same-sex crush as an adolescent and was punished for it by her mother. Dr. Starke thus determined that because of the resulting guilt, Hallie could not form proper relationships as an adult. Miraculously, through this revelation, Hallie was "cured" of her lesbian tendencies and able to enjoy a normal heterosexual life.

From the mid-1960s to mid-1970s, the dominant images of gay men on TV were the limp-wristed, effeminate queen who walked with a swish and the villainous sexual predator (Alwood, 1996). NBC's *Rowan and Martin's Laugh-In* featured the first of these types. In 1970, it became the first network television show to regularly address the subject of gay men and their lifestyles by creating the stereotypically effeminate character Bruce, who was subjected to constant antigay jokes. An episode of ABC's dramatic series *Marcus Welby, M.D.* in 1974 centered on the gay male as villain. "The Outrage" depicted the brutal rape of a junior high school boy by his male science teacher, reviving the old stereotypes that gay men prey on young children and should not be allowed to teach (Alwood, 1996). Another episode of the show, aired the previous year, featured yet another common role for sexual minorities: the pathetic mentally ill victim. "The Other Martin Loring" portrayed homosexuality as a serious mental illness that dooms men to unfulfilling, unhappy lives, despite the fact that in 1973 the American Psychiatric Association removed homosexuality from its list of mental disorders.

Network television's first sympathetic portrayal of a gay individual occurred on the groundbreaking situation comedy *All in the Family* during its first season. In February 1971, the episode "Judging Books by Covers" had lead character Archie Bunker, not the most open-minded person in the world, discovering that a friend of his, a former football player, is gay. The episode broke ground by challenging notions of how a gay male should look and act (Steve, the football player, appears to be a typically macho guy) and by portraying homophobia, not homosexuality, as the problem.

Reconsideration of the nature of homosexuality in the mid-1970s (it was no longer considered a mental illness by health professionals), combined with the growing gay rights movement, affected the way the topic was approached on television. Television medical dramas treated homosexuality during this period with a generally liberal, although possibly misguided, attitude (Tropiano, 2002). Sexual minorities were treated with pity rather than condemnation. They were to be tolerated, if not really accepted. Because there was less scientific belief in homosexuality as an illness, these shows linked sexual confusion to specific medical conditions, such as ulcers or a bad heart. Before a patient's condition could be treated, his or her sexual orientation frustration had to be eliminated. The television law-and-order dramas popular during that period also sent mixed messages about sexual minorities (Tropiano, 2002). Cop shows such as *Police Woman, N.Y.P.D.*, and *The Bold Ones* simultaneously reinforced and challenged negative stereotypes by featuring gay characters on both sides of the law. On one hand, gay men were portrayed sympathetically as victims of blackmail and violence. However, they were also depicted as deranged, knife-wielding psychopaths whose deviant sexuality was considered a part of their criminal behavior. Because of these negative portrayals, media watch groups such as the Gay Activists Alliance and the National Gay and Lesbian Task Force were formed and actively challenged the three major networks to be more sensitive about gay characters and avoid harmful stereotypes. They protested episodes such as *Marcus Welby's* "The Outrage" and a *Police Woman* episode, "Flowers of Evil," about killer lesbians.

As the mental health community was reconsidering the nature of homosexuality in the 1970s, the issue of transsexualism was also getting more notice. The topic had first entered public consciousness in 1952 when former U.S. Army Sergeant George Jorgensen had sex reassignment surgery in Denmark and became Christine Jorgensen. A medical television drama first tackled the complex subject in 1975, when *Medical Center* aired a two-part episode titled "The Fourth Sex." Robert Reed, a then-closeted gay man who later starred in *The Brady Bunch*, won an Emmy nomination for his guest-starring role as Dr. Pat Caddison, a celebrated vascular surgeon who travels to Los Angeles for a sex change. The show focused on the effects of such a controversial decision on Caddison and his family, as well as the reaction of those in the hospital. Although the episodes centered on the "problem" transsexuality presents for those involved, it did not resort to sensationalism and did much to introduce the public to a generally unfamiliar topic (Tropiano, 2002).

Although the 1970s saw an increase in the number of GLBT characters on television series—and they were usually treated sympathetically—sexual minorities were almost always peripheral characters who appeared in single episodes. Gay or lesbian characters were defined primarily by their sexual orientation, and their main purpose was to allow series regulars to deal with the "problem" of homosexuality. Often the approach was liberal: The aim was to expose the ignorance and fear generated by homophobes and to challenge myths that gay men are unhappy, promiscuous sexual predators who can be identified on the basis of their appearance and behavior (Tropiano, 2002). These shows never featured gay or lesbian main characters, and often the plotlines were predictable: the "coming out" episode, featuring a friend or colleague of a main character; the "mistaken identity" episode, in which a straight character is mistaken for gay; or the "pretend" episode, in which a character only pretends to be gay, usually to get next to someone of the opposite sex. The sitcom *Three's Company* was based on such a farce and allowed for years of stupid sexual innuendoes and double entendres.

Continuing gay male characters finally began to appear in the late 1970s. Jody Dallas, a flamboyant gay man considering a sex change operation, was played by Billy Crystal on the controversial comedy series *Soap* on ABC (1977–1981). Jody soon attempted suicide; however, after his lover left him, and by the time the show ended, Jody had not had the sex-change operation and was even preparing to marry a woman.

The late 1970s also witnessed homosexuality as the subject of several made-for-TV movies. In 1978, two such movies were based on the real-life experiences of lesbians and gay men who had faced discrimination because of their sexual orientation. *Sergeant Matlovich vs. the U.S. Air Force* told of one of the first successful challenges to the U.S. military's ban on homosexuals, and *A Question of Love* followed a lesbian mother's child custody case.

❖ AIDS ON TV

The positive representational strides achieved by gay men and lesbians in the late 1970s and early 1980s suffered a series of setbacks in the middle of the decade as AIDS emerged as a health threat and was linked in the news and entertainment media to gay men (Hart, 2000). The first major national newspaper story about what would become known as AIDS appeared in the *New York Times* in July 1981. At first the illness was known as gay-related immune deficiency because it was originally identified in homosexual men. Although the name was changed to acquired immune deficiency syndrome (AIDS) after it was understood that anyone, gay or straight, could become infected with HIV, television programs continued to perpetuate the association between gay men and AIDS by consistently framing AIDS as a gay disease (Alwood, 1996).

The first prime-time drama to tackle AIDS was a December 1983 episode of *St. Elsewhere* titled "AIDS and Comfort." In the show, a respected—and supposedly heterosexual—Boston city councilman was diagnosed with AIDS and subsequently revealed his sexual history with men. He went public with his illness and refused to resign his office. The show focused on the public response to the councilman's decision, as well as the hospital staff's reactions to having an AIDS patient in their care, reflecting a major public concern about the possible ease of contracting AIDS. On November 11, 1985, NBC aired a made-for-television movie, *An Early Frost,* about a young gay lawyer with AIDS who returns home to tell his family about both his sexual orientation and his medical condition. Written by Ron Cowen and Daniel Lipman, who would later create the American version of *Queer as Folk,* the movie combined a coming-out story with AIDS education to inform viewers about the disease and shatter myths surrounding transmission of the virus. Although the movie presented a sympathetic character and attempted to educate the public about AIDS transmission, it had some critics. Gross (2001) argues that the movie—and other AIDS-centered television—focused too much on the response of the heterosexual biological family and none on the response of the gay "families of choice" that so many sexual minorities create for themselves and receive support from. Televised portrayals of AIDS had other problems, too. The constraints imposed on prime-time, episodic television were partly to blame. The fact that regular characters must be around for the next week's show usually prevents them from contracting a most likely fatal disease. Also, the economic reality that forces television shows to appeal to the largest possible audience discourages writers and producers from challenging societal norms, such as homophobia (Netzhammer & Shamp, 1994).

Gay men were already more visible than lesbians on television, and the focus on AIDS in the 1980s only worsened the situation. One group that has consistently fought for improved representation of lesbians on TV is GLAAD, the Gay and Lesbian Alliance Against Defamation. Formed in 1985, GLAAD regularly meets with television network executives and local station managers to encourage the production of more accurate and realistic portrayals of lesbian and gay male lives. For more than 15 years, they have sponsored the annual GLAAD Media Awards to focus attention on those responsible for positive and accurate depictions of sexual minorities in the media. In the late 1980s, members of GLAAD were especially distressed at the treatment of lesbians on television:

One of GLAAD's primary areas of concern at present is the almost uniform negative depiction of lesbians in movies and on television. That these depictions present an extremely unbalanced and inaccurate picture of lesbian lives is an understatement. In our view, such depictions help foster a climate in which discrimination against lesbians and gay men is taken for granted and in which violence against lesbians and gay men is, not surprisingly, on the rise. (GLAAD, 1991)

The first recurring lesbian character on a television show was not until 1988 in *Heartbeat,* a short-lived medical series that featured a lesbian nurse (Gail Strickland) who lived with her partner (Gina Hecht). Three years later, TV saw its first lesbian kiss. C. J. Lamb (Amanda Donohoe), a bisexual lawyer on *L.A. Law,* kissed a female colleague on the lips, an act that outraged religious groups and some advertisers but that improved ratings for the show.

❖ THE GAY '90s

Sexual minorities gained more visibility and respect on American television in the 1990s. Major network prime-time shows began to include gay and lesbian characters that more accurately reflected the wide range of roles that gay men and lesbians actually occupy (Hart, 2000), and things changed so drastically that *Entertainment Weekly* in 1994 said television had entered the "Gay '90s."

In the early 1990s, three popular shows introduced gay or lesbian characters in continuing roles, which was even more of a historic event because their sexuality was not the primary issue every time they appeared (Gross, 2001). In 1990, the highly rated *Roseanne* introduced the character of Leon Carp, Roseanne's openly gay boss, played with wonderfully dry humor by Martin Mull. Viewers then met Roseanne's friend Nancy (Sandra Bernhard), one of the few bisexual characters anywhere on the small screen. The prime-time 20-something soap opera *Melrose Place,* which debuted in 1992, featured among its ensemble cast Matt Fielding (Doug Savant), a man who was openly gay but who was almost never shown as being romantically or physically involved with another man. Although the other characters on the show were extremely sexually active, Matt was usually cast as "the good friend" who rarely had a date, much less any sex. Finally, during the 1992 season, the hour-long comedy-drama *Northern Exposure* told the story of the founding of Cicely, Alaska, where the show was set, by a lesbian couple, Cicely and Roslyn. *Northern Exposure* also featured two gay secondary characters, Ron and Erick, who owned a bed and breakfast in Cicely. Two years later, Ron and Erick married during a religious ceremony on the show, although the kiss sealing the marriage was not aired.

Roseanne again made headlines in 1994 when it was revealed that ABC executives did not want to air an episode of the show in which Roseanne Barr's character kissed another woman. ABC changed its mind, deciding to air the kiss and even promoting it as the "lesbian kiss" episode. More than 30 million viewers watched on March 1 as Roseanne, trying to prove that she was "cool" and open-minded, kissed guest star Mariel Hemingway for four seconds. An even more controversial same-sex kiss had aired the previous spring. The drama *Picket Fences* featured a kiss between two teenage girls, one of whom was the series regular Kimberly, in a sensitive show about emerging adolescent sexuality and homophobia. Network officials, afraid of public response to the kiss as it was originally shot, had the scene reshot in the dark. But it was still a first—rarely were television adolescents allowed to explore the possibility of homosexuality. As the authors of a study about television's portrayal of teenagers note: "The treatment of adolescent subjects on network television is exceedingly heterosexist; continuing adolescent characters are always heterosexual, and the adolescent audience is addressed as if it were composed exclusively of heterosexual characters" (Kielwasser & Wolf, 1992, p. 350).

Television featured its first lesbian wedding in January 1996 on *Friends*, a show that over the years seemed very willing to approach gay-themed topics. In "The One with the Lesbian Wedding," Ross's ex-wife Carol married her lover Susan, and Ross struggled with his feelings about losing his wife to a woman. But when Carol's parents refused to attend the ceremony, Ross magnanimously agreed to walk his ex down the aisle. Carol was a recurring character on the show, and one of the main characters, Chandler, had a father (played, interestingly enough, by actress Kathleen Turner) who was a drag performer.

This sharp upturn in quality and quantity of GLBT characters in the mid-1990s may have been a response to changing social attitudes about homosexuality, but it was also a calculated attempt to attract what network executives consider a high-quality audience. Becker (2003) labels this group "slumpies": socially liberal, urban-minded professionals, gay or straight, in the 18 to 49 age range. They are hip, cosmopolitan, professional adults who pride themselves on being tolerant of—even seeking out—images of sexual minorities on TV. The images they want to see, according to Becker, are those of white, urban, affluent, well-educated gay men and lesbians, which reduces the visibility of sexual minorities of color or of lower socioeconomic status. The appearance of two sitcoms, *Ellen* and *Will and Grace*, with sexual minorities in major roles did nothing to disprove this criticism, but they were groundbreaking nevertheless.

❖ ELLEN'S COMING OUT

Gay men have gotten more TV airtime than lesbians, but the most hyped, anticipated, and possibly influential gay moment on television was actually a lesbian moment. *Ellen* (originally titled *These Friends of Mine*) premiered on ABC in 1994 with standup comedian Ellen DeGeneres starring as Ellen Morgan, a wacky but endearing bookstore owner. Rumors of DeGeneres' lesbianism had occasionally appeared in the media, but she refused to publicly address them. The character of Ellen Morgan, meanwhile, seemed ambivalent about the dating and mating that are plotlines common in situation comedies. Things changed during the 1996–1997 season. *TV Guide* reported at the beginning of the season that network officials were considering having Ellen Morgan come out. The writers teased viewers with hints during the season's opening episodes. Then it happened. Amid unprecedented media coverage, in addition to protests from antigay organizations such as The American Family Association, the "Puppy Episode" aired on April 30, 1997, during the spring sweeps period. Ellen Morgan came out of the closet to her friends, family, and viewers in a star-studded episode featuring Laura Dern as Ellen's love interest, k. d. lang, Oprah Winfrey, Demi Moore, Gina Gershon, Dwight Yoakam, Melissa Etheridge, and Billy Bob Thornton. Ellen Morgan's revelation was accompanied by one from Ellen DeGeneres. In interviews on ABC's *20/20*, on *Oprah*, and in *Time* magazine, the comedian proclaimed herself to be what most everyone had figured out by then: a lesbian. She appeared on *Time*'s cover with the straightforward headline "Yep, I'm Gay."

Although DeGeneres insisted that she did not mean for her coming out to become a major political statement, that is what it became. She was for months the focus of a media frenzy, applauded by gay audiences and groups such as GLAAD for her honesty and heavily criticized by many conservative and religious organizations. She was even called "Ellen Degenerate" by evangelist Jerry Falwell. The postouting episodes of *Ellen* focused on the main character's exploration of her new identity and included more than one same-sex kiss. The show was acclaimed by many, but overall ratings dropped as *Ellen* was criticized for being "too gay" (Gross, 2001). The show was canceled in 1998. Ironically, DeGeneres, now the host of a successful talk show, has been criticized for not being gay or political *enough* on her latest show.

It might seem unusual that *Will and Grace,* the first successful network series to feature gay characters in a gay milieu, premiered the same year that *Ellen* was canceled. The time was right, however. Premiering on September 21, 1998, on NBC, *Will and Grace* was the first television series that focused on the intimacies of a gay male urban culture *and* the first to achieve significant critical and commercial success with an openly gay lead character. The show stars Eric McCormack as Will Truman, a successful and handsome gay Manhattan lawyer, and Debra Messing as his best friend Grace Adler, a straight, beautiful, sometimes neurotic interior designer. Sean Hayes plays Jack, Will's flamboyant, flighty, and stereotypically gay friend. In the early episodes, Will was extremely low-key about his sexuality, which led to criticism that he was not gay enough. Jack, on the other hand, was from the beginning presented as the stereotypical flamboyant oversexed queen. He is a frequent butt of humor on the show, but one of the characters that audiences like most (Cooper, 2003). Unlike *Ellen, Will and Grace* did not provoke advertiser boycotts or denunciations from right-wing Christian groups but instead received critical praise and strong ratings. It maintained considerable popularity in its first five seasons, winning numerous awards, including People's Choice Awards, Golden Globes, a GLAAD Media Award for Outstanding TV Comedy Series, and multiple Emmys. GLAAD has praised the show for presenting two different and likable representations of gay men and for presenting their sexuality simply as part of who they are as individuals.

But *Will and Grace* is not without its critics. It has been faulted for not showing Will in many romantic or sexual situations and for not focusing on larger gay political issues (Cooper, 2003). Others argue that the show lacks any lesbian voice and equates gayness with a lack of masculinity (Battles & Hilton-Morrow, 2002). Also, like many series with GLBT characters, *Will and Grace* had been criticized for confining the portrayal of gay men to those who are white and upper middle class, making the characters more acceptable to a mainstream heterosexual audience at the expense of alienating a large portion of the gay community (Battles & Hilton-Morrow, 2002).

Those looking for strong lesbian characters were not without hope in the late 1990s. *Buffy the Vampire Slayer,* about a high school girl who fought demons and vampires, premiered in 1997 on the fledgling network The WB and developed a small but loyal fan base. The show included three sympathetic lesbian characters during its 7-year run. The primary one was Willow, played for all seven seasons by Alyson Hannigan. She appeared in almost every episode and was, for the most part, a very positive character, an assertive, self-confident woman. Her character broke ground in terms of physical displays of affection between women and the normalizing of lesbians and lesbian relationships. Willow's 2.5-season relationship with the character of Tara was the longest-running lesbian relationship on network television, and in a controversial episode, "Seeing Red," Willow and Tara were even shown naked in bed after sex, something that had not been done on network television before. The show also featured the first lesbian sex scene on network TV (during its last season, and after switching networks to UPN): It was between Willow and Kennedy (Iyari Limon), who was also unusual in that she was a recurring Latina lesbian character. Willow was not without her detractors, however. She was portrayed as heterosexual at the beginning of the show's run and then suddenly as a lesbian in later seasons, all without any consideration that the character may have been bisexual.

❖ REALITY TV

Reality television is considered a phenomenon born in the 1990s, but the first reality show, *An American Family,* actually aired in 1973 on PBS. The series followed the lives of the Loud family of Santa Barbara, including the eldest son, Lance, who did not hide his homosexuality from his family or the cameras. Outrageous, funny, and self-centered, Lance became the star of the show and introduced the American public to its first real gay TV star.

It was Pedro Zamora, however, who truly captured viewers' hearts through reality television. *The Real World,* which premiered in 1992 on MTV, featured a group of young strangers who came together to live in a house and have their lives filmed by a camera crew. From its first year, the show included sexual minorities. The third season, set in San Francisco, introduced America to the 22-year-old Zamora, a gay Cuban American from Miami who had been diagnosed with HIV at age 17.

The show chronicled Zamora's relationship with Sean Sasser, an African-American gay man, and the two exchanged rings in a marriage ceremony during one episode. Zamora's health deteriorated during the season, and on November 10, 1994, millions tuned in as Pedro Zamora left *The Real World* at the close of the show, which had been filmed months before. The next day, Zamora died at age 22.

A number of reality shows have featured GLBT characters. In its first season on CBS, the wildly popular *Survivor* featured a gay contestant, Richard Hatch, who was loved and hated by millions and shocked the country when he was crowned the sole survivor. A gay male couple, Chip Arndt and Reichen Lehmkhul, were the winners of CBS' *The Amazing Race 4* in 2003, and in *Survivor*'s ninth season, which debuted in September 2004, there were not one, but two lesbian-bisexual women in the competition.

Gay men became the stars of reality TV with the premiere of the Bravo channel's *Queer Eye for the Straight Guy* in July 2003. The makeover show features the "Fab 5," who each week take a style-challenged heterosexual male and turn him into Prince Charming. *Queer Eye* debuted to record-breaking ratings for Bravo and widespread critical acclaim. The first season resulted in 24 episodes, a best-selling book, soundtrack, music video, endorsement deals, magazine covers, and talk show appearances. A more controversial gay-themed reality show, *Boy Meets Boy*, premiered in July 2004, also on Bravo. It is a gay male dating show with a twist: It secretly includes straight men among the pool of dating prospects. GLAAD expressed some initial concern that adding straight suitors to the pool could be demeaning to the gay men on the show, but GLAAD executives decided that Bravo's track record with *Queer Eye* and other gay-themed programming was evidence that *Boy Meets Boy* would be respectful. But the Traditional Values Coalition, a conservative organization of 43,000 churches, was outraged. "Clearly they've hit a new low," said Andrea Lafferty, the Washington-based group's executive director. "What's next after *Boy Meets Boy*? Boy Meets Sheep?" (Traditional Values Coalition, 2004).

Into the Majority: *Queer as Folk* and *The L Word*

The television world was rocked in December 2000 with the premiere of Showtime's *Queer as Folk (QAF)*. Generating almost as much media buzz as Ellen Morgan's coming out, the first gay drama series on U.S. television was what GLAAD called culturally groundbreaking.

QAF, based on a British show of the same name, follows the lives and loves of five gay males, ranging in age from 17 (during the first season) to 30-something. Brian, Justin, Michael, Emmett, and Ted are joined on the show by lesbian partners of 8 years, Melanie and Lindsay, the mother of two young children. *QAF*'s sexually explicit weekly episodes include both positive and negative images of gay men and lesbians. There is camaraderie among the lead characters, supportive families, and members of the gay community, as well as sensitive portrayals of coming-out struggles and the repercussions of gay bashing. The show is not afraid to tackle controversial subjects such as bug chasers (gay men who seek to become HIV-positive), straight-bashing gay men, teen hustlers, and lesbians who sleep with men. However, there is also considerable promiscuity and drug use among the main characters, and although the show is set in Pittsburgh, a city comprising more than 90,000 African American residents, there is rarely a person of color seen in any episode. All of the major characters are white.

QAF shocked audiences from the beginning. In the opening episode, Brian, a gorgeous, sex-obsessed advertising executive in his late 20s, meets the virginal 17-year-old Justin. During a steamy and explicit sexual encounter with the teenager, Brian is summoned to the hospital as his son is being born to his longtime friend Lindsay and her lesbian partner, Melanie. Cocreator Ron Cowen says *QAF* is the antidote for all of the seemingly asexual gay and lesbian characters on television:

> *QAF* threw down the gauntlet and set a standard for all portrayals of gay characters in its wake. Sure, there were and will continue to be gay characters who have no discernable sex life and who are just there for laughs. But the fact that *QAF* exists makes that kind of two-dimensional portrayal feel exactly like what it is: incomplete. (Jones, 2004, p. 58)

Lesbians had to wait 2 years for their own drama, and it was again Showtime that came through. *The L Word* premiered on January 18, 2003, and focused on the personal, professional, and sex lives of a group of lesbian and bisexual women in Los Angeles. Like *QAF*, the show features lots of explicit same-sex sex, although there have been some heterosexual sex scenes because of the presence of bisexual characters. Also like *QAF*, all of the main characters are beautiful, although there is more ethnic diversity on *The L Word*. The show has been very popular with lesbian audiences and has been renewed for a second season. There have been critics, however. The main criticism is the "type" of lesbian portrayed. Almost all of the women are traditionally feminine and good looking, which has led one critic to call *The L Word* "butch phobic" (Lo, 2004).

❖ THE ISSUE OF RACE

Although most people would agree that the overall representation of sexual minorities on television has improved since the days of gay men as victims or villains, there is still some way to go, particularly in the area of ethnic diversity. As critics have noted, most GLBT characters have been white and relatively affluent. Ethnic minorities, especially those from lower income settings, are rare. There have been exceptions, of course: In 1995, Dr. Dennis Hancock, played by Vondie Curtis-Hall, joined the cast of the medical drama *Chicago Hope* and revealed his homosexuality to his colleagues. Hancock was a strong force on the show, his compassion often standing in contrast to the money-centered attitudes of the hospital administration. The following year, RuPaul became the first (and still, the only) openly gay African-American drag queen to host his own national talk show when *The RuPaul Show* premiered on VH-1 in October 1996. Also in that year, the sitcom *Spin City* premiered on ABC, starring Michael J. Fox as Michael Flaherty, an assistant to mayor Randall Winston (Barry Bostwick). Carter Heywood, played by African-American actor Michael Boatman, was the city's openly gay director of minority affairs and got some of the show's best lines, often serving as a moral compass for other members of the mayor's administration. *Spin City* and *Chicago Hope* are no longer on the air, but the edgy and quirky HBO drama *Six Feet Under,* about a semifunctional family that runs a funeral home, features a secondary character, Keith, who is gay and African American. Keith is the on-again, off-again lover of main character David, who is white. The show has received praise for its portrayal of a biracial gay couple and the homophobia and racism they often face.

The summer of 2004 witnessed the premiere of America's first African-American gay series, although it was not actually on television. *Noah's Arc,* written and directed by Patrik-Ian Polk, went straight to sale on DVD. The show, sponsored in part by the gay equality organization the Human Rights Campaign, follows a quartet of men living in Los Angeles. Polk said in interviews promoting the show that he was tired of Hollywood's refusal to feature positive African-American gay and lesbian characters on TV or in the movies, so he took matters into his own hands, creating a mix of drama, comedy, and shocking sexuality. He refused to wait for a network to pick up his show.

Lesbian and bisexual women of color have been even more invisible on television, although recent seasons have been more colorful. Rosetta Reid (Jennifer Lewis) and Danny Gates (Cree Summer) starred on the short-lived 1995 drama *Courthouse,* and Showtime's irreverent comedy *Rude Awakenings* in 1998 featured an African-American lesbian in the character of Jackie (Rain Pryor). In the 2001–2002 season, two more lesbian women of color were introduced: Sandy Lopez (Lisa Vidal) on *ER,* the first Latina lesbian primary or secondary character on a TV series, and Original Cindy (Valerie Rae Miller), an African-American lesbian on Fox's science fiction show *Dark Angel.* A few more appeared the following season, including on HBO's series *The Wire,* which featured a lesbian detective played by African-American–Korean-American actress Sonja Sohn. *The L Word* has two lesbian women of color, both major characters: Bette (Jennifer Beals), who is of mixed race (African-American and white), and Marina, played by American Indian actress Karina Lombard. *Soul Food* on Showtime has a recurring African-American lesbian character, Eva, played by Terri J. Vaughn. And finally, *Nip/Tuck* on FX features Liz, played by Latina actress Roma Maffia, as the clinic's lesbian anesthetist. Viewers are still waiting for a network television series featuring an ensemble cast comprising more than a mere smattering of GLBT characters of color.

❖ WHERE ARE THE BISEXUALS?

Television seems to have a love-hate relationship with bisexuality. On one hand, network executives have sometimes preferred bisexual characters over gay males or lesbians because bisexuals can have romantic encounters with members of the opposite sex and not risk boycotts or loss of advertising revenue. The creator of the prime-time soap opera *Dynasty,* Esther Shapiro, recalls that ABC was so nervous about the introduction of gay character Steven Carrington in 1981 that it was easier to make him bisexual just so he could get uncontroversial opposite-sex romantic action (Weintraub, 2004). Still, there have been very few truly bisexual characters on television. Instead, many characters have questioned their sexuality and even dabbled in same-sex relationships, but most have returned to the safe fold of heterosexuality. Women bisexual characters, with the "potential" to have sex with anyone, have even been used as a tool to attract straight male viewers, such as with Sophie on *That '80s Show* or Jane on *Coupling*. This is also a criticism of Jenny on *The L Word*. Jenny (Mia Kirshner), who at first considered herself to be heterosexual but ended up in bed with the beautiful Marina, has been shown in numerous sex scenes, both lesbian and straight. Her presence has been resented by some lesbian and bisexual viewers, who consider Jenny nothing more than an excuse for another sex scene. *The L Word* does have one truly bisexual character, journalist-writer Alice Pieszecki, played, ironically, by the only lesbian cast member, Leisha Hailey.

The one character still virtually invisible on television is the bisexual male. There are males who identify as heterosexual but who sometimes have sex with men, but self-identified bisexual males are not on the screen. The situation is so noticeable that the Web site AfterEllen .com, which monitors and critiques images of lesbian and bisexual women on television, refers to male bisexuality as TV executives' "kryptonite."

❖ FUTURE TRENDS

Sexual minorities have recently become visible on TV through vehicles other than the traditional television series. Gay-themed specials have become hip with cable channels such as the Discovery Channel, MTV, VH-1, and Bravo. Entertainment documentaries about same-sex weddings, transsexuals, the down low (a phenomenon in which African-American males identify as heterosexual but engage in sex with other men), and other gay-related topics can be regularly found in the television listings. Specials such as VH-1's *Totally Gay* and *Totally Gayer* and Bravo's *TV Revolution: Out of the Closet* even look within, an example of television examining how television portrays sexual minorities.

Another trend is the idea of "sexual fluidity." Characters that cannot or choose not to label their sexual orientation are becoming more common. Rather than automatically labeling themselves bisexual, these characters are examining their sexual identity and questioning whether labels are needed. Jenny on *The L Word* and Lindsay, a lesbian on *Queer as Folk* who had an affair with a man, are two examples.

One of the surest signs that gay-themed programming is gaining in popularity is that shows such as *Queer Eye* and *Queer as Folk* are being copied and even spoofed. Comedy Central's spoof *Straight Plan for the Gay Man* brought lots of laughs from regular *Queer Eye* fans and introduced some nonviewers to the makeover show. *Queer Eye for the Straight Girl*, a genuine follow-up to the wildly popular original show, premiered in 2005 on Bravo.

Possibly the clearest indication that television representation of sexual minorities is still in the growth stage is the launching of LOGO, the first gay-themed American basic cable television channel. In May 2004, MTV chairman and CEO Tom Freston announced plans for MTV Networks to launch LOGO on February 17, 2005. The channel was to debut with about 25% original programming and 75% acquired or licensed programming. In addition, LOGO announced a partnership with GLAAD to begin airing the annual GLAAD Media Awards beginning in 2005. The only U.S. network geared to the GLBT market before LOGO was HERE TV, a pay service available only on satellite systems.

Freston said the name LOGO was chosen because it signified the many meanings of identity, and the channel's vision is always to reflect the diversity of the LGBT experience (Hernandez, 2004). The channel's main target audience is LGBT viewers from 25 to 49 years old, but MTV executives are banking on a wider audience that includes many straight viewers. Freston said he knows some people will be uncomfortable with such a channel, and he has been proven correct. The Traditional Values Coalition has already protested the channel and plans to boycott any advertisers.

Regardless of some protests, LOGO's chances for success look promising. Although issues such as same-sex marriage rights and gays in the military still have the power to polarize Americans, television has forged ahead. Representation of sexual minorities on television may not have reached a state of perfection, but things in the 21st century have certainly progressed faster than most people could have imagined in the previous century.

❖ DISCUSSION QUESTIONS

1. In your opinion, which scenario is most damaging for the sexual minority of color: (a) No representation on network television or (b) negative or misrepresentation?

2. What are the individual and societal implications of television's portrayal of sexual minorities as primarily white, educated, and affluent?

3. How has the portrayal of heterosexual sexuality on television differed from the portrayal of homosexual sexuality?

❖ HOMEWORK ASSIGNMENTS

1. Watch reruns or new episodes of the various *Law & Order* television shows. How are GLBT characters portrayed differently than they were in cop shows of the 1970s? Does this represent progress?

2. Look at a week's worth of primetime TV show descriptions. Are some networks more likely than others to feature gay-themed topics? What types of shows (medical dramas, comedies, etc.) are most likely to have gay-themed content?

❖ REFERENCES

Alwood, E. (1996). *Straight news: Gays, lesbians, and the news media.* New York: Columbia University Press.

Battles, K., & Hilton-Morrow, W. (2002). Gay characters in conventional spaces: *Will and Grace* and the situation comedy genre. *Critical Studies in Media Communication, 19*(1), 87–105.

Becker, R. (2003). Prime-time television in the Gay '90s. In M. Himes (Ed.), *Connections: A broadcast history reader* (p. 323–341). Belmont, CA: Wadsworth/ Thomson Learning.

Cooper, E. (2003). Decoding *Will and Grace:* Mass audience reception of a popular network situation comedy. *Sociological Perspectives, 46*(4), 513–533.

Gay and Lesbian Alliance Against Defamation. (1991). Images of lesbians in television and motion pictures. Retrieved May 9, 2005, from http://www .glaad.org/publications/archive_detail.php?id=307

Gerbner, G. (1998). Cultivation analysis: An overview. *Mass Communication & Society, 1*(3/4), 175–194.

Gross, L. (2001). *Up from invisibility: Lesbians, gay men, and the media in America.* New York: Columbia University Press.

Hart, K-P. (2000). Representing gay men on American television. *Journal of Men's Studies, 9*(1), 59–78.

Hernandez, G. (2004, July 6). Just how far will LOGO go? *The Advocate,* p. 62.

Jones, W. (2004, July 6). *Queer as Folk:* The ultimate episode guide. *The Advocate,* pp. 40–60.

Kielwasser, A. P., & Wolf, M. A. (1992). Mainstream television, adolescent homosexuality, and significant silence. *Critical Studies in Mass Communication, 9,* 350–373.

Lo, M. (2004, April). *The L Word's* first season thrills, frustrates. Retrieved May 9, 2005, from the AfterEllen.com Web site: http://www.afterellen.com/TV/thelword/firstseason.html

Mackie, D. M., Hamilton, D. L., Susskind, J., & Rosselli, F. (1996). Social psychological foundations of stereotype formation. In C. N. Macrae, C. Stangor, & M. Hewstone (Eds.), *Stereotypes and stereotyping* (pp. 41–78). New York: Guilford Press.

Netzhammer, E. C., & Shamp, S. A. (1994). Guilt by association: Homosexuality and AIDS on prime-time television. In R. J. Ringer (Ed.), *Queer words, queer images: Communication and the construction of homosexuality* (pp. 91–106). New York: New York University Press.

Russo, V. (1987). *The celluloid closet: Homosexuality in the movies.* New York: Harper and Row.

Signorile, M. (1993). *Queer in America: Sex, the media, and the closets of power.* New York: Random House.

Traditional Values Coalition. (2004). TVC leaders speak out on Bravo homosexual dating show. Retrieved August 2004 from http://www.traditionalvalues.org/modules.php?name=News&file=article&sid=954

Tropiano, S. (2002). *The prime time closet: A history of gays and lesbians on TV.* New York: Applause.

Weintraub, J. (2004, May 19). Bravo tunes in to TV's many changes. Retrieved May 9, 2005, from the JS Online Web site: http://www.jsonline.com/enter/tvradio/may04/230487.asp

❖ ADDITIONAL RESOURCES

AfterEllen.com. (2004). AfterEllen.com—Reviews and commentary on lesbian and bisexual women in entertainment and the media. Retrieved May 9, 2005, from http://www.afterellen.com

Gay and Lesbian Alliance Against Defamation. (2004). GLAAD: Fair, accurate and inclusive representation. Retrieved May 9, 2005, from http://www.glaad.org

Media Awareness Network. (2005). Representations of gays and lesbians on television. Retrieved May 9, 2005, from http://www.media-awareness.ca/english/issues/stereotyping/gays_and_lesbians/gay_television.cfm

NLGJA Stylebook

ACT UP: The acronym for AIDS Coalition to Unleash Power, an activist organization with independent chapters in various cities. ACT UP acceptable in first reference. See **AIDS**.

AIDS: Acquired immune deficiency syndrome, a medical condition that compromises the human immune system, leaving the body defenseless against opportunistic infections. Some medical treatments can slow the rate at which the immune system is weakened. Do not use the term "full-blown AIDS." Individuals may be HIV-positive but not have AIDS. Avoid "AIDS sufferer" and "AIDS victim." Use "people with AIDS" or, if the context is medical, "AIDS patients." See **HIV**.

bisexual: As a noun, an individual who may be attracted to either sex. As an adjective, of or relating to sexual and affectional attraction to either sex. Does not presume nonmonogamy.

civil union: The state of Vermont began this formal recognition of lesbian and gay relationships in July 2000. A civil union provides same-sex couples some rights available to married couples in areas such as state taxes, medical decisions, and estate planning.

closeted, in the closet: Refers to a person who wishes to keep secret his or her sexual orientation or gender identity.

coming out: Short for "coming out of the closet." Accepting and letting others know of one's previously hidden sexual orientation or gender identity. See **closeted** and **outing**.

commitment ceremony: A formal, marriagelike gathering that recognizes the declaration of members of the same sex to each other. Same-sex marriages are not legally recognized in the United States. (In April 2001, The Netherlands became the first nation to offer legal marriage to same-sex couples who are citizens or legal residents.)

cross-dresser: Preferred term for person who wears clothing most often associated with members of the opposite sex. Not necessarily connected to sexual orientation.

cruising: Visiting places where opportunities exist to meet potential sex partners. Not exclusively a gay phenomenon.

domestic partner: Unmarried partners who live together. Domestic partners may be of opposite sexes or the same sex. They may register in some counties, municipalities, and states and receive some of the same benefits accorded married couples. The term is typically used in connection with legal and insurance matters. See **gay and lesbian relationships.**

don't ask, don't tell: Shorthand for "Don't Ask, Don't Tell, Don't Pursue," the military policy on gay men, lesbians, and bisexuals. Under the policy, instituted in 1993, the military is not to ask service members about their sexual orientation, service members are not to tell others about their orientation, and the military is not to pursue rumors about members' sexual orientation. The shorthand is acceptable in headlines, but in text the full phrase adds important balance.

down low: Term used by some bisexual men of color to refer to men who have sex with other men without the knowledge of their female partners. Sometimes abbreviated as DL. See **MSM.**

drag: Attire of the opposite sex.

drag performers: Entertainers who dress and act in styles typically associated with the opposite sex (*drag queen* for men, *drag king* for women). Not synonymous with transgender or cross-dressing.

dyke: Originally a pejorative term for a lesbian, it is now being reclaimed by some lesbians. Caution: still extremely offensive when used as an epithet.

"ex-gay" (adj.): The movement, mostly rooted in conservative religions, that aims to change the sexual attraction of individuals from same-sex to opposite-sex.

fag, faggot: Originally a pejorative term for a gay male, it is now being reclaimed by some gay men. Caution: still extremely offensive when used as an epithet.

FTM: Acronym for "female to male." A transgender person who, at birth or by determination of parents or doctors, has a biological identity of female but a gender identity of male. Those who have undergone surgery are sometimes described as "post-op FTMs" (for postoperative). See **gender identity** and **intersex.**

gay: An adjective that has largely replaced "homosexual" in referring to men who are sexually and affectionally attracted to other men. Avoid using as a singular noun. For women, "lesbian" is preferred. To include both, use "gay men and lesbians." In headlines where space is an issue, "gays" is acceptable to describe both.

gay and lesbian relationships: Gay, lesbian, and bisexual people use various terms to describe their commitments. Ask the individual what term he or she prefers, if possible. If not, "partner" is generally acceptable.

gender identity: An individual's emotional and psychological sense of being male or female. Not necessarily the same as an individual's biological identity.

heterosexism: Presumption that heterosexuality is universal and/or superior to homosexuality. Also: prejudice, bias, or discrimination based on such presumptions.

HIV: Human immunodeficiency virus. The virus that causes AIDS. "HIV virus" is redundant. "HIV-positive" means being infected with HIV but not necessarily having AIDS. AIDS doctors and researchers are using the term "HIV disease" more because there are other types of acquired immune deficiencies caused by toxins and rare but deadly diseases that are unrelated to what we now call AIDS. See **AIDS.**

homo: Pejorative term for homosexual. Avoid.

homophobia: Fear, hatred, or dislike of homosexuality, gay men, and lesbians.

homosexual: As a noun, a person who is attracted to members of the same sex. As an adjective, of or relating to sexual and affectional attraction to a member of the same sex. Use only if "heterosexual" would be used in parallel constructions, such as in medical contexts. For other usages, see **gay** and **lesbian.**

intersex (adj.): People born with sex chromosomes, external genitalia, or an internal reproductive system that is not considered standard for either male or female. Parents and physicians usually will determine the sex of the child, resulting in surgery or hormone treatment. Many intersex adults seek an end to this practice.

lesbian: Preferred term, both as a noun and as an adjective, for women who are sexually and affectionally attracted to other women. Some women prefer to be called "gay" rather than "lesbian"; when possible, ask the subject what term she prefers.

LGBT: Acronym for lesbian, gay, bisexual, and transgender.

lifestyle: An inaccurate term sometimes used to describe the lives of gays, lesbians, bisexuals, and transgender people. Avoid.

lover: A gay, lesbian, bisexual, or heterosexual person's sexual partner. "Partner" is generally acceptable. See **gay and lesbian relationships.**

MSM: Acronym for "men who have sex with men." Term used usually in communities of color to describe men who secretly have sex with other men while maintaining relationships with women. Not synonymous with "bisexual." See **down low.**

marriage: Advocates for the right to marry seek the legal rights and obligations of marriage, not a variation of it. Often, the most neutral approach is to avoid any adjective modifying the word "marriage." For the times in which a distinction is necessary, "marriage for same-sex couples" is preferable in stories. When there is a need for shorthand description (such as in headline writing), "same-sex marriage" is preferred because it is more inclusive and more accurate than "gay."

MTF: Acronym for "male to female." A transgender person who, at birth or by determination of parents or doctors, has a biological identity of male but a gender identity of female. Those who have undergone surgery are sometimes described as "post-op MTFs" (for postoperative). See **gender identity** and **intersex.**

obituaries: When reporting survivors, list partners of gay, lesbian, bisexual, or transgender deceased in an order equivalent to spouses of heterosexual deceased.

openly gay or lesbian: As a modifier, "openly" is usually not relevant; its use should be restricted to instances in which the public awareness of an individual's sexual orientation is germane. Examples: Harvey Milk was the first openly gay San Francisco supervisor. *Ellen* was the first sitcom to feature an openly lesbian lead character. "Openly" is preferred over "avowed," "admitted," "confessed," or "practicing."

outing: (from "out of the closet") Publicly revealing the sexual orientation or gender identity of an individual who has chosen to keep that information private. Also a verb: "The magazine outed the senator in a front-page story." See **coming out** and **closeted.**

pink triangle: Now a gay pride symbol, it was the symbol gay men were required to wear in Nazi concentration camps during World War II. Lesbians sometimes also use a black triangle.

Pride (Day and/or march): Short for gay and lesbian pride, this term is commonly used to indicate the celebrations commemorating the

Stonewall Inn riots on June 28, 1969. Pride events typically take place in June. See **Stonewall.**

queen: Originally a pejorative term for an effeminate gay man. Still considered offensive when used as an epithet.

queer: Originally a pejorative term for gay, now being reclaimed by some gay men, lesbians, bisexuals, and transgender people as a self-affirming umbrella term. Still extremely offensive when used as an epithet.

rainbow flag: A flag of six equal horizontal stripes (red, orange, yellow, green, blue, and violet) signifying the diversity of the lesbian, gay, bisexual, and transgender communities.

seroconversion: Scientifically observable alteration of blood or other bodily fluids from HIV-negative to HIV-positive. The verb is "seroconvert." See **HIV.**

seronegative: Synonymous with HIV-negative. See **HIV.**

seropositive: Synonymous with HIV-positive. See **HIV.**

safe sex, safer sex: Sexual practices that minimize the possible transmission of HIV and other infectious agents.

sexual orientation: Innate sexual attraction. Use this term instead of "sexual preference." See **lifestyle.**

sexual preference: Avoid. See **sexual orientation.**

sodomy: Collective term for various sexual acts that some states have deemed illegal. Not synonymous with homosexuality or gay sex. The legal definition of sodomy is different from state to state; in some states, sodomy laws have applied to sexual acts practiced by heterosexuals. The U.S. Supreme Court decided in June 2003 that state sodomy laws targeting private, consensual sex between adult same-sex or opposite-sex partners violate the U.S. Constitution's Due Process Clause.

special rights: Politically charged term used by opponents of civil rights for gay people. Avoid. "Gay civil rights," "equal rights," or "gay rights" are alternatives.

Stonewall: The Stonewall Inn tavern in New York City's Greenwich Village was the site of several nights of raucous protests after a police raid on June 28, 1969. Although not the nation's first gay civil rights demonstration, Stonewall is now regarded as the birth of the modern gay civil rights movement.

straight (adj.): Heterosexual; a person whose sexual and affectional attraction is to someone of the opposite sex.

transgender (adj.): An umbrella term that refers to people whose biological and gender identity or expression may not be the same. This can include preoperative, postoperative, or nonoperative transsexuals, female and male cross-dressers, drag queens or kings, female or male impersonators, and intersex individuals. If an individual prefers to be called transsexual, drag queen or king, intersex, etc., use that term. When writing about a transgender person, use the name and personal pronouns that are consistent with the way the individual lives publicly.

transition: The process by which one alters one's sex. This may include surgery, hormone therapy, and changes of legal identity.

transsexual (n): An individual who identifies himself or herself as a member of the opposite sex and who acquires the physical characteristics of the opposite sex. Individual can be of any sexual orientation. To determine accurate use of names or personal pronouns, use the name and sex of the individual at the time of the action.

transvestite: Avoid. See **cross-dresser.**

Contact Information for Gay and Lesbian Organizations

ACLU Lesbian and Gay Rights Project: Special division staffed by legal and civil rights experts working for equal treatment of lesbians, gay men, and bisexuals. 125 Broad St., New York, NY 10004; (212) 549-2627; fax: (212) 549-2650; http://www.aclu.org; lgbthiv@aclu.org.

ACT UP: Chapter-based activist group. ACT UP Philadelphia: P.O. Box 22439 Land Title Station, Philadelphia, PA 19110–2439; (215) 731-1844; fax: (215) 731-1845.

AIDS Action: Lobbies for programs and research funding. (202) 530-8030; fax: (202) 530-8031; http://www.aidsaction.org; aidsaction@aidsaction.org; media contacts: Marsha Martin, executive director, ext. 3044, or Donna Crews, government affairs and public policy, ext. 3040.

Bisexual Resource Center: P.O. Box 1026, Boston, MA 02117-1026; (617) 424-9595; brc@biresource.org.

Cathedral of Hope: Christian church based in Dallas, with primary outreach to lesbian, gay, bisexual, and transgendered people. (214) 351-1901 or (800) 501-HOPE; fax: (214) 351-6099; http://www.cathedralofhope.com; hope@cathedralofhope.com.

Children of Lesbians and Gays Everywhere (COLAGE): National organization supporting young people with LGBT parents. 3543 18th St. #1, San Francisco, CA 94110; (415) 861-5437; fax: (415) 255-8345; http://www.colage.org; colage@colage.org; media contact: Felicia Park-Rogers, executive director.

Dignity USA: LGBT Catholics. 1500 Massachusetts Ave. NW, Suite #11, Washington, DC 20005-1894; (800) 877-8797 or (202) 861-0017; fax: (202) 429-9808; http://www.dignityusa.org; dignity@aol.com.

Family Pride Coalition: Support for lesbian, gay, bisexual, and transgender parents and their families. (202) 331-5015; fax: (202) 331-0080; http://www.familypride.org; info@familypride.org; media contact: Corri Planck, communications director, (202) 331-3775, corri.planck@familypride.org.

FTM International: Educational organization serving female-to-male transgender people and transsexual men. (415) 553-5987; http://www.ftmi.org; info@ftmi.org.

Gay, Lesbian, and Straight Education Network (GLSEN): Chapter-based group working to create safer schools. 121 W. 27th St., Suite 804, New York, NY 10001; (212) 727-0135; fax: (212) 727-0254; http://www.glsen.org; glsen@glsen.org.

Gay and Lesbian Alliance Against Defamation (GLAAD): Promotes fair, accurate, and inclusive media coverage. (800) 429-6334; cell: (917) 239-0647; fax: (212) 629-3322; http://www.glaad.org; glaad@glaad.org; media contact: Glenda Testone, news media director, testone@glaad.org.

Gay and Lesbian Medical Association (GLMA): Represents health professionals and their patients. (415) 255-4547; fax: (415) 255-4784; info@glma.org.

Gay and Lesbian Victory Fund: Works to elect gay and lesbian officials. (202) 842-8679; fax: (202) 289-3863; http://www.victoryfund.org; Victory@victoryfund.org.

Gay Men's Health Crisis: AIDS and HIV service provider. The Tisch Building, 119 W. 24 St., New York, NY 10011. GMHC Hotline: (800) 243-7692; in New York City: (212) 807-6655; http://www.gmhc.org; hotline@gmhc.org. Press and media: Lynn Schulman, (212) 367-1210; lynns@gmhc.org.

Gay Men of African Descent: 103 E. 125th St., Suite 503, New York, NY 10035; (212) 828-1697; fax: (212) 828-9602; http://www.gmad.org; media contact: Jay Doss, director of development, (212) 828-1697, ext. 123, jdoss@gmad.org.

Gender Public Advocacy Coalition (GenderPAC): National organization working to end discrimination and violence caused by gender stereotypes. 1743 Connecticut Ave. NW, 4th Floor, Washington, DC 20009; (202) 462-6610; fax: (202) 462-6744; http://www.gpac.org; gpac@gpac.org.

Human Rights Campaign (HRC): Political action committee. (202) 628-4160; fax: (202) 347-5323; http://www.hrc.org; hrc@hrc.org; media contact: Mark Shields, communications associate director, (212) 216-1564, mark.shields@hrc.org.

Institute for Gay and Lesbian Strategic Studies (IGLSS): Independent think tank that addresses LGBT issues. P.O. Box 2603, Amherst, MA 01004-2603; (413) 577-0145; http://www.iglss.org; media contact on deadline: (413) 549-1055.

International Foundation for Gender Education: Information provider and clearinghouse for referrals. IFGE, P.O. Box 540229, Waltham, MA 02454-0229; (781) 899-2212; fax: (781) 899-5703; http://www.ifge.org; info@ifge.org; media contact: Denise LeClaire.

International Gay and Lesbian Human Rights Commission (IGLHRC): (415) 561-0633; fax: (415) 561-0619; http://www.iglhrc.org; iglhrc@iglhrc.org.

Intersex Society of North America: (707) 633-6077; fax (707) 633-6049; http://www.isna.org; info@isna.org.

Lambda Legal Defense and Education Fund (LLDEF): (212) 809-8585; fax: (212) 809-0055; http://www.lambdalegal.org; pressqueries@lambdalegal.org; media contact: Eric Ferrero, communications director, ext. 227.

Latina/o Lesbian, Gay, Bisexual and Transgender Organization (LLEGO): (202) 408-5380; fax: (202) 408-8478; http://www.llego.org; moq@llego.org.

Log Cabin Republicans: Chapter-based. (202) 347-5306; fax: (202) 347-5224; http://www.logcabin.org; info@logcabin.org.

Metropolitan Community Church: Fellowship of Christian churches with special outreach to gay, lesbian, bisexual, and transgender people. 8704 Santa Monica Blvd. Second Floor, West Hollywood, CA 90069-4548; (310) 360-8640; fax: (310) 360-8680; http://www.MCCchurch.org; info@MCCchurch.org.

National Center for Lesbian Rights (NCLR): Legal resource center. (415) 392-6257; fax: (415) 392-8442; http://www.nclrights.org; info@nclrights.org.

National Gay and Lesbian Task Force (NGLTF): Civil rights. (202) 393-5177; fax: (202) 393-2241; http://www.ngltf.org; ngltf@ngltf.org.

National Lesbian & Gay Journalists Association (NLGJA): Resource that works within the news industry; chapter-based. (202) 588-9888, ext. 11; fax: (202) 588-1818; http://www.nlgja.org; info@nlgja.org; media contact: Pamela Strother, executive director, pstrother@nlgja.org.

National Stonewall Democrats: Network of lesbian and gay Democrat clubs. P.O. Box 9330, Washington, DC 20005; (202) 625-1382; fax: (202) 625-1383; http://www.stonewalldemocrats.org; johnmarble@stonewalldemocrats.org.

National Transgender Action Coalition: Works for civil rights for all transgender, intersex, and gender-variant people. P.O. Box 76027, Washington, DC 20013; http://www.ntac.org; info@ntac.org.

New York City Gay and Lesbian Anti-Violence Project and the National Coalition of Anti-Violence Programs: Serves GLBT and HIV-positive victims of violence. 240 W. 35th St., Suite 200, New York, NY 10001; (212) 714-1184; fax: (212) 714-2627; http://www.avp.org; webmaster@avp.org.

Parents, Families and Friends of Lesbians and Gays (PFLAG): Provides support, education, and advocacy through 460+ chapters. (202) 467-8180; fax: (202) 467-8194; http://www.pflag.org; info@pflag.org.

Republican Unity Coalition: A gay-straight alliance of Republican leaders. P.O. Box 19206, Washington, DC 20036-9206; http://www.republicanunity.com; ccfrancis@aol.com.

Senior Action in a Gay Environment (SAGE): Social service and advocacy organization dedicated to LGBT senior citizens. 305 Seventh Ave., 16th Floor, New York, NY 10001; (212) 741-2247; fax: (212) 366-1947; http://www.sageusa.org; sageusa@aol.com.

Servicemembers Legal Defense Network (SLDN): Legal-aid and watchdog group. (202) 328-3244; fax: (202) 797-1635; http://www.sldn.org; sldn@sldn.org.

Sexual Orientation Issues in the News (SOIN): Resource center for journalism educators. Annenberg School for Communication, University of Southern California, 3502 Watt Way, Los Angeles, CA 90089-0281; http://www.usc.edu/annenberg/soin. Media contact: Roy Aarons, director of SOIN; raarons@aol.com.

World Congress of Gay, Lesbian, Bisexual, and Transgender Jews: Keshet Ga'avah: Chapter based. P.O. Box 23379, Washington, DC 20026-3379; (202) 452-7424; fax: (215) 873-0108; http://www.glbtjews.org; info@glbtjews.org; media contact: Scott Gansl, president, (609) 396-1972.

Index

About the Editors

Laura Castañeda is Assistant Professor of Journalism at the University of Southern California's Annenberg School of Journalism. She has worked as a staff writer, editor, and columnist for the *San Francisco Chronicle*, the *Dallas Morning News*, and the Associated Press in San Francisco, New York, and Mexico. Her freelance work has appeared in the *New York Times, BusinessWeek Online, Women's Wire, Online Journalism Review*, and in *Hispanic Business, Latina, Latina Style, Latin Girl, Columbia Journalism Review*, and *American Journalism Review* magazines. Academic articles have appeared in *Journalism Studies* and *Journalism and Mass Communication Educator*. She won the 2002 Baskett Mosse Award given by the Association of Educators in Journalism and Mass Communication, which recognizes outstanding young or mid-career faculty members. Her book, *The Latino Guide to Personal Money Management* (1999), was released in Spanish in 2001. She earned undergraduate degrees in journalism and international relations from the University of Southern California and a master's degree in international political economy from Columbia University, where she also was awarded a Knight-Bagehot Fellowship in business and economics reporting. She lives in Los Angeles with her husband, Art Buckler, and their daughter, Olivia.

Shannon B. Campbell is Assistant Professor of Public Relations in the Annenberg School of Journalism at the University of Southern California. She has presented research at more than 35 refereed conferences around the nation and the globe and is the author or coauthor of many book chapters and articles. A Freedom Forum Fellow, she has served as a consultant for the Internal Revenue Service (Jacksonville, FL), the federally funded One-Stop Service Centers Conference (Daytona, FL), and the Florida Fund for Minority Teachers. She has been an invited presenter at Rand Afrikaans University (Johannesburg, South Africa), Truman State University (Images of Blacks Symposium), and the Institute of Public Relations (International Symposium III). She received a B.S. in Communications Management from Southwest Missouri State University, an M.A. in Speech from Southern Illinois University, and a Ph.D. in Journalism from the University of Texas at Austin. She served as a senior research associate on the $3.3 million National Television Violence Study and the $1.4 million Urban AIDS Prevention Project. She has received grants to study African Americans and the tenure process in the state of Florida, the relationship between teen magazines and Generation-Y females' interpretation of the feminine ideal, and the gangsta rap musical genre.

About the Contributors

Sine Anahita is Assistant Professor of Sociology and Women's Studies at the University of Alaska Fairbanks. Her research interests center on gender and sexuality. She teaches classes on these topics, as well as on the sociology of aging, race and ethnic relations, rural sociology, and work and occupations. Specific research topics include the U.S. land-dyke (lesbian land) movement, gendered water inequalities, and the link between wolf control and masculinity in Alaska. She collaborates with other sociologists on the process couples undertake to become engaged and married and the politics of predator control. She lives in a log cabin on the edge of the Alaskan wilderness, along with her partner, dog, and seven cats.

Willow Arune, a graduate of the University of Alberta, practiced law in British Columbia. At the age of 50, she was able to realize her life's dream and became a woman, crossing the gender boundary. She now lives with her partner and pets in Prince George, BC. A life long student, she has assembled a collection of more than 400 titles of books by and about transsexuals and is an active correspondent with clinicians, writers, scholars, and other transsexuals around the world. An outspoken advocate of transsexual rights, she continues to write for such publications as *Transgender Tapestry* magazine and the Lambda Literary Foundation and has published articles in Canada, the United States, Germany, Australia, and New Zealand on transsexual history, literature, and civil rights.

Jamel Santa Cruze Bell is Assistant Professor of Media Studies in the Communication Department at Boston College. Her critical media approach is grounded in notions of social justice, and her research focuses specifically on media ethics and economics, as well as the social implications of non–majority group depictions. She has presented her research nationally, internationally, and in local communities. Her recent publications focus on media's role in framing dissident voices.

Thomas M. Conroy has a B.A. from Saint Peter's College, an M.A. in sociology from the University of Wisconsin, and a Ph.D. in sociology from Boston University, where he specialized in social constructionism and social problems theory. His dissertation was titled *The Creation and Transformation of Social Problems: Social Constructionism and Social Problems Theory.* He is currently a full-time lecturer in the Department of Sociology and Social Work at Lehman College, City University of New York, in the Bronx, where he teaches courses on research methods, political sociology, and the sociology of religion.

Marc J. W. de Jong is a Ph.D. candidate in the Sociology Department of the University of Southern California, where he currently is writing his dissertation on fundamentalisms and the U.S. news media. De Jong earned M.A. degrees from the University of Amsterdam, the University of London, and, most recently, the University of Southern California. His research interests center on the sociology of sex and gender, media, race, and crime and deviance. He expects to receive his doctorate in 2006 or 2007.

Rhonda Gibson is Associate Professor of Mass Communication at the University of North Carolina at Chapel Hill. She earned a doctorate in mass communication at the University of Alabama in 1993 and a bachelor of science degree in journalism from the University of Tennessee in 1986. Her current research focus is the effect of GLBTQ (gay, lesbian, bisexual, transgender, and queer) images in the mass media on audience attitudes toward sexual minorities. She started a course, "Sexual Minorities and the Mass Media," at the University of North Carolina in 2003.

Kevin Menken is a Ph.D. student in the Department of Speech Communication at Southern Illinois University–Carbondale, specializing in rhetoric, pedagogy, and media representation. A native of Bloomington, Illinois, he received a B.A. in Communication from the University of Illinois–Springfield in 1987 and earned an M.A. in Journalism in 1995 from the University of South Carolina, where he studied obituary comparisons of same-sex couples in newspapers. He has written for a dozen newspapers and magazines, covering business and features, and received two awards for commentaries written as a student journalist. He also taught mass communication courses at Georgia Perimeter College in Atlanta and advised the student newspaper for 3 years. His graduate work continues to center on media representations of different marginalized groups.

Kim Pearson teaches writing for journalism and interactive multimedia courses at the College of New Jersey. She has more than 25 years' writing and editing experience in both consumer and controlled-circulation publications. Most recently, she coedited *The Niagara Movement: Black Protest Reborn*, an interactive CD-ROM published by the Association for the Study of African American Life and History. Her Web log covers race, class, gender, religion, and sexuality topics at Professor Kim's News Notes (http://professorkim.blogspot.com). In 2000, she was named the New Jersey Professor of the Year by the Carnegie Foundation for the Advancement of Teaching and the Council for the Advancement and Support of Education. She holds an A.B. in Politics from Princeton University and an M.A. in Journalism from New York University, where she earned the Hillier Krieghbaum Science Writing Award. Her memberships include the Society of Professional Journalists and the Association for Education in Journalism and Mass Communications.

Damien W. Riggs is a Ph.D. candidate whose thesis focuses on the social construction of whiteness in Australia. In addition, he conducts research on both lesbian and gay psychology and critical health policy. He is also involved in foster career advocacy and training, as well as being a foster parent himself. He has published widely on both race and whiteness and lesbian and gay psychology, including a coedited collection (with Gordon Walker) titled *Out in the Antipodes: Australian and New Zealand Perspectives on Gay and Lesbian Issues in Psychology* (2004) and an edited collection titled *Taking up the Challenge: Critical Race and Whiteness Studies in a Postcolonising Nation* (2005). He is currently editor of the Australian Psychological Society's *Gay & Lesbian Issues and Psychology Review.*

Clare Sears is a doctoral candidate in sociology at the University of California, Santa Cruz. Her research interests include queer theory, gender studies, critical legal studies, California historiography, and urban studies. She is currently completing her dissertation, titled *A Dress Not Belonging to His or Her Sex: Cross-Dressing Law in San Francisco, 1860–1900*, which explores the operations of cross-dressing law in multiple cultural sites in 19th-century San Francisco, including the street, freak show, newspaper scandal, and courtroom.

Rodger Streitmatter is a former reporter and bureau chief for the *Roanoke Times & World News* in Roanoke, Virginia. He holds a Ph.D. in U.S. History and is currently Associate Dean and Professor in the

School of Communication at American University, where he teaches reporting as well as a course titled "Media & Sexuality." Streitmatter has published six books, including *Unspeakable: The Rise of the Gay and Lesbian Press in America; Empty Without You: The Intimate Letters of Eleanor Roosevelt and Lorena Hickok;* and *Sex Sells! The Media's Journey from Oppression to Obsession.*

John C. Watson is Associate Professor in the School of Communication at American University. He earned a bachelor of arts degree in mass communication at Rutgers College–New Brunswick and a J.D. at the Rutgers School of Law–Newark. He joined the American University faculty in 1998 after 21 years as an award-winning newspaper reporter and city editor. He won a Freedom Forum Ph.D. Fellowship in journalism and mass communication at the University of North Carolina–Chapel Hill. His research has been published in the *Journal of Mass Media Ethics, Communication Law and Policy,* the *Rutgers Race and the Law Review,* the *Thomas M. Cooley Law Review, Journalism History,* and *History of the Mass Media in the United States.*